Everyday Bias

Everyday Bias

Identifying and Navigating Unconscious Judgments in Our Daily Lives

Howard J. Ross

ROWMAN & LITTLEFIELD
Lanham • Boulder • New York • London

Published by Rowman & Littlefield
A wholly owned subsidiary of The Rowman & Littlefield Publishing Group, Inc.
4501 Forbes Boulevard, Suite 200, Lanham, Maryland 20706
www.rowman.com

16 Carlisle Street, London W1D 3BT, United Kingdom

British Library Cataloguing in Publication Information Available

Library of Congress Cataloging-in-Publication Data

Ross, Howard J.
Everyday Bias : Identifying and navigating unconscious judgments in our daily lives / by Howard J. Ross.
p. cm.
Includes bibliographical references and index.
ISBN 978-1-4422-3083-5 (cloth : alk. paper) -- ISBN 978-1-4422-3084-2 (electronic)
1. Prejudices. I. Title.
BF575.P9R67 2014
303.3'85--dc23
2014011226

Printed in the United States of America

Contents

Acknowledgments

When I began my professional career, I never set out to develop any expertise in the specific topics discussed in this book. My interest in social justice and my experience in social action almost inadvertently drew me to becoming a consultant. My fascination with the topic of the unconscious mind evolved over a number of years as I became more and more curious about why it was that I would continually interact with seemingly good people who would, nonetheless, demonstrate irrational behavior that created disparities in the way they treated people and ran organizations. Convincing people to develop an intention to be more equitable was challenging, but in the bigger picture never seemed all that difficult. What I found perplexing was why their behavior didn't change over a sustainable period.

In a way, my life has forced me to grow and evolve. The pain that my family suffered at the hands of Nazi aggression combined with growing up in a barely desegregated Washington, D.C., community contributed to creating a core sense of purpose to address injustice in society. The coincidence of being born when I was and growing up during a time of tremendous social upheaval placed me at the heart of the social change movement. My clumsiness in my early leadership roles forced me to study leadership. Early in my career my ignorance about how to grow a school that I was running led me to learn about organizational and cultural change. My own transition through personal struggles, particularly divorce, led me to learn more about myself and how people experience their world. The exploration of my spiritual life led me to explore the meaning of life. And my observations of my own biases completely confounded me, because I *knew* that I didn't want to be biased—yet I was, and am!

So I find myself an almost "accidental" specialist in the work that I have had the privilege to be part of for the past thirty years. In that sense I have many people to thank.

And so my work has taken me to forty-seven states and dozens of other countries. I've worked with people in the back rooms of grocery stores and in the board rooms of corporations; in hospital operating rooms and baseball locker rooms. I've worked in every kind of organization you can imagine, with people of every race, ethnicity, identity, age, and religion.

For my passion for equity and inclusion I am grateful to so many people whom I have learned from and worked with. My experience in diversity and inclusion has been influenced by hundreds of diversity professionals over the years, far too many to name here, and also by the students and staff of Operation Understanding DC, my students at Bennett College for Women, colleagues at the Human Rights Campaign, Leadership Greater Washington, the National Council for Community and Justice, and dozens of other social change organizations that I have had the privilege of working with over the years.

What I have learned about the brain and the mind has been influenced by so many great minds over time that it is hard to count them all. Some of those whose work has most enlightened me include: Robert F. Allen, Nalini Amba-dy, Dan Ariely, Ian Ayres, Mahzarin Banaji, Lera Boroditsky, Christopher Chabris, Amy Cuddy, Antonio Damasio, Edward De Bono, Joe Dispenza, Michael Gazzaniga, Anthony Greenwald, Jonathan Haidt, John Jost, Carl Jung, Daniel Kahneman, Ray Kurzweil, Jonah Lehrer, Matthew Lieberman, Konrad Lorenz, Beau Lotto, Arnold Meyersburg, Leonard Mlodinow, Walter Mischel, Michael Norton, Brian Nosek, Scott E. Page, Daniel Pink, Stephen Pinker, V. S. Ramachandran, David Rock, Dan Siegel, Daniel Simon, Sam Sommers, Claude Steele, Hal Stone, Sidra Stone, Amos Tversky, Shankar Vedantam, Kipling Williams, Tim Wilson, and Philip Zimbardo.

My personal and spiritual growth led me to a fascination with the perennial streams of learning, and I owe an enormous debt to the wisdom of the Baghavad Gita, the ancient Sufis, particularly the poets Rumi and Hafiz, and the teachings of the Buddha, who somehow seemed to identify patterns of the mind 2,500 years ago that science is just now coming to understand. Also a wide range of teachers, including Gerald Jampolsky, Fernando Flores, Buck-minster Fuller, Neem Karoli Baba, Werner Erhardt, Howard Thurman, Nancy Neall, Osho, Eckhardt Tolle, Ken Wilber, and Thich Nhat Hahn. And a special thanks goes to my dear colleagues, friends and soul mates Michael Schiesser and Neelama Eyres.

All of that provided the ingredients, but turning it into a book is another story. I want to especially thank my editor Mary Stanik who not only worked on basic editing, but also strategized the format with me and managed to capture my "voice" in a way that gave me great confidence and trust, both with this book and with my first. Thanks also to Dan Egol, who did an exceptional job of reading and offered tremendously helpful suggestions as well as research support; Howie Schaffer and Laura Malinowski, who also served as valuable readers and gave helpful feedback; and Jake Ross, who contributed research support. Also thanks to Jon Sisk and the rest of the folks at Rowman & Littlefield who are a pleasure to work with.

I am very grateful to the people of Cook Ross Inc., the company I co-founded in 1989, who are deeply committed to transforming the world one organization at a time: Dwight Anderson, Patricia Bory, John Cruzat, Dan Egol, Shayne Bauer-Ellsworth, Erik Granered, John Honor, Arsalan Iftikhar, Hannah Mack, Laura Malinowski, Nicole Martin, Armers Moncure, Rosalyn Taylor O'Neale, Eric Peterson, Reema Rahman, Kimberly Rattley, Brian Rhone, Shandra Richardson, Susana Rinderle, Howie Schaffer, Scott Shields, Pedro Suriel, Minjon Tholen, Carlo Veloso, and Jasmine Zhu. And especially my incredible business partner, Michael Leslie Amilcar.

My deepest gratitude goes to my family. My parents, Jack and Irene Ross, raised all of us to be thinkers and learners and to make a contribution to the world around us. I miss them. My stepfather, Bob Rosen, loved me for more than twenty years, and I am deeply grateful that he came into our lives. My sisters, Sharryn and Robbie, have always inspired my passion for social justice through their own good works. And special thanks to my sons, Matt, Jason, Gabe, and Jake, who are smart, loving and, simply, awesome, and to their wives, Monita, Kate, and Shauna, who contribute to my life in so many ways.

To my grandchildren, Hannah, Mayah, Sloane, Penelope, Davis, and Audrey, thank you for showering your Aaja with love.

And to my wife, business and life partner Leslie Traub. No words can possibly express how much my life has expanded because you are in it. If a river runs through our lives, there is nothing more important than knowing you are always in the boat beside me. You are at the core of everything. I love you.

Finally, to the Great Beloved, in all of the names. Thank you for my life and the chance to share it in a meaningful way.

Introduction

Blinded by the Light of Our Bias

We allow our ignorance to prevail upon us and make us think we can survive alone, alone in patches, alone in groups, alone in races, even alone in genders.
—Maya Angelou

Ninety-nine percent of who you are is invisible and untouchable.
—R. Buckminster Fuller

Did you know people in supermarkets buy more French wine when French music is playing in the background, and more German wine when the music is German? That white National Basketball Association (NBA) referees have been found to call more fouls on black players, and black referees call more fouls on white players? Or, that scientists have been found to rate potential lab technicians lower, and plan to pay them less, if the potential technicians are women? And that doctors treat patients differently when the patients are overweight, *and* that patients treat doctors differently when the doctors are overweight?

Most importantly, did you know that all of these behaviors, and many more, happen *without people realizing they are happening, and that these behaviors are demonstrations of biases*? Biases people don't know they possess. Biases that occur without people knowing why they occur.

Over the past twenty years or so, psychologists, cognitive scientists, neuroscientists, and social scientists have observed countless incidents and engaged in literally hundreds of tests that undeniably point to a human dynamic that ranges from the curious to the tragic.

Human beings are consistently, routinely, and profoundly biased.

We not only are profoundly biased, but we also almost never know we are being biased. The fact that we don't know it results in behaviors that not only include the ones described previously, but, as we'll discuss later, have even contributed to the deaths of innocent people.

During the course of the past five decades, people throughout the world have taken up the mantle of human equality in ways that have no historical precedent. In the United States, we have seen the civil rights movement, the women's movement, and the expansion of acceptance of and equal rights for lesbian, gay, bisexual, and transgender (LGBT) people. The public discourse has changed so dramatically during these past fifty years that in a great many social and professional circles, it is now completely unacceptable to voice openly bigoted statements. In South Africa, apartheid (the horrific system designed to subjugate black South Africans to permit the white minority to maintain power) has been gone for more than twenty years. In Europe, countries have moved toward elevating gender equity to formal public policy status. Many of the governments of these nations are studying the many facets of multiculturalism as waves of immigrants radically change the demographics of historically homogeneous countries.

We have established laws that limit people's biased behavior and hold them accountable for discriminatory behavior. We have hired chief diversity officers who have instituted diversity and inclusion guidelines and training programs for millions of people in schools, major corporations, small businesses, governmental agencies, not-for-profit institutions, and the military to teach us to be more "tolerant" of each other. We have established special holidays to recognize and honor the contributions made by previously unheralded individuals and movements. Large-scale summits and conferences meant to address equity issues take place around the world on an almost daily basis. We have written thousands of books (including mine), made numerous movies, developed social movements, organized protest marches, and produced countless *Oprah* shows, all in an attempt to try to understand the problem and then try to fix it. There is no question that, at least on a conscious level, the standard we set for our behavior has changed.

There is good reason for this change in our behavioral standards. More than ever, people realize that creating an inclusive, culturally competent society just makes good sense. Businesses recognize the impact of getting the best workers from an increasingly diverse workforce, creating the most engaged workplace environments which allow people to perform at the highest level while serving an increasingly diverse and global customer base. Healthcare providers recognize that removing bias and understanding the cultural patterns of patients not only creates greater equity, but also creates greater patient health outcomes. Educational institutions know that a diverse student body creates a better scholastic experience for their learners and that the quality of teaching improves when teachers demonstrate more inclusivity and less bias. Even politicians are realizing the limitations of an agenda that is built upon hatred toward one group or another.

And yet, despite all of these efforts and all of these good intentions, there are countless examples of how our biases still dominate our everyday thinking. How is it that with all of this effort, patterns of disparity continue in virtually every area of life? Medical and dental disparity gaps between whites and people of color in the United States, especially for African American, Latino, and Native American patients, have not changed significantly over the past five decades. Incarceration rates are still dramatically higher among African Americans than among the white population, and they are significantly higher in European countries among immigrant populations of color than among the native born. The salaries of women, compared to those for men in the same jobs, are changing in such a glacially slow fashion that at the current rate, we will not achieve gender equity in the salary sphere in North America and elsewhere in the world until we are well into the next century. Suicide rates for gay teenagers remain four times higher than those for heterosexual youth.

I could go on, because the data are overwhelming, but the question we need to ask is clearly staring us in the face. How can we have good intentions, engage in so many of the right kinds of behaviors, and still not get it right? In fact, many of the results of research that has been done on bias show that biased behavior is shockingly normal. Let's look at a few research examples that show how this behavioral tendency that exists in all of our minds shows up all around us.

Adrian North, David Hargreaves, and Jennifer McKendrick, members of the music research group in the psychology department at the University of Leicester in the United Kingdom, decided to find out whether the sound of music could influence people's choices when shopping.[1] They stocked the shelf of a normal supermarket with eight different bottles of wine. Four of the bottles were French and four were German. The wines were alternately displayed in different positions on the shelf, to ensure that the shelf placement would not affect the experiment. They were matched for cost and sweetness. Flags of their countries of origin were positioned near the bottles. On alternate days, French accordion music or German Bierkeller music was played as background in the store.

The results of this experiment were startling. When the French accordion music was playing, 76.9 percent of the French wine was purchased. When the German Bierkeller music was in the background, 73.3 percent of the German wine was purchased! Interestingly enough, when the forty-four shoppers involved in the experiment were questioned after their purchases, only 14 percent of them acknowledged that they noticed the music. Only one said it made any impact upon their purchases.[2] In similar studies, researchers have found that classical music playing in the background, as opposed to Top 40 popular music, can encourage people to buy more expensive wine and spend more money in restaurants.[3]

How fair are NBA referees? Justin Wolfers, an assistant professor of business and public policy at the Wharton School at the University of Pennsylvania, and Joseph Price, a Cornell graduate student in economics, decided to find out. They studied more than six hundred thousand observations of foul calls in games over a twelve-year period between 1991 and 2003. They worked hard to sort out a large number of non-race-related factors in the way fouls were called by referees. What did they find?

As it was, white referees called fouls at a greater rate against black players than against white players. They also found a corresponding bias in which black referees called more fouls against white players than black players, although the bias was not as strongly represented statistically as was the case with white referees and black players. The researchers claimed that the different rates at which fouls are called is large enough that the probability of a team winning is noticeably affected by the racial composition of the refereeing crew assigned to the game. Wolfers and Price also studied data from box scores. They took into account a wide variety of factors including players' positions, individual statistics, playing time, and All-Star status. They reviewed how much time each group spent on the court, and also considered differentials relating to home and away games.

In addition, the researchers reported a statistically significant correlation with performance relative to points, rebounds, assists, and turnovers when players were performing in games where the officials were primarily of the opposite race. "Player-performance appears to deteriorate at every margin when games are officiated by a larger fraction of opposite-race referees," Wolfers and Price noted. "Basically, it suggests that if you spray-painted one of your starters white, you'd win a few more games," Wolfers said.

David Berri, a sports economist, professor of economics at Southern Utah University, and a past president of the North American Association of Sports Economists, was asked to review the study. "It's not about basketball," Berri said. "It's about what happens in the world. This is just the nature of decision making, and what happens when you have an evaluation team that's so different from those being evaluated. Given that your league is mostly African American, maybe you should have more African American referees—for the same reason that you don't want mostly white police forces in primarily black neighborhoods."[4]

Jo Handelsman is a Howard Hughes Medical Institute professor of molecular, cellular, and developmental biology at Yale University, and the associate director for science at the White House Office of Science and Technology

Policy. Curious about some of the dynamics that might account for the fact that a disparity has existed for generations between the performance of men and women in the sciences, Handelsman and several colleagues designed a relatively simple experiment to find out if gender plays a role in the scientific staff hiring process. In a relatively straightforward attempt to explore the question, Handelsman reached out to science professors at three private and three public universities and asked them to evaluate a recent graduate attempting to secure a position as a laboratory manager. All of the professors were sent the same one-page candidate summary. The applicant was intentionally described as promising but not extraordinary. However, some of the applicants were named John, and some were named Jennifer. All other aspects of the applications were identical.

A total of 127 professors responded to the request. The results were both fascinating and troubling. When asked to evaluate the applicants on a scale of 1 to 7, with 7 being the highest score possible, candidates named John received an average score of 4 for perceived overall competence. "Jennifer" received a score of 3.3. When asked if they thought they were likely to hire the candidate, John was seen as the candidate not only more likely to be hired, but also the candidate the professors would be more willing to mentor.

The professors also were asked to propose a potential starting salary for the candidates. Candidates named John were thought worthy of $30,328 per year. The Jennifer applicants would get $26,508.

Perhaps most surprising of all, responses from female professors were virtually the same as those of their male counterparts![5]

We are sometimes led to believe that scientists are particularly rational, but in looking at these results, one might ask if scientists are more or less rational than anyone else. The results from this particular study do not seem to indicate as much.

David Miller, an associate professor of internal medicine at the Wake Forest University School of Medicine, decided to explore whether medical students' responses to patients were affected by the extent to which the students had a bias about obesity. Between 2008 and 2010, Miller and his colleagues tested 310 third-year students. The students came from twenty-five states within the United States and from twelve other countries. A total of 73 percent of the students were white and 56 percent were men.

The students were tested for their reactions to people of different weights using the Implicit Association Test (IAT), a computer-based testing system developed by researchers at Harvard University, the University of Washington, and the University of Virginia that I will discuss at greater length later in this book. The particular IAT that Miller and his colleagues used asked the students to pair images of heavier people and thinner people with negative or positive words, using a computer keyboard in a timed exercise.

The race, age, or gender of the students made no difference in their responses. According to the IAT results, 56 percent of the students tested had an unconscious weight bias that was characterized as either moderate or strong. A total of 17 percent of the students' results demonstrated bias against people who were thin, and 39 percent demonstrated bias against people who were heavy. And yet, two-thirds of the anti-fat students thought they were neutral bias, as did all of the anti-thin students.

Miller remarked in a Wake Forest University news release that "because anti-fat stigma is so prevalent and a significant barrier to the treatment of obesity, teaching medical students to recognize and mitigate this bias is crucial to improving the care for the two-thirds of American adults who are now overweight or obese"[6]

Ironically, researchers at the Bloomberg School of Public Health at Johns Hopkins University in Baltimore, Maryland, also studied the impact of weight on the doctor-patient relationship but from a different angle. They found that overweight patients tend to trust doctors more when they also are overweight, and that patients with normal body mass indexes tend to trust overweight doctors less.[7] "Our findings indicate that physicians with normal BMI more frequently reported discussing weight loss with patients than did overweight or obese physicians," said Susan Bleich, the study's lead author and an assistant professor at the Bloomberg School's health policy and management department. "Physicians with normal BMI also have greater confidence in their ability to provide diet and exercise counseling and perceive their weight loss advice as trustworthy when compared to overweight or obese physicians."[8]

Who's judging whom?

A story I once heard comes from the ageless tradition of the Sufis, the mystics of Islam. The story is a thirteenth-century fable about Nasreddin Hodja, Turkey's renowned ancient trickster. Nasreddin was walking across a border back to his country from a neighboring one. He walked along while pulling a donkey by a rope. On the donkey's back was a huge pile of straw. The border patrol guard, aware of Nasreddin's reputation for tricks, was sure he must have been smuggling something and so, determined to catch the cheat, he stopped him for questioning.

"What are you smuggling?" the guard asked Nasreddin. "Nothing," Nasreddin said. "I'm going to search you," said the guard, and he did just that, searching Nasreddin, unpacking the huge pack of straw on the donkey, and finding nothing. Frustrated, he let Nasreddin pass.

A few days later, Nasreddin was back again with another donkey full of sticks and straw, again he was searched, and again nothing was found. For months this continued, every other week. Same Nasreddin, with a donkey and a pile of worthless material, but nothing valuable was found.

Finally, one day the completely frustrated guard spoke up to Nasreddin. "Today is my last day on this job," said the guard. "I know that you have been smuggling something, but I have not been able to find it. It has been keeping me up at night to know what you are doing. I am leaving my job so I no longer want to get you in trouble, but please, for my peace of mind, tell me what you have been stealing."

"Okay then," Nasreddin said. "I have been smuggling donkeys."

In our struggle for fairness, for equality, for inclusiveness, have we been looking in the right places or have we been looking for trouble in bundles of straw?

This is an especially important question to ask at the present time, as I write this book more than six years since the start of the dramatic recession of 2008. This recession has not only devastated the world economy, but it has contributed to a regression in the very behaviors of bias I have discussed thus far. There is no real surprise here, as history has shown us time and again that economic stress creates a greater sense of threat and fear of "the other." On a societal scale, hate crimes go up when the economy goes down. On a global scale, dictatorial and fascist regimes are almost always preceded by economic upheaval, whether it is Hitler in Germany, Mussolini in Italy, Franco in Spain, or the Taliban in Afghanistan. These kinds of movements have almost always focused on identifying an "other" who has to be controlled, de-throned, or annihilated.

Consider the anti-immigrant sentiment that has swelled in the United States and Europe during the past decade. In the United States, the quintessential "nation of immigrants," a country in which virtually every person who is not of Native American origin comes from an immigrant heritage, anti-immigrant zeal is at its highest level in generations. In Denmark, the Netherlands, Sweden, Norway, and Germany, "nationalist" parties have risen with an all too familiar race-based fervor.

I have spent the past thirty years studying human diversity and engaging in direct interaction with hundreds of thousands of people. These sorts of reactions are not new to me. However, what has become apparent, and has been proven by research, is the pervasiveness of this phenomenon of bias and most especially, how completely unconscious most of us are about it.

Over the past decade we have been given scientific tools to study this question in ways that have not been previously available. While the brain still remains a great mystery, breakthroughs in the neurological and cognitive sciences are teaching us more than we have known in all of our history. Great developments in the social sciences are teaching us more than we have ever known about human behavior, both on individual and collective bases. Science is giving us insights that lead us to conclusions that are very different from those we might imagine possible.

And that is my purpose for writing this book. After a lifetime of working on and caring about these issues, I believe these new insights into human consciousness offer us the possibility of a new leap forward. The possibility of a deeper understanding of the human condition that may hold the potential for not only solving some of our specific problems, but transforming the way we relate as a species is one I believe must be embraced with vigor.

However, I want to be clear that I am not writing this book with any sense that I know how to fix people. In fact, the more I have studied unconscious bias, the more I have found myself recognizing my own. Let me give you an example of what I mean.

A while ago I was in Jackson, Mississippi, working with the deans and faculty members at Jackson State University, one of the nation's historically black colleges and universities. After working for two days I had to fly through Memphis, Tennessee, to LaGuardia Airport in New York to work with another client for the remainder of the week. I landed in Memphis and arrived at my gate for the last flight out that evening to New York. As I was sitting down and opening my computer to do some work, the gate attendant announced that our flight had been delayed for forty-five minutes. Almost immediately a voice bellowed from behind me in a deep Southern accent. "You talkin' to us lady?" I turned around and there he was, a man I would best describe as Santa Claus with an attitude. Mid-sixties, white, well-fed, white beard and hair, wearing overalls and a flannel shirt. In his hand was a car magazine. Boy, did I have him pegged. I smiled to myself and then went back to work.

Forty-five minutes passed, and it was time to board the plane. I had been upgraded to first class because of my airline miles, and I walked down the passage to my aisle seat when, lo and behold, who should be sitting at the window but "angry Santa" himself. I have to admit that I wasn't thrilled, but we did the "airplane greeting nod" I'm sure many of you are familiar with, and I sat down for the flight. As soon as we took off and were able to do so, I took out my computer and got back to work, preparing a course I would be teaching the next week at Georgetown University. My neighbor was reading his car magazine. At some point he got up to go to the restroom and when he returned he asked me, "What are you, a professor or something?" Girding myself a bit for a possible reaction, I explained what I did and that I wasn't really a professor but was just teaching a course. He barely reacted, and we went back to our parallel activities.

This continued until we approached New York, when the pilot announced our final descent and that the time had come to put away all electronics. Experienced flyers know this is the time when "airplane chat" often takes place, because it is now safe to start a conversation knowing you won't get stuck with somebody for two hours, someone you really might not talk to for even two minutes anywhere else. I turned toward the gentleman and asked him, "What takes you to New York?"

"I'm going to a professional meeting," he responded.

I immediately noticed the hearing aid he had in his right ear, which I hadn't seen before. Maybe that explained his reaction to the announcement?

"What do you do?" I asked.

"I'm a radiologist," he replied.

So here I was, a diversity consultant with thirty years of experience, and the guy who I had pegged with all of my socioeconomic stereotypes was, in fact, a doctor. But it didn't stop at that fact.

"Do you have a particular area of interest in radiology?" I inquired.

"Yes," he responded, getting very animated. "We're using active brain scans to learn about how the human brain responds to various stimuli, especially when people interact with different kinds of people."

In other words, he was an expert in one of the very fields that I am the most interested in. If it weren't for my immediate stereotyping of him, and all of the biases that it brought up in me, I might have learned as much about the brain in that two-hour flight as I had learned in my research during the past year!

Gulp!

We all have this mechanism built into the way we see the world. Through the course of this book, I'll be discussing why that is, what purpose it serves, and how the brain operates in that way. But before we get to that, let me give you a quick example. This is a story you may have heard.

A man and his son get on an airplane. The plane takes off and shortly thereafter is hit by a tremendous storm, which causes a crash landing. The father is killed instantly, but, miraculously, the son is injured but survives. An ambulance rushes him from the scene to the local hospital, where he is immediately taken to the operating room. After the boy is prepped for surgery, the surgeon approaches the operating table but then stops suddenly and says, "I can't operate on this boy—he is my son!"

Who is the surgeon?

This joke, or similar ones have been around for years and most people probably know the answer: The surgeon is the boy's mother!

Or is that accurate? Maybe, or perhaps it is the boy's other father, because he is the child of a gay male couple?

Our minds quickly go to the solutions that make the most sense and often miss other possibilities that are right in front of us. In later chapters I discuss in more detail how and why this happens.

My intention in writing this book is not to wag the finger of self-righteousness at you, the reader, or to act like this is something that I am immune to any more than anyone else. In fact, I am very clear that we are all, as human beings, in this boat together!

One of the challenges that we have had in dealing with patterns of unconscious bias is that we have evolved into a "good person/bad person" paradigm of looking at issues relating to differences. I discussed this at length in my first book, *ReInventing Diversity: Transforming Organizational Community to Strengthen People, Purpose and Performance.*[9] The whole way we have approached the work is built upon the assumption that good people treat people equitably, and it is bad people who do all of those terrible things that we read about in any manner of media. Often, this is especially true for people who come from a tradition of their own pain regarding "otherness." For example, my family is of Eastern European Jewish origin. We lost dozens of family members in the Holocaust. I grew up hearing lots of talk and concern about anti-Semitism from various relatives. But I also heard questionable comments from these same relatives about people of different races. I have heard African Americans complain about racism who then made homophobic or heterosexist comments. I have heard gays and lesbians make questionable comments about immigrants.

Do you know anybody who doesn't have something going on with some "other" group?

In fact, what the research shows pretty definitively (and I'll talk about some of this research in later chapters) is that most examples of bias, especially those that deferentially affect people in organizational life, are not conscious in origin at all. They are not decisions made because somebody is "out to get" somebody, but rather because all human beings have bias. Possessing bias is part and parcel of being human. And the more we think we are immune to it, *the greater the likelihood that our own biases will be invisible or unconscious to us!*

The challenge, of course, is that this is difficult for most of us to confront. Most people I know like to think of themselves as "good people." We like to think that we treat everybody around us fairly, at least most of the time, and we shudder to think that we might be biased in our nature. And yet it is apparent that to be biased is almost as normal as breathing, and that our hidden fears and insecurities often get expressed in the various ways we react and respond to each other. So, as we have evolved into a greater sense of shared understanding that it is not "right" to have bias, have we gotten to the point where we can have racism without racists, sexism without sexists, and so on? And if so, how does this require us to reinvent how we deal with these issues if we are going to create organizations and societies in which all people have an equitable chance of success?

There are some people who are concerned about the movement toward a greater understanding of unconscious bias. Some fear that the focus on bias from an unconscious standpoint may provide cover for people who can easily deny their prejudice by claiming it is unconscious. R. Richard Banks and Richard Thompson Ford of Stanford Law School at Stanford University state

The better explanation for the ascendance of the unconscious bias discourse is that assertions of widespread unconscious bias are more politically palatable than parallel claims about covert bias. . . . The invocation of unconscious bias levels neither accusation nor blame, so much as it identifies a quasi-medical ailment that distorts thinking and behavior. People may be willing to acknowledge the possibility of unconscious bias within them, even as they would vigorously deny harboring conscious bias. The unconscious bias claim thus facilitates a consensus that the race problem persists. Despite its ostensible political benefits, the unconscious bias discourse is as likely to subvert as to further the cause of racial justice. [10]

These are valid and reasonable concerns. The fact that somebody exhibits bias unconsciously does not change the impact of the behavior. Assume for the sake of argument that the referees mentioned earlier were motivated by unconscious bias as opposed to a conscious desire to help some of the players and hurt some of the others. Does it ultimately matter to the players if they foul out of a big game because of that desire? Obviously not. However, we do know that the way we perceive people's actions affects how we feel and how we choose to interact. In a recent study, Princeton University professors Daniel L. Ames and Susan T. Fiske found that "people saw intended harms as worse than unintended harms, *even though the two harms were identical* (emphasis added)." Ames and Fiske went on to suggest that as a result of this phenomenon, "people may therefore focus on intentional harms to the neglect of unintentional (but equally damaging) harms." [11]

At the same time, we know that one of the great barriers to getting people to look at our own biases is the shame and guilt that come when we feel like we are being made to look as if we have done something wrong, or that we are under attack. This shame and guilt cause defensiveness and reduce the chances of reaching people.

These biases make an impact upon each and every aspect of our lives. They affect the way we respond to threats. They make an impact upon the way doctors and patients interact. They affect the judgments we make about others. In organizational life, they influence how we interview people, whom we hire, whom we give job assignments to, whom we promote, and whom we're willing to take a chance on. In fact, they make their mark upon virtually every aspect of organizational life. They also affect the way teachers educate students and how parents treat their own children. Virtually every important decision we make in life is influenced by these biases, and the more they remain in the unconscious, the less likely we are to make the best decisions we are able to make.

My purpose in writing this book is to find a way to invite people into a conversation about our own bias. To recognize that who we are and who we want to be as a society will ultimately be defined by our ability to raise our consciousness level beyond our tendency to simply react to fear. I am not calling for people to ignore unconscious bias. On the contrary, I am hoping that by understanding it we can learn to work with it and reduce its ability to dominate our decision making. I know there are psychologists who say this is almost impossible. And yet, my experience in working with hundreds of thousands of people has been such that I know we can make inroads in our abilities to be more conscious.

There are some who may say, "Just tell me what to do!" Ah, if only life were that simple. If so, then all we would have to do to lose weight would be to learn about diets, but many of us know how well that has worked (or not). Albert Einstein reportedly once said, "If I had an hour to solve a problem and my life depended on the solution, I would spend the first 55 minutes determining the proper question to ask, for once I knew the proper question, I could solve the problem in less than five minutes." Transforming our fundamental ways of living and being in the world requires learning new information and behaviors. It also requires a shift in our mind-sets and emotions about the subject at hand. That's what I am attempting to create in this book. We will start by looking at what bias is and why it is so essential to us as human beings. We also will explore what the neurological and cognitive sciences are teaching us about how the brain processes bias. We will look at how unconscious bias affects some of the most fundamental aspects of our lives and the various ways it manifests itself. I will then share with you some of the resources that can help you learn about your own bias, and some of the ways that we are learning, individually and collectively, to reprogram our responses so that we can make better choices for ourselves, and our organizations and communities. And then, for those of you who want to look at ways that you can build more consciousness into the schools, businesses, hospitals, or other organizations that you work in, I have included an appendix with specific suggestions or ways to build more consciousness into your talent management processes. By the time you reach the end of this book, you will not only have a better understanding of what you think, but of *how* you think!

Let's get started.

Chapter One

If You Are Human, You Are Biased

Our conscious motivations, ideas, and beliefs are a blend of false information, biases, irrational passions, rationalizations, prejudices, in which morsels of truth swim around and give the reassurance albeit false, that the whole mixture is real and true. The thinking processes attempt to organize this whole cesspool of illusions according to the laws of plausibility. This level of consciousness is supposed to reflect reality; it is the map we use for organizing our life. —Erich Fromm, German psychologist and psychoanalyst

Interviews can be challenging to almost anybody and in almost any circumstance, but there are few circumstances more confronting than a medical school student admissions interview. Imagine. You have worked hard your whole life to be a good student, even an elite student. Medical school admissions are among the most competitive processes people will ever face. Virtually every other candidate you are competing against has an outstanding résumé with exceptional grades. The interview process weighs heavily on people's decisions because it often separates the merely good students from those who have the intelligence *and* the presence to be a good doctor.

The challenge, of course, is that interviews are subject to many unconscious biases based on any number of extraneous factors relating to the candidate being interviewed, the interviewer, and the environment in which the interview is being conducted. Two physicians at the University of Toronto, Donald Redelmeier and Simon Baxter, decided to explore one of these more extraneous factors. [1] They were curious about the observation as to how it seemed that prospective students interviewed on rainy days tended to get lower ratings in their interviews than people interviewed on sunny days.

Now I'm sure anybody reading this will agree that determining whether to accept students into medical school, or any other academic program for that matter, based on what the weather is on the particular day they are

1

scheduled for interviews, is the height of folly. How absurd would it be to base a decision on whether to admit a student, based on something so obviously random and out of the student's control?

Absurd, perhaps. Nonetheless, it happens.

Redelmeier and Baxter collected the results of medical school interviews that were conducted at the University of Toronto between 2004 and 2009. They compiled all of the scores from the interviews, almost all of which were conducted in the early spring. The scores ranged from 0 to 20.3. A score of 10 or less was considered "unsuitable," 12 "marginal," 14 "fair," 16 "good," 18 "excellent," and 20 was considered "outstanding." They then researched the Canadian National Climate Archive to track the weather on the days that the interviews were conducted.

Over the course of that time, Redelmeier and Baxter identified 2,926 candidates who were interviewed. The demographics of the interviewees were found to be unrelated to the results. However, those interviewed on rainy days were rated lower than those who were screened on sunny days. In fact, when they compared the results against the students' scores on their primary testing mechanism, the Medical College Admission Tests (MCATs), they found that the difference in interview scores was equivalent to the students reducing their MCAT scores by 10 percent! Given the intense competition between high-performing applicants, this is enough to determine whether or not, or perhaps, "weather or not," a student may get accepted, or even become a doctor at all.

Is it likely that interviewers responsible for choosing students for medical school said to themselves, "It's raining out so I think I'll give this student a lower score," or is it far more likely that they were unconscious to the impact that the weather made upon their mood? And the manner in which their mood influenced their perceptions of students?

It is not a far stretch to consider that similar environmental or other concerns might affect us when we are conducting hiring interviews in business or making other business decisions, grading student papers, or determining hundreds of other choices, including those that are seemingly insignificant as well as very significant.

Unconscious influences dominate our everyday life. What we react to, are influenced by, see or don't see, are all determined by reactions that happen deep within our psyche. Reactions which are largely unknown to us.

In a way, we all know this to be true. Most people have, at some point in their lives, asked themselves what made them do or not do a certain thing. We find ourselves curious as to why we don't always act in a way that is consistent with what we would like to do. Why do we eat too much, or lose patience with our loved ones, even as we had consciously appealed to our "higher" selves to do otherwise? We often have a hard time motivating ourselves to do things, even when we have determined that they are important. The comedian Flip Wilson built a whole career in the 1960s and 1970s upon the punch line of "the devil made me do it!," a line of thinking most of us can relate to in those moments when it seems like someone or something else is dictating our actions or choices.

We are constantly making decisions that are influenced by unconscious biases. In fact, even when our biases seem conscious, they may be influenced by a pattern of unconscious assumptions that we have absorbed throughout our lives. It is like a polluted river. We may do everything we can to clean the river as it flows downstream, without having any consciousness about the pollutants that are being dumped in it by a factory or sewage plant upstream.

Consider the biases that people clearly have in our society today toward LGBT people. We have gone through a decade in which we have seen breakthroughs in marriage equality: the end of "Don't Ask, Don't Tell" in the military; a dramatic shift in the presence of LGBT actors and actresses and themed programs in the arts; and, a lesbian elected mayor of Houston, Texas. And yet, bias against LGBT people continues to proliferate.

A May 13, 2013, Gallup poll found that 45 percent of the American public believes that same-sex marriages should not be valid.[2] Even after two July 2013 rulings by a conservative U.S. Supreme Court cleared the way for same-sex marriage in California and established, by declaring unconstitutional the Defense of Marriage Act, that same-sex couples were eligible for federal benefits under the law, overt discrimination and resistance to the rights of LGBT people still persist. Even in the entertainment industry, where most people see a great deal of open expression of sexual orientation, a Screen Actors Guild-American Federation of Television and Radio Artists study found that "the survey, based on responses from over 5,600 union members, showed nearly half of lesbian and gay respondents and 27 percent of bisexual respondents 'strongly agreed' that producers and studio executives believe that lesbian and gay performers are less marketable."[3]

However, are even these overt biases truly "conscious"? While there is no doubt many people are aware of the fact that they are uncomfortable or downright hostile to LGBT people, the cause for those animosities might still be very unconscious. From where do these biases come? Most of us were probably quite young when we started to hear that "boys should play with these toys, but not those." How old were most of us when we first saw modeling among the people around us about what was "normal" and what was "sick," "sinful," "gross," or other such descriptors? When we started going to our places of worship and hearing about biblical readings? When we heard people telling jokes about gays or lesbians?

As Brett Pelham, the associate executive director for graduate and post-graduate education at the American Psychological Association, has said, "virtually all bias is unconscious bias. We have learned to trust women to be nurturing and men to be powerful, for example, in much the same way that

Pavlov's puppies trusted ringing bells to predict the arrival of meat pow-
der. . . . Being biased is how we get through life without evaluating everything afresh every time we experience it."

Even when our biases are conscious downstream, their upstream causes
may be very much hidden in our unconscious. For a long time, it has been
our general belief that stereotypes and biases were the purview of bigoted
people. However, an explosion of studies about the unconscious over the past
two decades is revealing a truth that is very uncomfortable. All people use
biases and stereotypes, all of the time. And all of us do so without realizing
that we are doing it.

In any case, what is bias? Why do we have it?

Bias has been defined as "a particular tendency or inclination, especially
one that prevents unprejudiced consideration of a question."[4]

While we have generally thought about bias in relationship to people and
prejudice, we have biases in all aspects of our lives. We are biased toward
particular kinds of television shows or movies, certain foods or kinds of
foods, certain kinds of books or stories, etc. Virtually any preference we have
is likely to have some bias associated with us. And it is, for the most part,
unconscious.

This doesn't mean that every time we make a wrong determination about
somebody that it is based on bias. In that sense, it is important to distinguish
between what we might call "logical fallacies" and biases. People do sometimes follow faulty logic that leads to an error in reasoning. When we take a
position about something based on that faulty logic, we call that a fallacy.
Biases, on the other hand, result from times when we have some kind of
"glitch" in our thinking. These may result from social conditioning, belief
systems that we have been taught or exposed to, particular incidents that we
remember, or any number of other assumed "truths" that we have picked up
along the way.

The degree to which we see ourselves as "progressive" or "liberal" on
these issues, or the degree to which we may have been the victim of other
people's biases, has little or no impact on the unconscious biases we may
possess. Ironically, on an unconscious level, somebody (even a person of
color) who sees himself as liberal on racial issues, for example, may have
unconscious biases that are not much different from those possessed by an
overt racist. Or somebody who sees herself as progressive on gender issues
might still have hidden gender-based biases.

For instance, consider the attitudes that people have toward men and
women regarding who is more suited to having a career and who is more
suited to staying at home. When researchers at the University of Virginia
asked men and women to respond on a conscious level as to how strongly
they associated women with careers, the differences between men and wom-
en were quite pronounced. Women were almost twice as likely to see a

connection between women and careers and men almost twice as likely to not see that connection. However, when tested to see what their unconscious attitudes are to the same question, the disparity almost disappeared. It turns out that on an unconscious level, the differential is less than 20 percent. On an unconscious level, we all have absorbed the same stereotypes and have similar internal value systems, often completely inconsistent with our conscious values!

How might this difference in perception show up on a day-to-day basis? Perhaps, in assumptions that leaders make about a woman's willingness to travel and be away from her family, or take an overseas job assignment. Or in how willing a woman might be to ask for something that she needs, or a raise in pay. Or in how much a man might listen to a woman's point of view. Or how comfortable men or women feel about women with children working on flextime arrangements, *even when it is stated company policy to allow such arrangements*! The dissonance between our conscious value systems and our unconscious drivers can cause confusion to both ourselves and other people who are observing us.

These are often subtle perceptions. Like the story about the father and son in the airplane crash, we don't consciously say, "I'm going to ignore the possibility that the doctor could be the mother or the other gay father!" Yet, those images or thoughts don't occur to us as we contemplate the problem. Bias serves as a fundamental protective mechanism for human beings.

Psychologist Joseph LeDoux has referred to bias as an unconscious "danger detector" that determines the safety of a person or situation, before we even have a chance to cognitively consider it.[5] For example, in more primitive times, if we came across a group of people around the river drawing water, we had to decide instantly whether it was "them" or "us." The wrong choice might have led to our death. We learned, through evolution, that making those determinations quickly could save our lives. Unconscious bias comes from social stereotypes, attitudes, opinions, and stigma we form about certain groups of people outside of our own conscious awareness.

The same is true when we encounter other circumstances in life. We teach our children to have a "bias" about the danger in crossing streets. We want them to instinctively stop at the curb when they are chasing a ball or walking to school. We do the same when we are determining whether a stove is hot or cold. We cautiously touch it to test it. Our minds have been wired to protect us in this way.

The important part to realize is that we have these biases for a reason. Imagine if you didn't have any biases and you went out into the world. How would you know whether somebody approaching you was "friendly" or not? How would you determine how to relate to different circumstances? If somebody approached you with a knife in their hand, raised high in the air, would you look at them and say, "I wonder what that is and what you plan to do with it?" or would you immediately switch into "fight or flight" mode and defend yourself?

To manage and negotiate an extremely complex and busy world, we have developed the capacity to compartmentalize things and people we are exposed to on a regular basis. We put them in observable categories so we can quickly determine how they fit into our background of experience and then determine what we can expect from them in the future. Gender, race, sexual orientation, age, and so on, are all such categories. For instance, it makes it easier to know that somebody with gray hair is likely older, as opposed to not having any idea of the age of the person with whom we are dealing. It is not a big jump, then, for the mind to associate qualities and values to those categories, for example: good or bad; right or wrong; smart or stupid; safe or unsafe.

One of the most powerful ways we do this is by creating stereotypes. We begin to learn how to "read" different kinds of people. As we encounter them, we instantly compare them to other people we have encountered before. Were the others friendly, safe, and welcoming? If so, then we are likely to feel comfortable with these individuals. On the other hand, were the others hostile or unfriendly? Then the mind sends a different message: Be careful! Stereotypes provide a shortcut that helps us navigate through our world more quickly, more efficiently, and, our minds believe, more safely.

Of course, even when we haven't encountered a particular kind of person before, we may have the same judgments and assessments based on things that we have heard or learned about "people like that." As far back as 1906, William Graham Sumner, the first person to hold an academic chair in sociology at Yale University, identified the phenomenon of "in-group/out-group bias." Sumner wrote that "each group nourishes its own pride and vanity, boasts itself superior, exists in its own divinities, and looks with contempt on outsiders."[6] This phenomenon is magnified when the "in" group is the dominant or majority culture in a particular circumstance. Because the dominant cultural group in any environment usually creates the standard and acceptable norms and behaviors for that group, people from nondominant groups often will be seen as "different," "abnormal," "less than," or even "sick" or "sinful." Business cultures, to cite one example, are generally male dominant. Business leaders are overwhelmingly male. The cultures of companies have largely been around from a time when even more men were in leadership. This has created a male-dominated cultural model in most businesses. And yet most men don't look at their business cultures as wanting things to be done in "a man's way." They see it as wanting things to be done "the right way," without even realizing the gender influence in that categorization.

If we were to look at this thinking objectively, we could see a certain logic to it. If you were creating a mind and evolving it over the course of millennia, would it make more sense for that mind to be more sensitive, in encountering new people and experiences, to things that are potentially pleasant or things that are potentially dangerous? The obvious answer is that the one that might kill me is more important to spot than the one that might give me a "nice surprise." When we do not know much about this person, or these people, they can become potentially dangerous to us. Until proven otherwise. We are programmed to notice that potential threat before we notice "friend." To notice potential "danger" before we notice potential "pleasure." It helps keep us alive.

This isn't limited to people. We stereotype all kinds of things to try to figure them out. We see something and our mind automatically sorts it, consciously or unconsciously saying, "that reminds me of . . ." as a way of identifying what we are dealing with at that moment. Pelham and Blanton have studied this pattern of behavior, even as we relate to dogs.[7] If you show people pictures of a bulldog, a sheepdog, a poodle, and a pointer, and ask them which is "loyal," "prissy," "persistent," or "clumsy," you will get the same answers almost every time. Some of these stereotypes have even become part of our language (e.g., "he was as persistent as a bulldog!"). Of course we might say these are common characteristics in these breeds, but not every dog in any breed acts the same way, yet we still make the assumption. It is quicker and easier that way, and much more efficient for our brains. And it is mostly unconscious. While we have tended to look at the dynamics of unconscious bias most particularly concerning racial and gender identity, unconscious bias patterns exist in all areas of life and are influenced by factors that might surprise us. For example, it is no surprise that we make certain decisions based on our hand dominance. We may sit in a certain place because we are right-handed or left-handed and don't want to be constantly bumping up against the person next to us. A study from the Max Planck Institute for Psycholinguistics in the Netherlands seems to show that our responses to hand dominance may influence us more than we think.

In the study, which was led by Daniel Casasanto, researchers found that not only do people tend to choose more toward their dominant hand (in other words, if you are right-handed, you are more likely to choose something on your right side than on your left), but that we also respond to others based on their use of one hand or another.[8] In addition, we may be able to read people's positive and negative attitudes based on the hands they inadvertently use.

"In laboratory tests, right- and left-handers associate positive ideas like honesty and intelligence with their dominant side of space and negative ideas with their nondominant side," said Casasanto. "Right- and left-handers were found to associate positive ideas like *intelligence, attractiveness,* and *honesty* with their dominant side and negative ideas with their nondominant side." The researchers also analyzed the speeches of politicians to determine whether or not this pattern played out. Studying the 2004 and 2008 American presidential elections, they tracked 3,012 spoken clauses and 1,747 gestures from the four presidential candidates, two of whom were right-handed (John Kerry and George Bush), and two of whom were left-handed (Barack Obama and John McCain). In both cases, the dominant hand was more associated with positive statements and the non-dominant more associated with negative ones. In other words, if the candidate was right-handed, they used their right hand to gesture when they made a positive statement, and vice versa.

Now imagine hiring somebody because they happen to sit in the chair on the right side of your desk versus the one on the left side of your desk. That would be kind of a crazy way to decide who to hire, wouldn't it? And, of course, in addition to being patently unfair to the person who happened to be on "your wrong side," it also is a terrible way to make a talent management decision. Your chances of getting the best person have been reduced to a dice roll.

For the most part we have largely thought about bias from the standpoint of those incidents where people have a negative bias against somebody, which then has a destructive impact on that person's chances to be successful (e.g., a woman who doesn't get hired for a job because somebody has a negative gender bias about women). However, it is a much more complex situation.

These destructive uses of biases against a certain group (Q1 in figure 1.1) are the ones where we have focused most of our attention. We have, in fact, created laws to be sure that people are not discriminated against in this way. But they are not the only ways that bias plays out in our daily lives.

As odd as it may seem, there also are constructive uses of biases against certain groups (Q2 in figure 1.1). They can benefit us in many ways. We determine that people who have aggressive personality types might not be the best fit for a customer service job. Or that people who don't have certain technology skills and background won't be a good match for a job that requires computer proficiency. If we didn't have these filters, hiring would be almost oppressive, because we would start with a huge number of résumés and have to look at all of them more carefully than time might allow.

I know that many people would say those are "qualifications," and that looking for qualifications is not the same as having biases. In fact, qualifications are simply biases that we have agreed upon and codified. There are hundreds of examples of people who have performed in extraordinary ways who do not have the normal qualifications for their roles. If qualifications were the only measure of success, than college dropouts such as Steve Jobs and Bill Gates would still be unknown. However, understandably, we have determined that while there are occasional creative eccentrics like Jobs and Gates, it just doesn't make good sense to look at 150 résumés and not take education into account. So we use biases against the lack of those characteristics to "filter out" certain people who we might have determined are not a

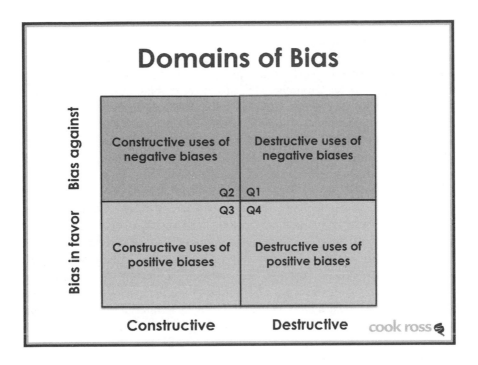

Figure 1.1.

good fit for the job. We do the same thing when we are in dangerous situations. For instance, we might be especially attentive to locking our car in a location with a higher crime rate.

All the same, it is important to note that we should be thoughtful and very conscious about how much we take these negative biases for granted. There are always exceptions, even to the most dependable of patterns (Jobs and Gates, for example!). So, while using negative biases can be helpful, we should never assume they are absolute. The annals of sport are filled with examples of players who were "too small to be successful" by "normal" standards. Yet they were able to succeed far beyond expectations. The same can be said for constructive uses of biases for a particular kind of person (Q3 in figure 1.1). We often look for certain circumstances or people because we have a history with them that tells us we can be more assured that they will meet our needs. People who have certain college degrees, or went to a certain college; certain personality types that fit a particular job or situation. Language skills, or any number of other "qualifications" that we have determined might make the person a better fit for the job. Once again, having these filters can be very helpful, but we have to be careful that we don't

develop blind spots that stop us from seeing exceptional people or circumstances that are "exceptions to the rule."

Finally, we also have to be mindful of the potentially destructive effects
of these "positive" biases (Q4 in figure 1.1). This can show up in several
different ways. For instance, we may place unrealistic expectations on somebody from a particular group because of a positive bias we have about "that
sort of people." I remember a Chinese student once telling me, "I'm so tired
of people expecting me to be good at math and sciences because I'm Asian.
It's just not my thing. I like the social sciences more. But everybody, from
my parents to my teachers seems to think I have to 'try harder' when my
math grades aren't straight As, even though I do really well in the courses
that matter to me."

Another way the potentially destructive effects of biases favoring a group
or person can show up is when one person suffers because we have a positive
bias toward somebody else. Imagine you are interviewing two candidates and
something about one of them reminds you of your sister. You may not even
realize it. It just occurs to you that "there is something about this person that I
like." As a result, you pay more attention to them, listen more carefully, and
are even warmer toward them in the interview. The interview goes great and
you want to hire the person. However, what may be lost in the "glow" of that
positive bias is that the other candidate never had a fair shot because of the
bias that you had in favor of the first person.

It would be great if we were totally conscious about every decision we
made and never used bias. However, such a thought is not only unrealistic,
but impossible. Our processing would slow to a near halt. The key is to
become more and more conscious about when our biases are serving our
greater objectives.

We develop biases toward people and behaviors all throughout our lives.
We learn that to relate in a particular way is "better" than another way, or
that we prefer people who act or look a particular way. We can sometimes
even develop patterns of behavior that work well enough for us in one domain that we unconscious and habitually use them in places where they do
not work nearly as well.

As an example, on May 5, 2013, the *Washington Post* reported:

> After they leave military service, veterans of the two wars (Iraq and Afghani-
> stan) have a 75 percent higher rate of fatal motor vehicle accidents than do
> civilians. Troops still in uniform have a higher risk of crashing their cars in the
> months immediately after returning from deployment than in the months im-
> mediately before. People who have had multiple tours in combat zones are at
> highest risk for traffic accidents.

This is obviously of great concern. The story went on to read:

The most common explanation is that troops bring back driving habits that were lifesaving in war zones but are dangerous on America's roads. They include racing through intersections, straddling lanes, swerving on bridges and, for some, not wearing seat belts because they hinder a rapid escape.[9]

This is one of the great challenges we have when our biases are unconscious. Without realizing it, we can apply the same behavior, or evaluation criteria that worked in one domain, and find that they are not at all helpful, or even tragic in another.

IS THERE ONLY ONE KIND OF BIAS?

Is bias basically something we have or don't have, or are there different kinds of biases? Amy Cuddy, an associate professor of business administration in the Negotiation, Organizations and Markets Unit at Harvard Business School; Susan Fiske, the Eugene Higgins professor of psychology and professor of public affairs at Princeton University; and Peter Glick, a professor of psychology at Lawrence University in Appleton, Wisconsin, studied these distinctions and created a valuable map for looking at the way we process bias.[10]

Cuddy, Fiske, and Glick were able to identify two distinct forms of bias. The first is bias based on warmth. In their terms, "our warmth scales have included good-natured, trustworthy, tolerant, friendly, and sincere."[11]

In short, do you consider the personal likeable? Is it somebody you feel comfortable being around? On the other hand, the second form is bias based on competence, which they classify as "capable, skillful, intelligent, and confident."[12] Looking at bias in this way can be very helpful. We may have inherent biases about groups of people, biases which are very strong, but are very different between the different groups. In extensive research, Cuddy, Fiske, and Glick found there were some groups people tended to respond to with a low degree of both warmth and competence (e.g., welfare recipients, homeless people, poor people, and Arabs). Others we may feel a high degree of warmth toward, but not see as very competent (e.g., the elderly and people with physical or mental disabilities). Still others we may see as very competent, but not feel very much warmth toward at all (e.g., Asians, rich people, and Jews). And finally, there are those for whom we feel a high level of warmth, and a high level of competence (e.g., housewives, Christians, middle-class Americans).[13] How we feel about each of these groups might yield very different behaviors.

Warmth seems to be the primary dimension in terms of how we respond to people. We are more likely to first emotionally respond to whether or not we like someone, and only secondarily respond to whether or not we believe they are competent. Cuddy and her study associates suggest this results in more active facilitation. They wrote that "perceived warmth predicts active behaviors: groups judged as warm elicit active facilitation (i.e., help), whereas those judged as lacking warmth elicit active harm (i.e., attack)."[14]

They also reported that "the competence dimension, being secondary (because it assesses others' capability to carry out intentions), predicts passive behaviors: groups judged as competent elicit passive facilitation (i.e., obligatory association, convenient cooperation), whereas those judged as lacking competence elicit passive harm (i.e., neglect, ignoring)."[15]

So the way the bias plays out may be very different, depending upon which dimension elicits a reaction from us. Consider whether you are dealing with somebody who is elderly, or has a physical disability, both types that tested in the high warmth, low competence dimension of the study. You may feel very warmly and loving toward them, but you may tend to treat them as being less competent than they are.

**Deb Dagit, Diversity Consultant and
former Chief Diversity Officer**

As a four-foot tall woman who either walks with a cane or uses a wheelchair, it is not unusual for people to express their surprise when they meet me.

I often find people intending to make sincere compliments that can be quite-off putting, like "When I first met you I was surprised to see that you were handicapped, but now I don't even think about you being a person with special needs." I would much prefer "person with a disability," which doesn't identify me *as* my disability. Others say things such as, "You must work for a really special company if they would hire someone like you in such a visible role." Some people continue to ask when I will be getting well enough to walk again, rather than be in my wheelchair.

Most people with disabilities consider their disability to be an important and valued aspect of their identity that does not need to be overlooked or forgotten in order to make us more acceptable and competent.

I remember leading a workshop for a client many years ago in St. Louis. We were conducting a three-day training in a hotel and had arranged to have several wheelchairs available for the participants to use at various times as they negotiated the hotel. Obviously, we were not pretending that this was the same as having a permanent disability, but we found that it could make a great impact upon people to consciously see what it was like to negotiate both the physical environment and being with people. One of the participants took the wheelchair overnight and called for room service for breakfast in the morning. The participant reported that when the room service waiter came with the food in the morning, he seemed visibly surprised to find somebody with a wheelchair in a room that was not handicap accessible. He proceeded to place the tray on the table, remove the chrome food cover, and started to cut the participant's food! The participant was stunned and asked the waiter what he was doing. The waiter said he was only trying to be of help. This example shows how we can feel very warmly toward people and still demonstrate behavior that is patronizing and demonstrates a judgment of less competence.

On the other hand, you may have enormous respect for someone's competence, thinking them extremely capable, and yet just not like them very much. This may result in a completely different kind of bias. You may not choose them to be on a team you are putting together to work on a project, or not invite them to lunches or other business gatherings, and in doing so affect their ability to be successful.

HOW RATIONAL ARE WE?

These findings also are important to consider as we think about our true orientation toward people versus the orientation that, especially in business environments, we sometimes believe we take. We like to think we are rational and that our emotions are secondary. This is not unusual in Western cultures. We have a long history of valuing the rational over the emotional. But, really, how rational are we?

Yale University law professor Daniel Kahan, along with psychologists Ellen Peters from Ohio State University, Erica Dawson from Cornell University, and Paul Slovic from the University of Oregon, decided to explore whether, for example, our politics might affect our ability to do something we consider very "rational" indeed: math problems.[16] Kahan gave more than one thousand participants in his study a tricky math problem to compute. In the first version, the question he posed involved the results of a clinical study of skin cream. Fifty-nine percent of the participants got the problem wrong.

Then he decided to add a more emotional component. He took the same numbers and framed them as a question about the effectiveness of laws against concealed handguns, a highly political and emotional issue. He and his colleagues found that "conservative Republicans were much less likely to correctly interpret data suggesting that a gun ban decreased crime in a city; for liberal Democrats, the exact opposite was true. The people who were normally best at mathematical reasoning, moreover, *were the most susceptible to getting the politically charged question wrong.*"[17]

We are trained to think we can talk people out of their points of view if we give them the right "evidence." But what this study demonstrated was that political biases distort our ability to reason logically. In the battle between emotion and rationality, emotion usually wins!

In a similar study, Brendan Nyhan, assistant professor of government at Dartmouth College, found that when voters are misinformed, factual information only makes them become more rigid in their point of view! Nyhan found these instances of facts making people more rigid:

- People who thought weapons of mass destruction were found in Iraq believed that misinformation even more strongly when they were shown a news story correcting that belief.
- People who thought George W. Bush banned all stem cell research kept thinking he did that even after they were shown an article saying that only some federally funded stem cell work was stopped.
- People who said the economy was the most important issue to them, and who disapproved of Barack Obama's economic record, were shown a graph of nonfarm employment over the prior year. It included a rising line that indicated about one million jobs were added. They were asked whether the number of people with jobs had gone up, down, or stayed about the same. Many, looking straight at the graph, said down. [18]

All of this might suggest that the age-old adage is true: "Never let the facts get in the way of a good story!"

A source of much of this thinking goes back almost twenty-five centuries to Plato. In one of his dialogues, the Phaedrus, Plato explained the way humans experienced the world through an allegory of a chariot. Describing love as "divine madness," Plato describes the charioteer driving a chariot pulled by two winged horses:

> First the charioteer of the human soul drives a pair, and secondly one of the horses is noble and of noble breed, but the other quite the opposite in breed and character. Therefore, in our case the driving is necessarily difficult and troublesome.

In this allegory, the charioteer represents our rational intellect, the part of our soul that must keep the horses, our passionate nature and our righteousness (extreme positive emotions) and our more lustful negative emotions in check. It is only when the charioteer is "in charge" that we can move forward toward enlightenment.

For 2,500 years, we have worshipped at the altar of the rational. Think about how embedded it is in our language. "Are you sure you're being rational about that? Aren't you being too emotional?"

However, as the study done by Cuddy and her associates suggests, we may be more governed by our emotions than we realize to be the case. In fact, the lack of awareness of that may get in the way of our ability to think as clearly as we might. The renowned neuroscientist, Antonio Damasio, discussed this in his book *Descartes' Error: Emotion, Reason and the Human Brain.*

In the book, Damasio described his encounter with a patient he called "Elliott." Elliott had a brain tumor removed that had caused ventromedial frontal lobe damage. The ventromedial prefrontal cortex is the part of the prefrontal cortex that processes risk and fear. It plays a major role in managing our emotional responses and decision making. Elliott, who had been a successful businessman and family man, was struggling. Despite the fact that he still registered very high intelligence (his IQ was in the ninety-seventh percentile), everything around him, his businesses, and his marriage, were failing. One would think that somebody without the pull of emotions would make very "rational" decisions. However, Elliott seemed to lack any motivation at all. Damasio wrote that "he was always controlled. Nowhere was there a sense of his own suffering, even though he was the protagonist. I never saw a tinge of emotion in my many hours of conversation with him: no sadness, no impatience, no frustration."

Damasio found that without access to his emotions, Elliott was incapable of making even the simplest of decisions. Each small decision seemed to take him forever. He took long periods of time to choose what to write with, whether or not to make an appointment, or decide where to eat lunch. He concluded that "Elliott emerged as a man with a normal intellect who was unable to decide properly, especially when the decision involved personal or social matters."

Damasio described Elliott as an "uninvolved spectator" in his own life. Once the emotional part of his brain had been disabled, he was virtually unable to make any decisions. [19]

We live with this inherent dichotomy between the rational decisions we think we are supposed to be making, and the real impact of our unconscious processing and our emotional reactions, which can remain under the surface, unobserved and, often, discounted. We want to think of ourselves as good people, but we still have these emotional impulses. This can create an enormous dissonance between what we think we see and evaluate and what's actually going on. In Freudian terms, the id, our instinctive impulses, react and feel one way, but our superego, our inner controller and manager, tries to keep them under control by burying them deep in our unconscious. We know, for example, that we are "not supposed to be biased," and so we convince ourselves that we are not, even sometimes in the face of evidence to the contrary.

In fact, one of the many remarkable contradictions we see in this research is that intelligent people with high self-esteem may be the most likely to develop blind spots about their biases. Philip Dodgson and Joanne Wood, both psychologists at the University of Waterloo, found that people with high self-esteem respond less to weaknesses than do people with low self-esteem. As a result they may be less likely to internalize negative thoughts or ideas about themselves. Not only that, but intelligent people often can rationalize their own bias as justified. The more sophisticated we are in coming up with explanations for our opinions, the more we see them as truth! [20]

In addition, the cultures we grow up in give us a particular set of standards and rules to live by, which inherently are defined by "not like them!" guidelines. Our standards become the foundation of our inner "book of rules," and others appear to us as simply wrong. Because our identities are formed around this ego identification, we see ourselves as "right" and the "other" as "wrong" or "flawed" in some way.

There is nothing wrong with this process. It is inherent in every human being, but it creates real mischief for us in understanding how we are responding to others because we are largely unaware of it. Let's now look at how the brain seems to make all of this happen.

Chapter Two

Thinking about Thinking

I'm entirely interested in people, and also other creatures and beings, but especially in people, and I tend to read them by emotional field more than anything. So I have a special interest in what they're thinking and who they are and who's hiding behind those eyes and how did he get there, and what's the story, really? —Alice Walker

Imagine you are walking down the street one morning, perhaps going to work. You walk past any number of people. And even though you are mostly lost in thought, certain people get your attention. The guy in the blue suit with the umbrella looks angry. The woman with the wire-rimmed glasses looks friendly. This person looks wealthy, another one poor. This person looks intelligent, that one, you're not so sure. Or perhaps you walk into a party alone. Who do you walk up to talk to, and why?

Check it out yourself the next time you are in a group of people. How long does it take before you start evaluating, judging, and classifying them as happy, sad, smart, dumb, attractive, unattractive, safe, dangerous? Do you make a quick judgment about their job? And how thoughtful are you when making these judgments? Our minds are filled with memories, conscious and unconscious, that we access to figure out the circumstances we find ourselves in.

In fact, this sort of thinking doesn't apply only to people, but to virtually anything we encounter. Stop for a moment and take a look around the room or place you are sitting in right now. Allow your eyes to focus on any inanimate object and see what memory comes up. Does the lamp remind you of one that was at your grandmother's house when you were growing up? Does the fire alarm remind you of fire drills in school? Does a picture on the wall remind you of one that was in a college dorm room? When was the last time you thought about any of those things? As it is, these memories are

17

stored in our unconscious. We are not thinking about them at all until something, or someone, jogs them into consciousness.

And there is something else to notice. What feelings do these memories bring up? Are they pleasant, happy, or warm ones? Or are they sad, upsetting, or even traumatic? Seeing those objects recalls both the memory and the feelings associated with those objects.

Over the course of our lives, we collect millions of memories, which get stored in both the conscious and unconscious parts of our brains. Some of them are pretty obvious and dependable, but most drift into an amalgamation of thoughts and feelings that are recessed in a sort of filing system in our brains. Circumstances we encounter can trigger those memories, often in ways that we're not aware of in full. These memories also get stitched together into a fabric that makes up our view of the "real" world. But how "real" is this world?

When I was young, we used to have "sock hops" after our junior high school basketball games. And in those days, we really did dance in socks so we wouldn't mess up the gym floor! Given that there were virtually no LGBT students who were "out," the boys would invariably line up on one side of the room and the girls on the other. It was almost always expected that the boys would ask the girls to dance, and so at some point you were expected to walk all the way across the gym floor, in front of all of your friends, and ask a girl to dance. If she said no, you had to walk all the way back, again, in front of all of your friends.

And on the whole walk back, what were you thinking? More often than not, it was something like "I'll never do *that* again!"

Flash forward twenty-five years. You are working for a company that is having an annual conference. You are asked to call an important community member to invite them to the event. You sit down at your desk and pick up the phone, and all of a sudden you feel a wave of nervousness sweep through you. The act of invitation has triggered a fear of rejection. It is almost like somebody entered your internal jukebox, hit "D7," and that song of fear began to play. Did you choose to feel a fear of rejection at that moment? Or did the fear of rejection simply "happen"?

These kinds of triggers are around us all of the time. A memory may be triggered, and we cannot say why it was triggered. I'm sure almost everybody reading this has had an incident when you were walking somewhere, driving a car or doing almost anything, and "out of nowhere" you start thinking about something you haven't thought about in a long time. Without our realizing it, something has jogged that memory. It might have been something that passed in our peripheral vision, or a smell or sound or bump in the road. Memories are constantly being triggered within us.

Here is one example of a seemingly "random" memory trigger. I was working out at the gym one morning and listening to my iPod. My iPod has more than 24,000 songs on it and sometimes I just put it on "shuffle" and songs will play at random. I might hear a song that I haven't heard in a few years. That was exactly what happened on this particular morning. A Neil Young song that I like came on; in fact, I even played it a second time. I listened to eight or nine more songs and then showered and dressed and got in my car. At the stoplight, I had a thought about a health food store that was a couple of miles down the road that my wife and I used to go to but that I hadn't been to in a good while. I decided to drive that way, not even remembering the store's name. When I pulled into the parking lot, I saw the store, which is named "Harvest Moon." Which happens to be the same name as the Neil Young song I played twice! Coincidence? I don't think so.

This is the way our minds work. Different things get linked together, along with all of the memories and feelings associated with those things. When we meet somebody and say, "There's something about that person that I like," that person is probably stimulating an old memory of somebody or something that was positive. If that memory link is to a negative stereotype that we have been exposed to in our past, the same applies.

Over the course of the past couple of decades, we have experienced an explosion in new research about the way our minds and brains work. The ability to use technology in new ways has permitted us not only to watch the brain in action in a more robust fashion than ever before, but also has allowed many more brains to be tested. This has helped us begin to understand the way we think in a much more acute way than ever before. And what we are seeing is anything but "logical."

As a diversity and human resources/management professional, my interest in this research is completely practical. How can we take what we have learned from the mind and use it to better understand our relationships and organizations, so that we can make more conscious decisions? What changes our behavior? One thing that feeds our predisposition to act unconsciously is our tendency to rush ahead before we truly understand what we are dealing with at that moment.

I like to use dieting as an example of behavior that is not always so well thought out because it is such an obvious one that applies to so many people. For years I struggled with my weight, fluctuating between gaining and losing as much as forty pounds. Even when I was heavy, I knew exactly what to do: eat less and exercise more. With the possible exception of a few people, that formula is pretty dependable. It wasn't until I looked behind the curtain, so to speak, that I began to understand *why I eat* (in my case, eating is related to stress and fatigue), that I had a chance to stick with a sensible weight-loss regimen.

To deal with an issue, we have to know what we are dealing with in the first place. So, let's talk about the real issues we deal with on a daily basis.

We have known for a long time that the world we see is shaped by our experience. In the simplest of terms, two people wander up to a snake. One says, "Cool! A snake!" The other immediately says (or feels), "Oh my God! I'm going to die!" The snake is no different, but each person's experience with the snake is obviously very different. And the background through which they see the snake shapes those experiences.

Throughout our lives, we are exposed to countless experiences, numerous teachings, and also certain paradigms that we have been told are "true." All of this makes up an ideological structure, a kind of internal "book of rules" through which we process the world we see. That book of rules can then both consciously and unconsciously influence our behavior, and in turn, what we experience. We develop a certain schema, which is a system through which we organize and perceive things that we encounter.

We all have schema. I play golf. If I am driving down the road past a row of trees, I only have to see about one square foot of a sand trap before I spot a golf course. If my wife or another person is in the car with me and they are not golfers, it's likely that they never will see it. Think of something similar that applies to you. Do you have a hobby or something you are particularly fascinated with or that you enjoy doing? Haven't you noticed how easily you spot things related to that when they occur around you?

Let me show you what I mean. Take a look at the picture on the following page. It was designed many years ago by Karl Dallenbach, one of the early pioneers of experimental psychology and the editor of the *American Journal of Psychology* for more than half a century. See if you can make out a discernible image.

Perhaps you saw something you recognize in the picture? Or maybe you did not. Now turn the page and look at the next image with the picture drawn in a way that is easier to see:

Can you see the cow? Now go back and look at the original picture. It is almost impossible to not see the cow, isn't it? Something that was invisible just minutes ago is now inescapably in your line of vision.

This experience is often referred to as perceptual organization, the ability of the mind to organize information around a common unifying idea. Once you have been shown that the cow is indeed there (by looking at the other picture), you can't not see it! Our brains are designed to organize around particular ideas, concepts, or variables that are important to, or known by us.

The same is true at work. Our professional skills focus our attention in similar ways. I remember a number of years ago I had a visit from my wife's brother. He happens to have a very successful house-painting business. I was telling him we were thinking of painting one of the rooms in the house and asked him a simple question. His response involved many more questions, questions I would never have thought to ask. What kind of paint? What kind of roller? To which I responded, "A paint roller!" Then there was the matter

Figure 2.1.

of how long to let the paint dry. How many coats? On and on. Knowing what questions to ask is often what gives us mastery. And that same body of distinctions can frame what we see or miss, and in doing so, can dramatically affect the nature of the way we see the world.

The more critical we perceive something to be part of our survival, the more we will automatically refer back to the instinctive ways of seeing that we have learned. My friend and colleague John Cruzat spent twenty years in the military, with most of those years spent in hostile environments. He can't help but scan rooftops, even as he walks down a perfectly safe street, because his war experience trained him to do that, even though it makes no real sense in the situation and environment he is in at present.

Still, when we are looking at those things that help shape our experiences and perceptions, what things are we *not* seeing?

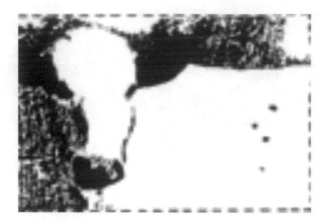

Figure 2.2.

If the job that we have can so easily shape our perception, how can the most fundamental identities that we live with throughout our lives, including our race, gender, sexual orientation, age, and so on, not do as much?

In real time, being able to make quick determinations about the people we encounter and the situations we are in is critical to our survival. It is built into the fundamental ways our brains function. Social identification is especially important because picking up social clues about the circumstances we are in not only helps us be successful, but more importantly, it keeps us safe.

However, in real life, what we think we see may not be clearly happening at all. Our perceptions, our memories, and our social judgments are all constructed by our unconscious mind from the limited information that we interpret through the expectations we have, the context that we see the situation in, and what we hope to get out of the situation.

So, what takes place in our minds when we observe a person or situation?

Often, our first mental reaction comes from the amygdala, the most primitive part of the brain, and, when looking at matters from an evolutionary standpoint, one of the oldest parts. There are two amygdalae in a normal human brain, each located within the temporal lobes. The amygdalae are a key part of our limbic system, which is a complex set of structures in the brain that control various important functions including emotion, long-term memory, and behavior. The amygdalae play a primary role in processing our emotional reactions, and they also are involved in beginning the process of linking those emotional reactions to memories.

Quite logically, the amygdala is especially sensitive to fear. I often like to think of the amygdala as a deer in the forest. If you have ever observed a deer in the wild, you notice that it is constantly scanning, highly sensitive to potential danger, and ready to respond accordingly. The amygdala has evolved in similar ways. As I noted earlier, from a survival standpoint alone, it makes sense for the amygdala to spot danger before pleasure. If something pleasurable is coming your way and you don't notice it, it is a nice surprise. Certainly no major harm is done. But if something dangerous is approaching and you don't notice it, you could end up dead! Something of that sort has a tendency to heighten the senses, doesn't it? The amygdala scans what we are seeing, hearing, smelling, tasting, or sensing with a particular sensitivity to circumstances or people that might be threatening. Some of these might be obvious to us, but overwhelmingly, they may be things that our conscious mind does not perceive.

We are exposed to as many as eleven million sensory triggers at any one time, yet we can only absorb about forty to fifty. We consciously notice a much smaller number than that, perhaps as few as seven. Given the immense number of stimuli we are exposed to at any one particular moment, how can we know what we are responding to?

As the amygdala picks up these signals, they get sent into a complext set of structures in the brain, which are generally referred to as the limbic system. The limbic system is responsible for a tremendous amount of our rapid, responsive and automatic functioning. The hippocampus, which will be discussed more at length later, processes the information, searches the 'database" of memories to identify the catalyzing person object, or circumstance and figure out what it is (e.g., gray hair/older). This happens so rapidly that it appears to be instantaneous. It keeps us walking, talking, and breathing, along with hundreds of other "automatic" responses that would almost paralyze us if we had to think about them every time we encountered a new environmental stimuli. The system determines the signifance of the occurrence and generates whatever emotions and motivational states it requires to respond. The hypothalamus then serves as a traffic control system, which sends signals through the cingulate gyrus and then the anterior cingulate cortex and tells the body how to respond. It is like a raging river of automaticity that helps us function on a minute-by-minute basis throughout our lives. Nobel Prize winner Daniel Kahneman called this System One Thinking. It is very instinctive, very fast, and often strongly driven by visceral, emotional responses.

This automatic response rapidly kicks our brain into reaction to whatever the amygdala senses. These almost instantaneous reactions are often drawn from past memories, and they provide us with the ability to respond and react quickly when necessary. For example, if somebody throws something at you, it is not the best time to stop and say, "Hmmm. What is the best thing for me to do in a situation like this?" If you do, the object could hit you. Instead, the anterior cingulate cortex sends a message to our nervous system that causes us to react to the potential threat and our hands fly up to protect ourselves, or we duck or dodge the object. Most people can probably remember the game of "flinch" that many of us played as children, in which one person would place their hands under another's and then either try to slap the other person's hands or pretend to do so. Remember how hard it was to stop the automatic impulse to pull one's hands away?

Our reaction to what we see is also strongly affected by the context in which we see it. Let me give you an example.

Now read the characters in figure 2.3 below:

So, is the middle character, a "B", or a "13"? Context determines whether it is a letter or a number. In fact, context determines almost everything we see.

Where bias is concerned, we usually see people in the context of the ideas we have developed about "those kind of people." One of the responses in this cycle that is especially central to our propensity toward bias is our tendency to sort people into "them" and "us" categories. This tendency has been documented for many years as the source of some of our most intense conflicts, whether it is in interpersonal relationships based on identity (gender, race, sexual orientation, etc.), or within countries (the North and the South in the American Civil War, Hutu versus Tutsi in Rwanda, Catholic versus Protes-

Figure 2.3.

Figure 2.4.

tant in Northern Ireland, etc.), by politics (Democrat versus Republican), by sports (Yankees/Red Sox or Michigan/Ohio State), and in countless other ways.

Our identities can easily become defined by our relationship with "the other," and our sensitivity to the feeling of "otherness" can change, depending upon the context we find ourselves in. An African American female attorney, working in a large law firm, may at one moment see herself as one of the lawyers when an issue arrives between the lawyers and the administrative staff, but then just as quickly react from her gender and racial identity when the dispute is between a white male lawyer and a black female executive assistant. We all have multiple identities through which we see the world at various different times, in various different ways.

**Allyson Robinson,
American Human Rights Activist**

I encounter bias on an almost daily basis. To the degree that people around me are aware that I am transgender, I am judged to be mentally unstable, morally corrupt, or just plain "weird." This becomes the primary, predominant lens through which some relate to me. Most people rely on negative stereotypes, misunderstandings, and misinformation. Gender dysphoria, the condition from which most transgender people suffer, is still poorly understood by the public despite the fact that physicians have been treating it successfully for over a century.

These biases lead to shockingly high rates of unemployment and poverty among transgender people in America, twice the rate of unemployment as our fellow citizens. Yet we are almost twice as likely to hold a bachelor's degree. This means that hiring managers are uncritically ruling out highly qualified transgender candidates—and their businesses pay the price of that bias.

Even among those who are well intentioned, unconscious bias expresses itself. When someone who never knew me as a male slips and uses a male pronoun to describe me, that pronoun opens a window into his or her thinking about me. Conversely, when someone to whom I've just disclosed my transgender status responds with, "I never would have known if you hadn't told me," he may feel as if he's paying me a compliment. In reality, they're telling me they expect people like me to fall short of their standard for womanhood or manhood.

As a general rule, we are more attentive to our identity and the feeling of otherness when we are in a nondominant group. It is worth noting, for instance, that the people who committed the horrid acts on September 11, 2001, are generally referred to as "Arab" or "Muslim" terrorists. Yet Timothy McVeigh and Terry Nichols, the two U.S.-born, white, Christian men who were convicted of the 1995 bombing in Oklahoma City, are rarely referred to as "white male" or "Christian" terrorists.

This phenomenon can even affect our own perception of our identity. Depending upon the circumstance we are in, our group identity may be more or less present to us. Let me describe a personal example.

My wife and business partner, Leslie, and I were recently asked to conduct a half-day workshop for an annual gathering of a group of Muslim leaders from the United States and the United Kingdom. The group's mission statement says it is "dedicated to promoting social integration and mobility." The group of nearly one hundred people included a member of the British Parliament, a top official from Al Jazeera, imams, academics and business leaders, and many other people representing various professions.

There is nothing unusual about my being asked to lead a half-day workshop on unconscious bias; after all, it's what I do for a living. It's why I am writing this book. I've conducted thousands of workshops during my career, but in the days approaching this particular workshop I noticed there was something different going on in my internal conversation about this one.

What bugged me was that I couldn't stop being concerned about how they would react to the fact that I am Jewish.

Now, I've been Jewish since the day I was born, and I have definitely been Jewish since I began my career. And I can't remember ever before having it be something I was consciously thinking about when going into a workshop. The circumstances, the context shifted my perception. I ended up sharing this very insight with the group and the session ended up going very well.

This tendency to determine quickly "us" and "them" is foundational to our survival, as I have discussed earlier. Knowing whether "they" are one of "us" keeps us safe. We, quite logically, are likely to be more positively disposed toward people who we feel safer around, and more negatively disposed to those we don't. However, those we identify with as "us" or who we see as "them" may be subject to very fluid interpretations because all of us have any number of different identities. I am a man, I am Jewish, I am white, I am of a certain generational group, and so on. My colleague Dan Egol, who is of mixed race, describes such fluid interpretation this way:

> For people who are of mixed race or multiracial/ethnic, that can complicate the way we experience otherness. Our physical representation may not coincide with how we identify and how people view us may not match how we identify. We may not have an "other" or everyone may be the other, depending on the situation. For example, when I am walking around Columbia Heights—a predominantly Latino/African American neighborhood in Washington, D.C., I "pass" as white and know physically how I come across since I am light-skinned. People who don't know me can mistake me for a white person based on my appearance, but I prefer to be in Columbia Heights because the Spanish language and culture is very comforting to me. There is a disconnect between how I relate to the space and how people see me as a racial outsider. The "us/them" paradigm gets complicated because my physical traits betray my cultural connection to the community. While I see myself as similar to the majority community, I doubt I am ever seen that way by that same majority community.

Regardless of what situation we are in, the tendency toward the "us versus them" way of seeing the world is strong within us. In fact, researchers have discovered that this tendency begins early in life.

Neha Mahajan, a psychologist at Temple University, and Karen Wynn, professor of psychology and cognitive science at Yale University and director of Yale's infant cognition laboratory, have studied the development of this "us/them" phenomena in relation to young children.[1] Mahajan and Wynn chose thirty-two babies, all of them just under one year of age. The researchers gave the babies a choice between three foods, Cheerios in one bowl, or graham crackers or green beans in another. They noted which snack each baby preferred.

The babies were then shown two researcher-controlled puppets that were given the same food choices the babies had been given and were simulated to appear as if they were making a choice between the foods. Finally, when the infants were given a choice between the two puppets, twenty-seven of the thirty-two babies chose the puppets that had made choices similar to what the babies had picked. Even at this early age, we have developed the capacity to identify "us." In fact, in other studies, Wynn was able to see that children have a sense of a moral code, identifying "right" and "wrong" when they were as young as five months old. Other researchers from the United States, the United Kingdom, and China have demonstrated that babies demonstrate preference for people of their own race when they are as little as three months old![2] Wynn and her team conducted an even more remarkable second experiment. They took the puppets the babies had chosen and those that weren't and play acted that each of them was treated either well or not by another set of puppets. The babies were then offered a choice between the second set of puppets. They chose the puppets that treated the one they had earlier associated with more positively, and also the ones that treated the ones that they had earlier rejected more harshly!

They were demonstrating bias against the "other" and they were not even a year old!

This tendency toward "us versus them" creates the phenomena we call xenophobia, a fear of "the other" that we see, for example, strongly represented in the anti-immigrant feelings that have emerged in the past few years.

This is not to say we are born without the facility for empathy. On the contrary, we have the capacity to feel so closely aligned with people that we can almost feel their pain or sadness in our bodies. Most of us have had the instant reaction to seeing somebody have an accident, either in person or while watching a movie or television show. We can feel the reaction in our body, a visceral flinching as if we were feeling the pain ourselves.

We know that something similar happens when we see very young babies relate to their parents. There is a natural tendency for the babies to imitate parental behavior, to "mirror" the actions that they see. The Austrian Nobel Prize–winning zoologist Konrad Lorenz was one of the cofounders of the field of ethology, which is the biology of behavior. Lorenz was particularly interested in studying how animals began to develop their identities and their way of being "imprinted" to their parents upon birth. Lorenz famously showed this in various experiments. One of the best known involved Lorenz substituting himself for the parents of goslings upon their hatching. He found that they related to him as their parent throughout their lives.

But if connecting to "our people" is so important, how do we connect so deeply with others? The answer may lie in a discovery that occurred in Parma, Italy, in the late 1980s.

Five University of Parma neurophysiologists, Giacomo Rizzolatti, Giuseppe Di Pellegrino, Luciano Fadiga, Leonardo Fogassi, and Vittorio Gallese, were observing a group of macaque monkeys to attempt to understand how certain neurons controlled hand and mouth movements. Food was placed close enough to the monkeys so that they could reach for it. Electrodes tracked the ventral premotor cortex of the monkey's brains so the scientists could observe how the brain responded when the monkey picked up the food. However, something unexpected changed the focus of the experiment.

One of the researchers casually reached into the bowl of peanuts that had been placed in front of the monkey and took one. Suddenly, and completely unexpectedly, the tracking system began to record signals from neurons that were identical to those it tracked when the monkeys were eating the peanuts themselves! The researchers called these "mirror neurons."

The discovery has been somewhat controversial in the twenty years since it was published, but many people have begun to see in it as a doorway to our understanding of human empathy. V. S. Ramachandran, director of the Center for Brain and Cognition at the University of San Diego, has become one of the strongest scientific advocates of the importance of this discovery to our understanding of empathy. He has called mirror neurons "the basis of civilization," because they may explain why it is that we feel such a deep connection and both physical and emotional reaction to the experience of others, and in particular, pain. He also has suggested that an understanding of mirror neurons may provide a window into our understanding of human self-awareness.[3]

Others have attributed this capacity to a phenomenon that has its roots in the philosophical debates of René Descartes and others and is called "theory of mind." Theory of mind is the ability to attribute beliefs, intentions, wants, and knowledge to others, and to understand when others have beliefs that are the same or different from our own. While empathy and theory of mind are often used interchangeably, it is unclear whether these are exactly equivalent because theory of mind seems to be more of a function of the brain's temporal lobe and the prefrontal cortex, and empathy relies more on the sensorimotor cortices as well as the limbic system. Nonetheless, both speak to the ability to sense the feelings, needs, and circumstances of others. It appears that most people have some capacity for theory of mind and, interestingly, women seem to have a stronger capacity for it, on the whole, than men.

Still, there are other times when we may feel so distant from that experienced by people, even those to whom we are the closest. It seems that our brains may be selective in their ability to be empathetic, depending upon whether we see another person as "them" or "us." Xiaojing Xu, Xiangyu Zuo, Xiaoying Wang, and Shihui Han, researchers in psychology and radiology at Peking University, found that the empathetic neural responses in the anterior cingulate cortex decreased significantly when participants viewed faces of other races.[4]

Mina Cikara, assistant professor of social and decision sciences at Carnegie Mellon University, Emile Bruneau, a postdoctoral fellow with the Social Cognitive Neuroscience Laboratory at the Massachusetts Institute of Technology (MIT), and Rebecca Saxe, associate professor of cognitive neuroscience at MIT, have written that "these tendencies to care about and help one another form the foundation of human society. When the target is an out-group member, however, people may have powerful motivations not to care about or help 'the other.'" They went on to say that "out-group member suffering elicits dampened empathetic responses as compared to in-group members' suffering." They even suggested that when faced with out-group suffering, people may feel Schadenfreude, or pleasure gained from another's pain.[5]

Why is this so important? Most everyone feels empathy for someone in their life. In fact, a complete lack of empathy makes it very difficult for us to live together in a civilized society. People without any capacity for empathy are often quite incapacitated socially, if not outright dangerous. But what if it is harder for us to feel empathy for those who are not like us? That doesn't bode well for us to establish connection with each other in an increasingly diverse world.

We might ask then, why is it so important for us to be connected to others? In 1943, Abraham Maslow explored this notion when he published his now historic paper, "A Theory of Human Motivation."[6] Maslow's model, which has been familiarly referred to as "Maslow's Hierarchy," suggests there are five levels of needs that human beings strive for, and that it is difficult, if not impossible, for us to achieve one level without being satisfied that the one before it has been achieved.

The first, or bottom level in Maslow's model, generally depicted as a triangle or pyramid, refers to our "physiological" needs: breathing, food, water, sleep, sex, and the like. The second is "safety": resources, physical security, a way to make a living, health, a place to live, and the like. The third is "belonging": a sense of connection to community, family, friendship, and love. The fourth is "esteem": a sense of confidence, self-esteem, respect from others, and a sense of achievement. Finally the fifth, and uppermost on the pyramid, is "self-actualization," which Maslow describes as including creativity, problem solving, empathy, and morality, among other "higher" forms of consciousness.

Maslow's model has been the foundation for much of psychology for more than seven decades since its inception. My guess is that most readers have heard of it, even though you may not know all of its details. However, it has not gone without challenge. There have been many, including Geert Hofstede, professor emeritus of organizational anthropology and international management at the University of Maastricht in the Netherlands, and a pioneer in the study of cross-cultural interaction, who have suggested that Maslow's model may shift from culture to culture depending upon the particular social norms and memes of the culture that a person is raised in. Others have disagreed about where certain of the characteristics might fall within the model.

However, recent research has indicated that for as much as Maslow's model has contributed, he may have missed the most fundamental fact: that our primary need is what I briefly discussed earlier, the idea that is often called "belongingness."

Naomi Eisenberger, an associate professor of psychology at the University of California, Los Angeles (UCLA), Matthew Lieberman, professor and laboratory director of social cognitive neuroscience at UCLA, and Kipling Williams, professor of psychological sciences at Purdue University, have gone so far as to take this question into the study of brain functioning. By studying brain imaging in test subjects who were participating in social activities and then excluded, the researchers found that social exclusion triggers activity in the same region of the brain associated with physical pain.[7]

This primacy of belongingness has been explored for a long time. Harry Harlow, a University of Wisconsin psychologist who worked with Maslow for a time, conducted a series of studies with rhesus monkeys in the 1950s, in which he presented two different kinds of surrogate "mothers" to see how baby monkeys would react with each "mother." One was a cloth surrogate made to look and feel like a rhesus monkey, with cloth fur. The other was made of wire mesh but was constructed in such a way so as to feed the babies with a bottle. Overwhelmingly, he found the babies preferred being with the cloth monkeys. He suggested that the need for social closeness is primary.

Edward Tronick, the university distinguished professor of psychology at the University of Massachusetts in Boston, demonstrated this when he conducted what he called the "Still Face Experiment." Tronick set up a situation in which parents were videotaped interacting with their children in normal ways, including talking, laughing, and playing. At some point the parent was asked to freeze their facial expression and not react to the child. The reaction on the part of the infant is almost immediate. The babies looked initially confused, then tried to do whatever they could to get a reaction from the parent, finally getting more and more upset. Tronick said "what's really striking about the still face experiment is that the infants don't stop trying to get the parents' attention back. They'll go through repeated cycles where they try to elicit attention, fail, turn away, sad and disengaged, then they turn back and try again. When it goes on long enough, you see infants lose postural control and actually collapse in the car seat." The children also demonstrated physiological changes, for example, increase in the stress-inducing hormone cortisol and increased heart rate.[8]

Studies aside, there is logic to all of this research. Think of the most vulnerable time in a human being's existence: birth. Newborn human babies need contact with their parents or some caretaker longer than most species on the planet. We are not like zebras who jump up and walk within minutes of being born. When my granddaughter, Audrey, was born just a few months ago, she was completely incapable of surviving, *unless she belonged to somebody who would care for her most basic needs.*

We see signs of the primacy of belongingness all around us, if we look hard enough. Parents who sacrifice their own needs for their children. Soldiers who throw themselves on grenades to save their comrades. People who put themselves at great risk, in Nazi Germany and other places, to save innocent lives. There is a strain of altruism that runs deep in us.

Part of what has us so drawn to this identification with others is a desire to be part of the particular groups with which we identify. This desire to fit in, to identify ourselves by the group that we are a part of, leads to all kinds of seemingly "irrational" human behavior. It can be a positive force when it involves people joining together to put their own needs aside, as in the case of tens of thousands of Americans who gave to the Haiti earthquake relief fund, even as our own recession was hitting full bottom in 2010. Or it can be a negative force when "good" people go along with, or refuse to stop genocidal behavior in Nazi Germany, Rwanda, and other places. We seemingly are social beings by our nature.

This tendency to be drawn to those whom we identify with the most has been called "homophily," a term created by sociologists in the 1950s that loosely translates as "love of the same."

So we are forever in a tug of war between our tendency toward "us versus them" and xenophobia, and our mirror capacity for empathy or homophily.

We do, of course, as humans, have the ability to consciously make decisions that are less instinctive and more "thoughtful." Many of these decisions occur in our prefrontal neocortex, perhaps the "newest" part of our brain, at least when viewed on an evolutionary level. The prefrontal neocortex is where our higher functioning thoughts tend to manifest. For example, our deeper reasoning capacity, our ability to formulate and use language, our sensory perceptions, and our more conscious thinking take place in the prefrontal neocortex. Kahneman referred to the activity that takes place here as System Two Thinking, or the slow brain.

All mammals have some capacity for prefrontal neocortex thinking, but on the whole, humans seem to have dramatically greater capacity for this kind of thinking than almost any other mammal. For example, humans possess at least twice as much of this thinking as chimpanzees. The prefrontal neocortex also gives us the capacity for metacognition, the ability to think about thinking. As humans, we have the ability to have thoughts like, "What made me think about that?" A rather unremarkable thought for a human, but one that is not nearly as common in other animals.

Consider, for instance, when you put your dog outside and it then sees a squirrel. Do you get a sense that it says to itself, "Should I chase the squirrel?" Probably not, eh? More likely the dog reacts and goes into instinctive hunting mode. Of course, we as humans can do the same thing at times, but we are far more likely than other mammals to first consider our actions.

Of course, it takes far more energy to think consciously; more blood flow, more glucose, and so on. That is why sitting in contemplation or working hard at thinking, studying, or solving a problem can be so tiring. Think about the times you have sat around a library in a comfortable chair without much physical exertion and still left feeling as exhausted as if you had been exercising at a high rate of intensity.

As a result, our capacity for our more "conscious," or "slow brain" activity is dramatically less than our automatic "fast brain" reactions. It is probably hundreds of thousands of times as active. We might use the metaphor of a sea mammal, or perhaps a whale. The whale largely lives under the water, but every once in a while it needs to surface for air. During that time, it might catch a quick glimpse of the world above the water before it quickly goes under again. Similarly, most of our thinking is automatic.

We have the capacity to develop biases and blind spots in both ways of thinking, yet our capacity to "see ourselves in action" almost always occurs in the prefrontal neocortex. This occurs when we slow down and can *really* observe ourselves.

We can easily see how having an experience that we have had before would create a rapid response. For example, if you touch a hot stove and get burned, it is likely that you might be hesitant and especially careful the next time you are near a hot stove. However, new research seems to suggest that our brains are much more proactive. We unconsciously extrapolate from one experience to others that, for whatever reason, our brains think are similar.

At Columbia University, Elliott Wimmer, a postgraduate doctoral scholar, and Daphna Shohamy, an associate professor of psychology, study the cognitive neuroscience of learning, memory, and decision making. They have recently shed new light on how the brain makes these associations.

Wimmer and Shohamy scanned the brain and found that a big factor in this phenomenon is the hippocampus, another part of the limbic system, which is connected to the amygdala. It has been known for quite some time that the hippocampus helps consolidate information from short-term to long-term memory. But Wimmer and Shohamy found something else that explains many of our reactions.[9]

As we experience life, we are constantly being put into positions where we must make choices between things that we have never experienced before. Many times we don't even hesitate in making these kinds of decisions. Wimmer and Shohamy found that not only does the hippocampus help us make decisions about things that we have been exposed to, but that it also "enables the spread of values across memories."[10]

While using functional brain scans to watch the brain in action, they gave their test subjects monetary rewards for certain behaviors. These rewards led to a predictable activation of related memories. However, they also found that the hippocampus then made association with other behaviors or activities that had not been rewarded but were stored in the memory base. When offered an opportunity for choice, the test subjects were biased toward selecting items they had not been rewarded for, but that the hippocampus had somehow associated with those for which they had received rewards.

To better understand this phenomenon, let's put it in a normal experience. Let's say I am walking down the street and a man wearing a bright yellow windbreaker is coming in the opposite direction. As we approach each other, he suddenly punches me in the stomach and hits me in the back of the head, grabs my wallet, and runs away. I recover and move on. Weeks later I am driving in my car and out of the corner of my eye I notice a person walking on the street wearing a yellow windbreaker and all of a sudden I feel a sense of danger. I may not have consciously noticed the person, just captured him in my peripheral vision, but the connection is made, and the memory, with its associated feelings, is transferred.

Put the same dynamic is a business meeting. I was born in 1951. I grew up in what we might call the *Leave It to Beaver* era. I'm sure that most people reading this remember the sitcoms of the 1960s and beyond, including *Father Knows Best*, *Ozzie and Harriet*, all of them similar to each other. Father left in the morning for work, leaving mother at home with the children and the household duties. Then he came home at the end of the day to solve the family's problems. In the mind of somebody from that era, it is not hard to imagine a conscious or unconscious link between women and domestic chores.

Now let's move on to a modern business meeting. Several men gather for the meeting and then a woman enters the room. Without thinking one of the men says, "Hey Margaret, do you know if there is any coffee around here?" Without anyone even thinking about it, Margaret has become June Cleaver from *Leave It to Beaver*.

Our brains are constantly searching to understand what we see and to predict what we can expect. Once again, this makes perfect sense from a survival standpoint. The more predictable things are, the easier it is to defend ourselves, or to be successful. Lars Muckli, a psychologist at the Institute of Neuroscience and Psychology at the University of Glasgow, calls these "cortical predictions." The brain takes in information, considers the context, references learned associations, and then predicts what to expect. Muckli has written that "we are continuously anticipating what we will see, hear, or feel next. If parts of an image are obstructed we still have precise expectation of what the whole object will look like."[11]

This transference of memories creates what Jeff Hawkins, the founder of Palm Computing and Handspring, calls a memory-prediction framework. He believes that the neocortex connects with the hippocampus and the thalamus, which regulates consciousness and alertness, and matches what is being seen to what has been seen before in order to predict what it will mean for the future.[12]

This thinking can be demonstrated very easily. Fill in these sentences:

- Winston tastes _____ .
- I wish I were a(n) _____ .
- Melts in your mouth, _____ .
- You're in good hands _____ .
- Double your pleasure, double your fun with _____ .
- Like a good neighbor _____ .

If you grew up in the United States, you may not have gotten all of them, but my guess is that you got most of them, even though we haven't heard these phrases in years. The lines could easily have been intended to read:

- Winston tastes his soup and it is way too salty!
- I wish I were an eagle so that I could soar high in the air.
- Melts in your mouth, so you don't need a napkin.
- You're in good hands, so you can relax now.
- Double your pleasure, double your fun by staying two weeks at our resort instead of just one!
- Like a good neighbor, John picked up my trash can when it got blown over by the storm.

Is that what you thought? I doubt it. More likely you thought things should read as follows:

- Winston tastes good like a cigarette should.
- I wish I were an Oscar Mayer wiener.
- Melts in your mouth, not in your hands.
- You're in good hands with Allstate.
- Double your pleasure, double your fun with (clap, clap) Doublemint gum.
- Like a good neighbor, State Farm is there.

Or we can demonstrate the same dynamic visually. Look at the image on the next page.

Do you see the white square? Is it really there? Or is your mind assuming and expecting it to be there?

People say or do things and we are constantly "filling in the blank." As soon as they look at us, or start talking, we fill in the blanks. We also fill in the blanks based on expectations we have about "people like them." As Sukhvinder Singh Obhi, an associate professor in the Department of Psychology, Nueroscience, and Behavior at McMaster University says, "Our brains seem to have evolved to be good enough, most of the time."

This is why stereotyping is such a powerful phenomena. Before we ever have a rational thought, our brain is already starting to fill in the blanks about "that kind of person." We also, of course, relate to the people in question in a way that supports our fundamental sense of identity. Our minds want the world to reaffirm that which we already believe is true, consciously or unconsciously.

Consider, for example, that you are somebody who puts a lot of energy into calling people on their birthday. Imagine, then, that somebody you're close to forgets to call you on your birthday. What do you make it to mean? Do they not love you as much? Or do you sometimes forget people's birthdays yourself? In that case, you might not take such an omission to mean much at all.

One aspect of how this plays out is projection, a psychological defense mechanism first identified by Sigmund Freud. As a way of learning to cope

Figure 2.5.

with situations and maintain our sense of self, we often unconsciously project onto other people that which affirms what we believe to be true, either about them or ourselves. For instance, it is not unusual for somebody who believes that certain people do not like "people like me" to see behavior as negative toward them, even when that framing is different from the intent of others.

In a way, all of this makes perfect sense. If I have been led to believe, whether by a narrative that I have been exposed to or by personal experience, that Muslims do not like Jews, then I project that narrative onto the group *before they ever have a chance to interact with me.* I may then gather evidence to support that point of view by interpreting relatively benign behaviors (e.g., taking a chair I was planning on sitting in or not sitting next to me at lunch) as evidence of the very thing I believed to be true.

As a defense mechanism it makes a lot of sense. Once again, "better safe than sorry." All the same, that kind of thinking can obviously make interactions between people highly problematic. Some behavior like this is perfectly normal and healthy, but at times, especially when we are strongly emotionally threatened, our amygdalae can get "hijacked" and lead us to engage in ways that are destructive.

According to Freud, this happens because of the fundamental structure of the mind. In his model, every normal human being has a personality structure that is made up of three basic parts, of which we are all familiar: the id, the ego, and the superego. The id is our more impulsive, emotional function. The id does not have much in the way of values and standards, but much more in the way of wants and needs. It wants what it wants when it wants it, and it wants it *right now!*

The superego is the civilizing facet of the personality structure, which "controls" the id through various reminders of the book of rules that we have picked up during our life. "You should be nice to people." "You should work harder." "You didn't do that right." "You are being lazy!" All of these admonitions are internalized voices from our parents, our teachers, our religion, or other societal lessons that remind the "inner child" to behave.

For most people, the superego is very active. Think about your own inner thoughts. How many of them are constantly self-correcting? "Be careful about what you say in the meeting?" "Did you get it right?" "Don't let them know *that* about you!"

The ego somehow has to manage the often-conflicting interaction between these two "voices." We even speak about this when we say we "are of two minds." Where bias is concerned, our superego may know that we should treat each other fairly, but our id just likes those other people better, or feels more comfortable with them, more trusting of them, or feels like they are more competent.

Freud, of course, famously felt that the conscious aspect of the ego was like the tip of the iceberg, and the unconscious the larger part underneath.

However, more current research suggests that thought overstates our natural capability for consciousness. Our conscious may be more like a snowball on the tip of the iceberg! And when the ego cannot mediate successfully between the id and the superego, it can be a source of great anxiety for us, so we find a way to justify it. We'll often do this by developing a narrative that makes sense to us (e.g., "It's not bias against women that has me not wanting her to be my boss. I have no problem with women as leaders; it's just that she's not very competent!").

Projection occurs when we project the impulse or thoughts that we have about ourselves onto others (e.g., people who do not trust others will likely assume that others also do not trust others). People who steal are likely to assume that others have the capability of stealing. People who are dishonest will assume that others are lying. Or, in terms of diversity, people may say "it's not that I don't like them, they don't like us!" Such feelings are much more palatable and allow us to feel okay about ourselves while still safely keeping the "us" versus "them" dynamic firmly in place. For example, if you have been taught that racism is bad, and yet your id is uncomfortable with people of a different race, you may project all kinds of insidious motives onto them that justify your feelings.

This same phenomenon can occur when we have self-critical thoughts. For instance, a woman growing up in a society that tells her in any number of ways that she does not belong in a work environment as much as a man does may unconsciously be harder on other women she works with, and may also undermine her own performance by downplaying her abilities, *even though on a conscious level she desires to succeed.*

All of this can and will likely get triggered when we are afraid, because fear is such a primal emotion. When we are afraid, our amygdala takes over. On a physical level, the amygdala consumes most of the energy, effectively slowing down the ability of the prefrontal neocortex to act. Most of us have had experiences of this in the extreme when panic has set in, either in you or someone else. It is difficult, if not impossible, to make a thoughtful decision from that place. We react, pure and simple.

For most people, that reaction occurs through what we might call automatic fixations, behaviors that become habitually developed over time that we don't realize we are engaging in. In my experience these fixations occur in three major domains: projecting a particular image, or "looking good" at whatever I'm doing; taking a particular ideological point of view, or "being right"; or doing what I need to do to make myself physically and emotionally more comfortable.

It doesn't take much observation to see these patterns in others. Think of someone you know who shows off a lot (image), or stubbornly holds onto a point of view even in the face of vast evidence to the contrary (ideological), or simply removes themselves from an upsetting situation rather than trying to deal with it (comfort).

When we look at the ways the brain and the mind seem to work, we easily can be drawn into the ultimate existential question: Do we have free will? I am not going to try to answer that here, but suffice it to say, even if we have it, we use it very rarely. The behaviors I have been discussing are at best barely conscious. We seem to be far more robotic than we have ever imagined, and, as I discussed in the previous chapter, the more intelligent we are, the more likely we are to be able to convince ourselves that we are being "rational" when we are being driven by our more visceral impulses.

We all do it. The real question is whether we have the capability of doing anything about it. I'll address that question later in the book, but for now, let's look at how some of these dynamics can play out on a daily basis.

Chapter Three

The Many Faces of Bias

Our normal waking consciousness, rational consciousness as we call it, is but one special type of consciousness, whilst all about it, parted from it by the filmiest of screens, there lie potential forms of consciousness entirely different. We may go through life without suspecting their existence; but apply the requisite stimulus, and at a touch they are there in all their completeness. . . . No account of the universe in its totality can be final which leaves these other forms of consciousness quite disregarded. How to regard them is the question. . . . At any rate, they forbid our premature closing of accounts with reality. —William James, American philosopher and psychologist*

Many people are familiar with one of the most famous of all of the research studies ever conducted regarding how we pay attention to what appears to be right in front of us. Or not. Even if a gorilla is in the picture.

In the experiment, which was first performed in 1999 by Daniel Simons, a professor of psychology with the Beckman Institute for Advanced Science and Technology at the University of Illinois, Urbana, and Christopher Chabris, associate professor of psychology and codirector of the neuroscience program at Union College,[1] study participants were shown a video of two groups of students playing catch with a basketball. One of the "teams" is wearing white and the other is in black. Viewers were asked to count the number of times the team in white catches the basketball as they pass the ball among themselves. However, while the teams were weaving in and out, a person in a gorilla suit walked through the middle, turned and faced the camera, pounded on its costume chest, and then moved off screen. The incredible thing about the experiment is that about half of the video viewers were so focused on the task of counting the passes *that they never saw the gorilla!* Since 1999, the experiment's results have been replicated dozens of times by researchers all over the world. The results illustrate a classic example of the first of ten ways the unconscious mind filters our world. I'll discuss all ten in this chapter.

It is important to note that these patterns of how the unconscious mind affects our worldview are distinct in terms of the specific ways they affect our decisions and shape our view of the world. Yet, at the same time they also are interconnected patterns. We might want to think of them as various windows into the same mind. As you read through the descriptions, don't worry about memorizing them or struggling to figure out which is which and which is not. Instead, I recommend that you focus on the various ways they might show up in your life.

Selective attention, sometimes also known as *inattentional blindness*, is a mental process through which we selectively see some things but not others, depending upon our point of focus, or what we happen to be focusing on at a particular time. We are all very familiar with this pattern, even if we have never heard it described by name. Perhaps you were pregnant and suddenly noticed you were seeing pregnant women everywhere? Or you were considering buying a particular car, and it seemed as if you saw cars like it, or advertisements for them, all over the place. Our consciousness opens up to, and spots things, that are "on our mind" and may miss others even if they are right in front of our face. Just like that wandering gorilla.

Selective attention is helpful to us, and important to maintaining our ability to function in a world in which we are constantly being bombarded with stimuli. Almost everyone who has some kind of specialized job or hobby uses this framing structure to work more effectively. My editor notices typos or punctuation errors more easily than I do because her brain is "trained" by her experience to catch these items. Police officers spot potential criminal behavior in the midst of a crowd of thousands because their brains pick up on small behavioral traits that they have come to recognize as those related to criminals.

However, inattentional blindness also can cause us to miss things that are right in front of our faces. When we see things like this happen in lab experiments that include interloping gorillas, they are amusing. But what about when they take place in situations bearing potential life and death consequences (even if the smartest people possible are involved)?

Trafton Drew is an attention researcher at Harvard University Medical School who took the gorilla experiment to a whole new level.[2] Drew decided to check if the inattentional blindness effect would be true when it involved people who were extremely intelligent and highly trained in observation. He developed a research protocol in which he superimposed a small picture of somebody in a gorilla suit shaking its fist into a lung X-ray (see figure on the following page). The gorilla was roughly the size of a book of matches or *forty-eight times larger than an average cancer nodule*!

One would think, or hope, that doctors who have been rigorously trained to view the details of a lung scan, especially given the fact that people's lives could be on the line, would easily spot a picture of a gorilla superimposed on it. Shockingly, that was not the case. In fact, 83 percent of the radiologists did not notice the gorilla when they examined the scan to look for cancer nodules![3] The problem was not that they couldn't see the gorilla. It was right in front of their eyes. The problem was that their brains did not register what their eyes were seeing. Their minds were so focused on looking at cancer nodules that something as seemingly obvious as a picture of a gorilla, albeit in an entirely unfamiliar context, was essentially invisible!

Selective attention/inattentional blindness also accounts for why certain diversity-related behaviors might be obvious to some people and completely invisible to others. If you are a woman, for example, you may become sensitive to certain micro-behaviors that can affect a woman's success in the workplace. For instance, when you and a male colleague are interviewing a potential new hire, does the candidate seem to direct most of their answers to your male colleague? When you are in business meetings, do you tend to notice that when women offer comments or ideas, those comments or ideas are often ignored by most everyone in the meeting? But when a man makes

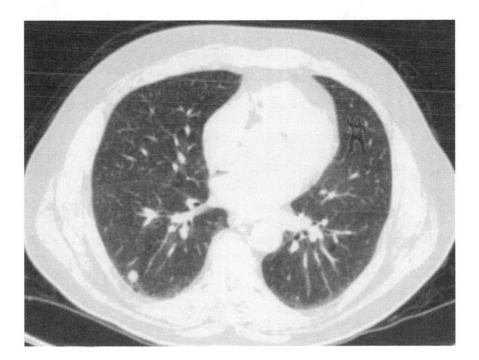

Figure 3.1.

the same statement a few moments later, do you notice that the chorus is falling over themselves to say it is a "brilliant" idea?

It is not by accident that people in nondominant groups pick up on these subtle behaviors more quickly and clearly than people in dominant groups. When we are members of dominant groups, which, in the United States, generally means whites, men, Christians, and heterosexuals (among others), we often don't easily see these behaviors. And we don't need to do so. Our culture is closely aligned with *the* culture. When we are in nondominant groups, it is essential to notice some of these subtleties to survive on a daily basis. We learn to spot them before they make a negative impact upon us.

Occasionally, something allows us to spot things that are right in front of us, things we did not see earlier. For example, LGBT people tend to develop this selective attention at a high level when it involves dynamics regarding sexual orientation. They often watch what is said and not said. They may even feel as if they must adjust their behavior to feel safe. If you're not LGBT and you want to get a sense of what I'm talking about, try an exercise my colleague Eric Peterson sometimes uses in trainings. Turn this dynamic around and imagine that you work in an environment where it is not considered acceptable to be heterosexual. Start noticing all of the things you might have to pay attention to which you previously never second-guessed. Do you have a picture of your boyfriend/girlfriend/husband/wife on your desk? How might you answer certain questions in a different way? Who would you take to the company holiday party? What would you say about what you did over the weekend? Dozens of other things might emerge, even if you were just "pretending." Those of us who are heterosexual are generally unaware that these dynamics inadvertently isolate our LGBT community members or members of other nondominant groups, even though these dynamics and behaviors are all around us.

In 1995, inattentional blindness became an issue in a court case when Kenneth Conley, a Boston police officer, was convicted of perjury and obstruction of justice. Conley was sentenced to nearly three years in jail when he claimed he did not see an assault that occurred in front of him while he was chasing a fence-climbing shooting suspect at two in the morning.[4]

Simons and Chabris attempted to reconstruct the circumstances to test whether or not Conley's claims that he didn't see the assault were viable. In their test, students were asked to take a four-hundred-meter run on the campus. While they were running, they were followed by another student who was running about thirty feet behind. The following student was instructed to count the number of times the person they were following touched their head during the run. While they were on the route, three other students staged a mock fight (including shouting) in which two of them pretended to beat up the third. They then tested how many of the runners saw the fight. When tested at night, only 35 percent of the runners noticed the fight. When tested in broad daylight, 40 percent did not see it. [5]

Just as we've seen in the medical and law enforcement examples I've noted, there are many things that take place around us on a daily basis that we only notice selectively. Whose ideas do we hear? Which do we miss? Who do we see doing something wrong, while we do not notice others? How many students do teachers observe differently, sometimes depending on their opinion of the student? Selective attention and inattentional blindness show up in every area of our lives. Think about it for a minute. What might you be missing in your own life? You might be missing something very important.

A second pattern is *diagnosis bias*, the propensity to label people, ideas, or things based on our initial opinions. Many studies demonstrate the way our quick decisions about people affect the way we treat these same people. Simply think of a time when you saw somebody, made an assumption about him or her, and acted according to your assumption. How many times have you made such assumptions about people? I would bet that you do just about any time you meet somebody new. When we encounter new people, we "scope them out," often without thinking we are doing so. We do so because we are "wired" to act that way. Our instant "diagnoses" of people definitely affect long-term relationships. Hence the expression of "there is no second chance to make a good first impression." Our impressions of people are often influenced by how they initially appear to us.

In my first book, [6] I wrote about a study conducted by two Princeton University professors, Alexander Todorov and Charles Ballew. Todorov and Ballew showed study participants pictures of competing candidates for the 2006 Senate and gubernatorial races for less than one second and asked them to judge their prospective competence and trustworthiness. The participants picked the eventual winners approximately 70 percent of the time, based on a one second "first impression." [7]

Think about how many times diagnosis bias might make an impact upon our lives. How might we respond to an interview subject, or a salesperson? Who do we consider "professional" in their appearance and how do we treat them based on that consideration? Believe it or not, this phenomenon even appears to affect medical diagnoses. Shaun Eack of the University of Pittsburgh reported that African American patients were almost three times as likely to be diagnosed as schizophrenic because the clinicians subjectively determined that the patients were not responding as honestly as white patients. [8] Studies in England have shown similar results in the diagnoses of Afro-Caribbean people by white psychiatrists, often based on the dubious notion that the patients are "strange, undesirable, bizarre, aggressive, and dangerous." [9]

Harold Kelley was a pioneer in social psychology and one of the fathers of attribution theory, a concept that examines how it is that the human mind explains the causes and behaviors associated with the things that we experi-ence. Kelly gave MIT economics students short biographies of prospective instructors and then told them they were going to be asked to evaluate the instructors. The students were not aware that they were given two different bios. Half of the students received biographies that described the instructor as "a very warm person," and the other half had information that indicated the instructor was a "rather cold person." After spending a class with the instruc-tor, the students were asked to evaluate the instructor. The researchers used different teachers, but the results were consistent. Students who were given the "warm" résumé consistently rated the instructor positively, describing the teacher as "more considerate, informal, sociable, popular, good natured, hu-morous and humane." Those who got the "cold" dossiers described those instructors as "self-centered, intolerant, humorless, formal, irritable, ruthless and unsociable." In addition, 52 percent of the students who got the "warm" bio participated in discussions, while only 32 percent of the "cold" ones did so.[10] The students appeared to make a quick diagnosis of the instructor based simply on what they had been told, seeing the instructor through the lens of that diagnosis.

A recent study sheds light on some serious consequences of diagnosis bias. Robert Fortuna, a health services researcher at the University of Roch-ester Medical Center, conducted a study using information on 2,298 patients who were twenty-one years of age and under who visited emergency rooms across the country with stomach pain, cramps, or spasms. What he found was very troubling indeed. Young black people were 39 percent less likely than whites to receive any painkillers and 62 percent less likely to be given a narcotic. In addition, black and Hispanic youth were 60 to 70 percent more likely than whites to be in the emergency room for more than six hours. It has been known for years that this pattern of medical treatment disparity was true among adults, but this was the first time it was established among children.[11]

How many times have you heard people say they "trust their gut" about their first impressions? Or that they make decisions about not hiring some-body because of some random factor: a soft handshake or poor eye contact? How reliable are those decisions? The research would seem to say that they are not very reliable at all.

We also make many of our decisions based on *pattern recognition*, which is the tendency to sort and identify information based on prior experience or habit. This is a fundamental protective mechanism of the mind. If we see something in a person that has been dangerous for us in the past (or that we think has been dangerous for us), we don't wait to determine whether or not it will threaten us this time. Instead, we immediately respond. This is much like staying away from a hot stove after having been burned by one before.

Pattern recognition can affect our reaction to various things, but it also can make an impact upon our very senses. One of my favorite examples of this sensory experience is this checkerboard example designed by Edward Adelson, the John and Dorothy Wilson Professor of Vision Science at MIT. [12] Look at this picture and see which block is darker, the one marked "A" or the one marked "B" (see figure 3.2)?

If you are like most people (and I will include myself in this group), block A is obviously darker. However, look now at the same picture with a gray bar put across it so that we can compare the two colors (see figure 3.3).

We now see that the blocks are the same color. The shadowing effect caused by the cylinder is designed to deceive our minds, but the biggest influence is the fact that most of us have seen checkerboards all of our lives and are so familiar with the black and white pattern that we mentally assume it to be true here as well. The incredible thing is that when you look back at the first picture, *it still looks different, even though you now know the two blocks are the same color*!

We generally want to see things as the same as other things we have seen. It is safer and more dependable to deal with them in that way. Stereotyping is a strong form of pattern recognition. When we see somebody coming toward us, it is safer to know what to do when we can relate them to other people we have seen before with similar physical characteristics. "People like that

Edward H. Adelson

Figure 3.2.

Edward H. Adelson

Figure 3.3.

_____ " is a natural response to wanting to know how to handle them, and ourselves in dealing with these people. And yet, such thinking is fraught with potential challenges. When we assume patterns are true (e.g., certain people are more likely to be criminals) the results can be tragic (and I'll talk about some of these results in the next few chapters). What are the patterns that your unconscious mind produces about people? What kinds of things do you assume to be true based on prior experience?

Let's look at a fourth pattern. On April 8, 2007, the _Washington Post_ ran a most interesting story by Gene Weingarten. Here is an excerpt:

> It was 7:51 a.m. on Friday, January 12, the middle of the morning rush hour. In the next 43 minutes, as the violinist performed six classical pieces, 1,097 people passed by. Almost all of them were on the way to work, which meant, for almost all of them, a government job. L'Enfant Plaza is at the nucleus of federal Washington, and these were mostly mid-level bureaucrats with those indeterminate, oddly fungible titles: policy analyst, project manager, budget officer, specialist, facilitator, and consultant.
>
>   Each passerby had a quick choice to make, one familiar to commuters in any urban area where the occasional street performer is part of the cityscape: Do you stop and listen? Do you hurry past with a blend of guilt and irritation,

aware of your cupidity but annoyed by the unbidden demand on your time and your wallet? Do you throw in a buck, just to be polite? Does your decision change if he's really bad? What if he's really good? Do you have time for beauty? Shouldn't you? What's the moral mathematics of the moment?

On that Friday in January, those private questions would be answered in an unusually public way. No one knew it, but the fiddler standing against a bare wall outside the Metro in an indoor arcade at the top of the escalators was one of the finest classical musicians in the world, playing some of the most elegant music ever written on one of the most valuable violins ever made. [13]

The musician was Joshua Bell, one of the world's great violin virtuosos, and this circumstance was a perfect example of the fourth pattern I am discussing in this chapter, *value attribution*. Value attribution is the inclination to imbue a person or thing with certain qualities based on initial perceived value. Bell was dressed in a baseball cap and a long-sleeved T-shirt. He opened his violin case and took out his $3.5 million violin, threw a few dollars in the case to encourage others, as thousands of other street musicians have done before. He then played for forty-five minutes. Almost nobody stopped to listen. Was it because they didn't like the music? Not likely. People all over the world pay more than $100 a seat to listen to Bell perform. They simply didn't assign a lot of value to this "street musician."

I remember something similar happening at one of my client sites, a food distributorship. One of their top suppliers, a multimillionaire agrobusiness-man paid a visit to the warehouse. But he wasn't dressed like you would expect. In fact, he was dressed more "like a farmer," wearing jeans and a flannel shirt, longish hair, and a beard. The warehouse workers almost threw him out before somebody recognized him as a big deal.

It is our nature to instantly assign value to people, without even realizing we're doing so. Are certain people "safer" than others? Are some more likely to look "smarter" or more "professional"? Do some languages or dialects sound "more articulate" than others? How about their accent, their height, their dress? Studies show that we assign value to all of these things and more. How does this pattern show up in your life?

The fifth pattern we'll look at is often called *confirmation bias*, a tendency for people to gather information or respond to a circumstance in a way that confirms their already established beliefs or ideas. If you have any question about this pattern, watch the evening news and see how "pundits" evaluate a political story. It is almost always very predictable. Something happens, and then the confirmation bias begins. Liberals interpret the story to prove their point, and conservatives interpret in a way that proves their point of view. Information is cherry-picked selectively to affirm the point each is trying to make. And in the end, everybody is right back where they began.

And we call that "thinking," right?

I'm not trying to be unfair to political pundits, because the truth is that we all do the same thing. We have a strong tendency to want to be right. In order to prove the things that we believe are true we can often unconsciously seek that information out while just as unconsciously disregarding evidence to the contrary. Ask people you know how they feel about the Patient Protection and Affordable Care Act, commonly called the Affordable Care Act or "Obamacare." See how many of them have an opinion that started with, "I like it," or "I don't like it," even before they understood fully what was in the act. That is, assuming they *do* understand the act.

And confirmation bias leads to confirmational behavior, through which we treat people in ways that have them perform consistent with our expectations. Studies have shown that teachers who believe children are good students treat them differently than those who think they are bad students. Employers also do the same with employees.

A beautiful example of this pattern at work is shown in the 1979 movie *Being There*, based on a novella by Jerzy Kosinski. In the movie, Peter Sellers plays the main character, Chance, a simple-minded gardener who lives in the home of an aging, wealthy man in Washington, D.C. When the man dies, Chance, whose entire body of knowledge seems to come from watching television, is forced to leave.

Chance is dressed in his former employer's nice clothing when a chauffeured limousine carrying a wealthy businessman's wife accidentally hits him on the street. The wife gives him a drink and when she asks who he is and he responds "Chance the gardener," she mistakenly hears the name "Chauncey Gardiner." Because of his dress, accent, and appearance, everybody assumes that this is an upper-crust, educated adviser of some sort. His innocent statements are taken for philosophy, his simplistic comments about gardening taken for allegories about the state of the world.

Pretty soon "Chauncey" finds himself advising the president of the United States, who happens to be a friend of the wealthy businessman. Chance becomes famous and appears on television talk shows. Polls show that the public loves his "simple wisdom." In the penultimate moment of the movie, after the businessman dies, other businessmen stand around discussing who should succeed the president after his term of office is complete, and, lo and behold, they all agree the new president should be Chauncey Gardiner.

Of course, this sort of thing happens every day in business. People are designated as "high potential," and then accordingly given opportunities to prove it. Or perhaps they are seen as questionable, and are not given the kind of stretch assignments that would allow them to prove otherwise. Yet, to the person making the determination, the determination is "logical" or "rational."

We all do this sort of thing. Every day. Each of us acting this way to different people, positively and negatively, for different reasons. It is as natural to us as breathing.

Before I introduce the sixth pattern, I'd like you to do a quick little exercise with me. All you have to do is respond to the following instructions as quickly as you can. Ready?

1. Say silk five times as fast as you can.
2. Now spell silk four times out loud.
3. Now say it again six times.
4. Now spell it out loud five times.
5. Now say it again seven times.

Now, quickly, what do cows drink?

If you did the exercise at top speed, and you are like most people (about 75 percent), the first thought that came to your mind when I asked the question, "What do cows drink?" was probably "milk."

Now we all know cows don't drink milk; they drink water. But the mind quickly goes all milky because of the auditory association with the word "silk." The repetitions of the word "silk" prime the mind for the word "milk." This is a simple example of the priming effect.

Priming is the implicit tendency to respond to something based on expectations created by a previous experience or association. There are times when we are very aware of priming. When I was young, I used to like to watch golf tournaments on television. I would sit and watch the tournament and invariably, as soon as it was over, I would be in the backyard playing golf. The same thing happens to me today when I go to hear live music. As soon as I get home, no matter how late it is, I feel a strong desire to pick up my guitar and play a few songs. There also are times when we are unaware of what is priming us, as we saw in the case of the study about rainy days and medical school interviews in chapter 1.

All of this makes perfect sense and ties into our earlier conversation about selective attention. Given that my brain could be focused on any number of things at a particular time, why wouldn't it shift into the mode of a focus on golf or music if I had just been immersed in those things?

The same thing also can happen in less pleasant ways. Imagine there was a story on the news about a plane crash. Do you believe that most people would be more or less nervous if they were heading to the airport after watching the story unfold? Kind of a no-brainer, isn't it? We are, in fact and in mind, being primed all of the time.

Researchers have found that we are primed by any number of experiences. For example, Nicolas Guéguen of the Université de Bretagne Sud in France has studied dozens of ways that indicate the colors or scents people are wearing, the slightest touch they make or feel, or other subtle factors can influence habits regarding dating, tipping, hitchhiking, or any number of other behaviors.

We can even be primed to see things that are not present at all. Many of you are undoubtedly familiar with the following experiment, which involves showing people the following words:

- slumber
- dream
- bed
- quiet
- nap
- pillow
- night
- blanket
- pajamas
- snooze

Now take away the list and take one of those words and add "kitchen" and "sleep" to the list and show them to the group, asking people which of the words they remember. Invariably, a large percentage of the group will "remember" that the word "sleep" was on the list, even though it was not there at all! The association with all of the related words primes the mind to think of but one thing: sleep.

The priming effect is centrally connected to most of our other mental lenses because our minds are primed to have us see certain things and not others. We are primed to value certain things and attribute certain behaviors to certain people. In fact, one might say that our life experience primes us to do almost everything we do. The challenge is that we often don't know what is priming us or how it is priming us.

The next pattern to pay attention to might be referred to as *commitment confirmation*, or *loss aversion.* Our minds can become very much attached to a particular point of view, even when it may be obviously wrong, especially when it provides us a way to save face, appear right, or allow us to glorify ourselves. This can lead to a form of confidence bias or self-motivated reasoning.

Here's a good illustration of confidence bias. Results from a University of Nebraska study[14] showed that 94 percent of professors rated themselves "above average" in comparison with their colleagues. Do you notice something amiss in those numbers? It may seem to be apparent, but this illusion of self is quite common. Similar studies have shown that most students consider themselves above average, and that shoppers generally see themselves as having gotten a good deal when they have not saved any money at all. Doctors have been found to believe that they made the proper diagnosis four times as often as they have. Public health workers are three times more likely to believe they know how to handle an emergency than they are. Medical students believe they are better communicators than either their teachers or patients. And the list goes on and on. We have a largely unconscious tendency to see ourselves in a positive light.

This unconscious tendency contributes to commitment confirmation and loss aversion. We want to win and we want to see ourselves as winners. As such, the mind often reconstructs our memories in ways that permit us to remember the positive aspects of ourselves far more than the negative areas. There are obvious exceptions to this idea. Some people have such low self-esteem and such a strongly critical superego that they judge themselves harshly in every way. But even in those cases, people are likely to deceive themselves. This is a trait that is especially common in more individualistic cultures such as the dominant one in the United States.

Think about how this thinking applies in businesses and other organizations. How often have you seen somebody refuse to admit they made a wrong hire, or developed a mistaken strategy? The mind finds ways to self-justify these decisions rather than accept that we are wrong. Think about the cost of this sense of "overconfidence." Might such thinking have, possibly, resulted in the loss of loved ones and the extension of the war in Iraq, because American military officials underestimated what it would take to win? How many chief executive officers or boards of directors have overpaid when they purchase companies that are struggling, because they are convinced they can turn the company around when others have failed?

This dynamic even affects our willingness to look at bias in ourselves. We want to think of ourselves as fair people, especially those of us who are committed to fair treatment of all people. The stronger the commitment, the more likely it is to blind us to reality. When we get feedback that we may have a bias, what is our reaction? "Me? Not me!" We then justify why we had the thought or made the decision. "Well, it's only because they (fill in the blank), not because I am biased!" This, of course, often seems like denial, and it is to some degree. But in the mind of the person with such a belief, *they actually believe that they are right.*

The same thing can happen when we have a sense of not being treated fairly. For example, such treatment may influence the degree to which we believe ourselves to be victims of prejudice. If you have believed that you are the victim of racism, sexism, homophobia, heterosexism, anti-Semitism, or any other bias, at some point you may become identified with that belief. The very foundation of your identity is built on believing that is true and in developing all of the protective mechanisms associated with that belief. Acknowledging that it may not be true can threaten the ego structure. "If I'm not that," the mind unconsciously says, "who or what am I?"

We have all seen this behavior play out so obviously in others. It's a good idea to ask how it plays out in us.

While most of the patterns I have been discussing are primarily external, the eighth pattern is especially insidious because it is internally focused but is often just as invisible to us. *Stereotype threat*, or *internalized bias*, is the experience of anxiety or concern in a situation where a person has the potential to confirm a negative stereotype about their social group. This has often been referred to as "internalized oppression" and was, perhaps, most famously demonstrated by Drs. Kenneth and Mamie Clark in their classic experiment with black children who preferred to play with white dolls. This important experiment is known to have influenced the U.S. Supreme Court in the 1954 *Brown v. Board of Education* school desegregation ruling. In more recent studies, Claude Steele found that simply asking African American students to answer one additional question before taking their SAT tests significantly lowered their scores. The question was: "What is your race?" For many of the African American students, being reminded of being black seemed to internalize negative performance bias.

When we first look at this bias, especially in conjunction with the dynamics of the kinds of confidence bias we just examined, it makes no logical sense. Why would we embrace someone else's negative stereotypes about ourselves? And, if we chose the things we were reacting to, we wouldn't embrace these negative thoughts. But of course, we adopt these thoughts quite automatically and not by conscious choice.

Any member of a nondominant group is exposed to the same negative stereotypes and social messaging about that group as dominant group members. People from nondominant groups see the same images on television or in the newspaper. They hear the same jokes, the same things being said in their homes, places of worship, or schools. Variations on the same data come in, and unless they have developed an extraordinary ability to deflect this information, it becomes part of their way of looking at the world.

In 2007–2008, I had the extraordinary experience of being asked to serve as the professor of diversity in residence at Bennett College for Women, a historically black college in Greensboro, North Carolina. All of my students were young black women. As part of their coursework, I asked the students to take the IAT, a test created by psychologists Anthony Greenwald of the University of Washington, Mahzarin Banaji of Harvard University, and Brian Nosek of the University of Virginia. The IAT is a computer-based test that is designed to give feedback as to unconscious positive and negative associations with particular groups. My students took several of the different tests, but all were asked to take the one that tested "white" versus "black." The results were striking. A total of 60 percent of the students had more positive associations with whites than blacks. Such results are not unusual. The students grew up in a culture that demonstrates far more positive messages about whites than blacks, and they simply unconsciously absorbed what they had seen and heard.

This dynamic can especially, and strongly, influence the performance of women. If we consider the external biases about women in the workplace, relative to men, how do those notions affect women's workplace performance? In my consulting practice I have noticed a pattern. More and more organizations are experimenting with various kinds of flextime arrangements to accommodate parents. In reality, most of these arrangements are designed for working mothers. And yet, a relatively small percentage of the women who might use these programs take advantage of the programs. Why is this so? Perhaps this comment from one of my clients can shed some light.

> I know the flextime program is available but something about it made me hesitant. I didn't realize what it was until I took the Implicit Association Test that was designed to measure attitudes toward men and women in business. My results surprised me. I showed a strong negative association with women in the work environment. That made no sense to me! I went to Yale. I am a great lawyer. Yet it seems like my unconscious still thinks I don't belong here! The more I thought about it, the more I realized my hesitancy to take the flextime option was probably influenced by that unconscious belief. I am afraid that if I use the program, others will think the same thing about me that I think about myself!

This self-defeating behavior is sad. It also can be tragic. When young gay men and women grow up in a culture that denigrates them for their sexual orientation, they can internalize such negative messages. And those beliefs probably contribute to the fact that four times more gay teenagers take their own lives than straight ones.

The ninth pattern is *anchoring bias*, sometimes referred to as *focalism*, the common tendency to rely too heavily or "anchor" on one trait or piece of information when making decisions. Nobel Prize winner Daniel Kahneman and his research partner Amos Tversky famously identified this bias. The initial "anchor" often determines the remainder of our thinking about the person or subject to be confronted. For instance, do you automatically assume, without questioning, that people who come from elite schools are better qualified than others? Or that certain personality types are "more professional"?

Within the past several years, researchers have become very interested in this dynamic. They have produced some pretty fascinating findings, especially in the domain of business economics. This is because some of the strongest anchoring techniques in the world are developed on Madison Avenue. For example, here's an experiment I have tried with groups. It's one you might want to try yourself. I show an audience a picture of a beautiful vacation destination. One half of the audience closes their eyes and the other half is shown a picture with a list of amenities that states the normal price of the site is $4,995 per night. Then the groups switch and the second group is shown the same picture. But this time, the price is listed at $49.95 per night. I then ask each of them to write down how much they would be willing to pay. Without fail, the first group is willing to pay far more than the second. Having seen the price anchors a standard price that primes the mind for what they would be willing to pay.

Kahneman and Tversky famously conducted a similar experiment in 1974 in which they asked a group of people to guess what percentage of countries from Africa were part of the United Nations.[15] However, before the participants responded, the researchers spun a roulette-style wheel, which was engineered to always end up on either ten or sixty-five. They then asked the participants to say whether they believed the percentage of countries was higher or lower than the number on the wheel, and to then tell them the actual percentage.

What they found was fascinating. On average, people who landed on ten when the wheel spun guessed that about 25 percent of Africa was part of the United Nations. People who landed on sixty-five said they thought the figure was about 45 percent!

How does anchoring show up where diversity is concerned? We are constantly using anchoring to lead our decision making without realizing or questioning it. How often do we measure somebody by "first impressions" based on how they dress, what their accent is, how "articulate" they are, or even by the strength of their handshake? All of these traits can, of course, be influenced by race, culture, nation of origin, or gender. Yet we don't notice the subjectivity because the importance of those traits is "anchored" in our mind. I have even read that Henry Ford would not hire anybody who salted their food before tasting it.

Meghan Busse, Ayelet Israeli, and Florian Zettelmeyer, researchers at Northwestern University's Kellogg School of Management, collaborated with an online car repair service to determine why different customers received different price quotes when they call an auto-repair shop.[16] The researchers called 4,603 auto-repair shops to price a radiator replacement for a 2003 Toyota Camry. They considered three conditions: one where customers knew the standard rate to replace the radiator; a second in which the customers had no idea how much it should cost; and a third where customers had a price in mind that was too high. It turned out that those who thought the repair should cost more than the market rate were quoted higher prices than other people. The other two groups were both offered the market price unless, as it turned out, they were women.

The researchers discovered that women were offered a higher price than men when both had indicated that they had no idea of what it should cost. When the researchers broke down their results by gender, they found that women are worse off if they indicate they have no idea what a radiator replacement should cost. Why was there a discrepancy? Is it that repair shops don't like women or are seeking to cheat women?

The researchers came to another conclusion. They believed that when the car repair people, almost all of them men, heard that the customer was a woman, they "anchored" to a belief that the customer was not informed about cars.

Every one of us has many anchored heuristics, or experience-based techniques, that we use for making decisions. What are yours?

Arsalan Iftikhar, Civil Rights Lawyer, Global Media Commentator and Founder of TheMuslimGuy.com

As an American born and raised Muslim, there are manifestations of bias that I notice every day. As a tall, brown-skinned man, I often experience the bulging eyeballs of some passengers when I walk onto an airplane for a flight. I find myself reacting by dressing with non-threatening colors (like pink) and making sure to smile at every person on the flight, as if to say "You have nothing to worry about with this brown dude."

It is much harder for many American Muslim women today, especially those who choose to wear the *hijab* (or headscarf) on a daily basis. My mother and sister both wear the *hijab*, and I have noticed the "looks" we have gotten as a family when we are in public places like shopping malls or restaurants.

Many American Muslims tend to cringe when people refer to us as "moderate Muslims" in everyday conversations. We prefer the term "mainstream Muslims" because the term "moderate Muslims" is viewed by many people in our community pejoratively as "acceptable" or "satisfactory" Muslims, as opposed to "mainstream Muslims," which more accurately defines the majority of the Muslim community around the world.

The final pattern I want to discuss is a function of the social primacy that I referred to earlier, and that is *group think*. So many of our personal biases are not personal at all. They are deeply influenced by the cultures and groups with whom we associate. This becomes obvious when we look at the hundreds of historical examples where normal people got caught up in a sort of collective societal madness and turned on their fellow citizens. We are deeply influenced by our group associations and beliefs.

All of us have a tendency to want to fit in. This sense of connection and belonging is vital to our existence, both emotionally and on a practical basis as well. Life is easier when we fit in with the group around us than when we seem to be swimming upstream against the culture. Any of the biases we have been discussing can, in that sense, take on a life of their own when a group begins to buy into them because we now have agreement for that point of view. When members of the group are too conscious of the opinions of others and begin to emulate each other and conform rather than think differently, these biases become almost automatic. In most cases, this is indicative of a circumstance where there is no conscious decision-making process in place.

Think about how many times this occurs in your family, organization, and community. We like "people like that," but not "people like *that*!" We all agree that people who go to certain schools are better. That people who are more extroverted are "a better fit," or that certain personality types are "our kind of people." At some point we stop thinking because the group thinks for us.

As I said earlier, it is helpful to distinguish these patterns but not to get too stuck in worrying about which is which and which is not. The most important realization is that we live every day in a maelstrom of biases generated by all of these dynamics. And the result can be circumstances that affect our lives in dramatic ways. Let's now look at a circumstance in which some of these biases may have played out and with tragic consequences.

Chapter Four

Life, Death, and Unconscious Bias on a Rainy Night

For the record, suspicion can kill, and prejudice can destroy. And a thought-less, frightened search for a scapegoat has a fallout all its own, for the children and the children yet unborn. And the pity of it is that these things cannot be confined to the Twilight Zone. —Rod Serling

I've mentioned in earlier chapters about how some manifestations of uncon-scious bias have resulted in tragic, and even deadly, circumstances. The story I now wish to discuss is a classic example of the potential life and death impacts of our unconscious bias. It is a story that became all too familiar to many people worldwide in early 2012. Despite the story's notoriety, it is worthwhile to recount all of its many intricate details because it is striking how few people know the facts about what took place.

On the night of February 26, 2012, Trayvon Benjamin Martin, a young African American man who had just turned seventeen, was walking through a Sanford, Florida, townhouse community, where he was visiting his father's fiancée and her son. Martin was eating candy, drinking from a can of juice, and talking to a friend on his cell phone while famously wearing a "hoodie," a hooded sweatshirt. He was unarmed.

The Retreat at Twin Lakes, the neighborhood where Martin was walking that night, is a 260-unit gated community. Its resident population is highly diverse. At the time of Martin's walk, the population was approximately 49 percent non-Hispanic white, 23 percent Hispanic, 20 percent black, and 5 percent Asian. In the fourteen months prior to February 26, 2012, police had been called to the community more than four hundred times. Crimes reported had included eight burglaries, nine thefts, and one shooting. There also were other reports of attempted break-ins and vandalism.

George Zimmerman, a twenty-eight-year-old, mixed-race Hispanic Sanford resident, had been selected some time earlier by the community to serve as its neighborhood watch coordinator. As of February 26, 2012, Zimmerman had been licensed to carry a firearm for approximately two-and-one-half years. Just three weeks earlier, Zimmerman had called the police to report a "suspicious" young man who was gone by the time the police arrived at the Retreat at Twin Lakes. Four days later, the same young man was arrested for allegedly stealing a laptop computer from a home in the community.[1]

At 7:09 that night, Zimmerman called the Sanford police nonemergency number to report "a suspicious person" in the community. Zimmerman stated that "We've had some break-ins in my neighborhood, and there's a real suspicious guy." He went on to describe Martin as "just walking around, looking about" and said, "This guy looks like he is up to no good or he is on drugs or something." Zimmerman also reported that Martin had his hand in his waistband and was walking around looking at homes. On the police recording, Zimmerman is heard saying "these assholes, they always get away."[2]

What made Martin appear "suspicious" to Zimmerman? Why was Zimmerman under the impression that Martin was "up to no good" or "on drugs or something?" Might his mind have been primed by earlier incidents that had taken place in the community or his personal life that caused him to see Martin as dangerous? And who, exactly, was he referring to as "these assholes" when he spoke to the police operator? Could such language have been an example of diagnosis bias at work? Would he, for example, have had the same reaction to a middle-aged white man who was dressed and walking exactly the same way? Or might his confirmation bias have prevented him from seeing that sort of person at all?

A couple of minutes into the call, the urgency of the situation seems to have increased. Zimmerman said "he's running," and the dispatcher then asked: "He's running? Which way is he running?" Zimmerman then followed Martin in his car. When asked by the dispatcher if he was following Martin, Zimmerman responded in the affirmative, only to be told by the police, "We don't need you to do that."[3]

When Police Officer Timothy Smith arrived at 7:17 p.m., just a few short minutes after the initial call, he found the unarmed Trayvon Martin lying face down, unresponsive, only seventy yards from his father's fiancée's home. Zimmerman was standing over the body, still armed. Officer Smith handcuffed Zimmerman and removed his weapon. Officers Ricardo Ayala and Anthony Raimondo began to administer CPR to Martin. Sanford paramedics arrived and continued CPR, but their efforts were not successful. At 7:30 p.m., only twenty-one minutes after the start of the now historic initial call, Trayvon Benjamin Martin was pronounced dead from a gunshot wound to the chest.[4]

Early on the morning of February 28, Martin's father, Tracy Martin, filed a missing person's report. At 9:20 that morning, police officers arrived at Tracy Martin's fiancée's condo with photographs of his dead son.

After his arrest, police questioned George Zimmerman for five hours. He passed a voice stress analysis test to determine if he was lying. His back was wet and covered with grass, and he was bleeding from his nose and the back of his head.[5]

On March 12, 2012, Sanford Police Chief William Lee asked the state attorney general's office to review the case. Lee had found insufficient evidence to arrest Zimmerman for a crime.[6] "In this case," Lee said, "Mr. Zimmerman has made the statement of self-defense. Until we can establish probable cause to dispute that, we don't have grounds to arrest him." When he was criticized for the investigation, Lee defended himself and the department, saying "We are all taking a beating over this . . . this is all very unsettling. I'm sure if George Zimmerman had the opportunity to relive Sunday, February 26, he'd probably do things differently. I'm sure Trayvon would too."

How might this scene have played out if the roles were reversed, and the shooter was a seventeen-year-old African American man, and the deceased was a twenty-eight-year-old, light-skinned mixed-race man? Was this an example of commitment confirmation on the part of the police?

Of course, this was only the beginning of the national drama that would unfold over the weeks and months that followed. One day later, on March 13, Chris Serino, the lead investigator for the Sanford police, recommended charges for Zimmerman of negligent manslaughter to the state's attorney, although he did not believe there was sufficient evidence to prove the charge and said that he was only filing the charge so that the prosecutor's office could continue the investigation.[7]

The *capias* (a court order requiring the arrest of a named person) that Serino filed stated that "the encounter between George Zimmerman and Trayvon Martin was ultimately avoidable by Zimmerman, if Zimmerman had remained in his vehicle and waited for the arrival of law enforcement or conversely, if he had identified himself to Martin as a concerned citizen and initiated dialogue in an effort to dispel each party's concern." The order went on to state, "There is no indication that Trayvon Martin was involved in any criminal activity at the time of the encounter." After an initial review, the state attorney general's office determined that there was insufficient evidence to charge Zimmerman and did not file any charges based on the *capias* request.[8]

Serino was interviewed by the *Orlando Sentinel* on March 16 and said his investigation had turned up no reliable evidence that cast doubt on Zimmerman's account of the incident, which suggested he had acted in self-defense. "The best evidence we have is the testimony of George Zimmerman, and he says the decedent was the primary aggressor in the whole event, everything I have is adding up to what he says."⁹

"The best evidence we have . . ." which, of course, did not include the testimony of the only other person who was there, because he was dead. Was this statement evidence of confirmation bias?

Two days after the shooting, Trayvon Martin's father, immediately skeptical of the police account of what had happened, retained civil rights attorney Benjamin Crump to generate media attention about the case and to pursue legal action. Publicist Ryan Julison and attorney Natalie Jackson also joined the Martin family effort. By March 7, the case began to receive major national media attention. Shortly thereafter, Crump sued to have the police calls made public. Tracy Martin and Trayvon's mother, Sybrina Fulton, began to give media interviews, and protests calling for Zimmerman's arrest cropped up all over the country.

Civil rights leaders nationwide weighed in. Television host Reverend Al Sharpton said that "Forty-five days ago, Trayvon Martin was murdered. No arrest was made. The chief of police in Sanford announced after his review of the evidence that there would be no arrest. An outcry from all over this country came because his parents refused to leave it there."¹⁰ Reverend Jesse Jackson was quoted as saying that Martin had been "murdered and martyred."¹¹ Even President Obama weighed in. "When I think about this boy, I think about my own kids, and I think every parent in America should be able to understand why it is absolutely imperative that we investigate every aspect of this," Obama said. He also said that all of America had some "soul searching" to do over the incident, adding that "if I had a son, he would look like Trayvon."¹² Spike Lee tweeted what he thought was the address to Zimmerman's residence to more than 250,000 followers, only to find that he had the wrong Zimmerman and had inadvertently tweeted the address of an innocent elderly couple, an incident for which he later publicly apologized to the couple and compensated them for his mistake.¹³

Were all of these reactions based on a full inquiry into the evidence, or were they triggered by a history of incidents such as this that had occurred in the past? What would the protests have looked like if the circumstances were exactly the same, except that Martin was white and Zimmerman was black? Were these reactions potentially driven by pattern recognition, given the history of all too similar incidents that had occurred in the past? Did groupthink begin to take hold?

Martin's attire became a focal point of the controversy. Fox News commentator Geraldo Rivera created a firestorm when he said, "I think the hoodie is as much responsible for Trayvon Martin's death as George Zimmerman was."¹⁴ "The "hoodie" became a ubiquitous symbol, and cries of "I am Trayvon" resonated across the mainstream news media, social media, in schools, neighborhoods, and even in the halls of legislatures. Students all over Florida staged walkouts. Tens of thousands of people calling for Zimmerman's arrest attended rallies all over the country. There was even a "Million Hoodie March." Politicians, celebrities, and professional athletes all appeared in public wearing hoodies. Bags of Skittles and cans of Arizona Iced Tea became symbols of solidarity with Martin and his family.

Millions of hoodies are sold every year. I own four of them myself. Does that make all of the owners suspect, or just those who look a "particular" way? Is value attribution at work here? Or selective attention?

But there were others who weighed in from different perspectives. More than a year after Martin's death, *Washington Post* columnist Richard Cohen wrote, "I also can understand why Zimmerman was suspicious and why he thought Martin was wearing a uniform we all recognize. I don't know whether Zimmerman is a racist. But I'm tired of politicians and others who have donned hoodies in solidarity with Martin and who essentially suggest that, for recognizing the reality of urban crime in the United States, I am a racist. The hoodie blinds them as much as it did Zimmerman."[15]

Former U.S. Secretary of Education William Bennett criticized those who wanted Zimmerman arrested by saying "a mob mentality seems to be in the ascendance." He added: "the tendency in the first days by some, including Al Sharpton, Jesse Jackson and an angry chorus of followers, was to rush to judgment with little regard for fairness, due process, or respect for the terrible death of a young man."[16] Shelby Steele, a senior fellow at Stanford University's Hoover Institution, said the tragedy of Martin's death was being exploited by a generation of "ambulance-chasing" black leaders who have promoted "our historical victimization as the central theme of our group identity."[17] Economist and commentator Thomas Sowell criticized the media for implying that Zimmerman had continued to follow Martin after the police dispatcher told him such action was not needed. He wrote that the media mostly left out Zimmerman's answer of "OK" because "too many people in the media see their role as filtering and slanting the news."[18]

There was more. Herman Cain, former Godfather's Pizza chief and 2008 Republican presidential candidate, complained about the "swirling rhetoric" and "war of words."[19] Other conservative news commentators expressed opinions as well. Sean Hannity of Fox News had Zimmerman on his program to give his side of the story. And Fox News contributor Bernard Goldberg said "if George Zimmerman did something good . . . they wouldn't refer to him as white Hispanic, he'd just be Hispanic."[20]

Were all of these reactions based on this incident alone, or were they also triggered by other incidents and experiences of the past, or even political and ideological positions that needed to be justified? Might commitment confirmation have caused people on all sides to see the evidence through the window of an "established point of view" that they already possessed?

Reactions escalated when it became known that various NBC news programs ran segments which inaccurately depicted what Zimmerman had said in his police call. One ran the clip as "this guy looks like he's up to no good or he's on drugs or something. . . . He's got his hand in his waistband, and he's a black male."[21] Others ran the story differently, saying "this guy looks like he's up to no good. He looks black." However, in the actual recording, the interaction between Zimmerman and the operator is: "This guy looks like he's up to no good. Or he's on drugs or something. It's raining and he's just walking around, looking about." The police operator then asked: "Okay, and this guy, is he black, white or Hispanic?" and Zimmerman answered that "he looks black."[22] It is not until later in the conversation that Zimmerman actually said, "He's got his hand in his waistband, and he's a black male."[23]

NBC issued an apology for "an error made in the production process that we deeply regret."[24] Producers and reporters who were involved were fired or disciplined. Other news organizations criticized NBC for trying to sway public opinion by portraying Zimmerman as a racial profiler. A *Washington Post* reporter, Erik Wemple, wrote that "the difference between what *Today* put on its air and the actual tape? Complete: In the *Today* version, Zimmerman volunteered that this person 'looks black,' a sequence of events that would more readily paint Zimmerman as a racial profiler. In reality's version, Zimmerman simply answered a question about the race of the person whom he was reporting to the police. Nothing prejudicial at all in responding to such an inquiry."[25] Zimmerman later sued NBC News for defamation.

Is this the only time that the major news media have given us partial information or erroneous information about a criminal case? How willing are we to accept information when it fits a narrative that we already believe? Is confirmation bias at work once again? Or do we selectively see and hear some things and not others?

On March 22, 2012, State Attorney Angela Corey was assigned to the case by Florida Governor Rick Scott. She announced that her department would decide whether or not to press charges instead of convening a grand jury investigation. "I always lean toward moving forward without needing the grand jury," Corey said. "In a case like this, I foresee us being able to make a decision, and move on it on our own."[26] Governor Scott also assigned the case to the Florida Department of Law Enforcement. Florida Attorney General Pam Bondi stated that "no stone will be left unturned in this investigation."[27] On a parallel track, the U.S. Department of Justice announced that the Federal Bureau of Investigation (FBI) would open its own investigation as to whether or not Trayvon Martin's civil rights were violated.

In interviews later released by the FBI, Serino was reported to have said that he had felt pressure from several officers within his department to charge Zimmerman, even though he "did not believe he had enough evidence at the time to file charges." He said he believed that Zimmerman's actions were not based on Martin's race, but rather on the way Martin was dressed, the circumstances of the encounter, and the fact that there had been a slew of previous burglaries in the Sanford neighborhood. He stated that interviews with Zimmerman's coworkers and neighbors were all complimentary of Zimmerman. He also accused one of the officers who had put pressure on Serino of being friendly with Tracy Martin, and suggested that people within the Sanford police department may have leaked evidence to the media. [28]

On March 17, the Sanford police released additional recordings of calls that had been made on the night of the shooting. One alleged witness came forth in an apparent attempt to support Zimmerman's version of the story. The witness said that "the guy on the bottom, who had a red sweater on, was yelling to me, 'Help! Help!,' and I told him to stop, and I was calling 911." The witness went on to say that when he got to his home and looked back down on the scene, "the guy who was on the top beating up the other guy, was the one laying in the grass, and I believe he was dead at that point." [29]

Another apparent witness was a thirteen-year-old boy, who was walking his dog and saw a man on the ground shortly before the shooting and identified him as wearing red. [30] The boy's mother later disputed her son's testimony and claimed that the police pressured him into choosing the color the man was wearing. She also stated that the police did not interview her son until five days after the incident, and that an investigator told her that he did not believe the shooting was in self-defense.

When the Volusia County medical examiner released the autopsy report, the report revealed that Trayvon Martin's blood and urine contained trace levels of tetrahydrocannabinol (THC), the active ingredient in marijuana. The medical examiner reported that trace levels of THC can remain in the body weeks or even a month after ingestion and, as such, could not be considered significant enough to have played any role in Martin's behavior on February 26. [31]

Did the assertion that Martin had smoked marijuana in the past influence people's perception of him as "criminal"? Was the assertion an example of anchoring bias?

As the media coverage of the story expanded, so did the stories of various pro-Martin and pro-Zimmerman witnesses, with many of the stories appearing in the media. One witness named Mary Cutcher, who appeared to support Martin, said "there was no punching, no hitting going on at the time, no wrestling." [32] Another said he saw two men on the ground and that he "felt that they were scuffling." He added that he saw the man who he thought was "Hispanic" who "didn't appear hurt or anything else." [33] A statement from yet another described "a black male wearing a dark colored 'hoodie' on top of a white or Hispanic male who was yelling for help." The black male was reportedly punching the other man "MMA (mixed martial arts) style." After hearing a noise described as "a pop," he saw the black male "laid out on the grass."[34] Later, in another interview, the alleged witness said he no longer was sure who was calling for help.

The state's prosecutor recorded a sworn interview on April 2 with Rachel Jeantel (who was not identified to the public at the time the interview was released), the friend Martin was speaking to on his phone on the night of February 26, 2012. She said Martin had told her that a man was following him from his vehicle. Martin said that he had lost the follower, but then he reappeared. Jeantel said that she told Martin to run for his townhouse. She then said she heard Martin ask, "What are you following me for?" She added that the question was followed by another voice that asked, "What are you doing around here?"[35] She went on to say, "I was trying to say 'Trayvon, Trayvon. What's going on? I started to hear a little of Trayvon saying 'Get off! Get off!'" when the call ended.[36] Her attempts to call him back went unanswered.

Were both Jeantel and Martin experiencing stereotype threat?

On June 21, 2012, Zimmerman's attorneys released the interviews he had conducted with the police. He acknowledged that he had followed Martin and said that after the police told him they didn't need to have him do that, he was returning to his car when he was confronted by Martin. Zimmerman maintained that Martin punched him, knocked him down, and began beating his head into the sidewalk. Zimmerman said he called for help, and that Martin covered his mouth. He then said that when Martin saw the gun Zimmerman was carrying, he said something to the effect that "you're going to die," and after a struggle for the gun, Zimmerman told police he shot Martin in self-defense.[37] An ABC News report stated that a medical report compiled by Zimmerman's family physician diagnosed Zimmerman with a closed fracture of his nose, two black eyes, lacerations to the back of his head, a minor back injury, and bruising in his upper lip and cheek.[38]

On April 11, 2012, approximately six weeks after the incident, George Zimmerman was charged with second-degree murder. Prosecutors alleged that Zimmerman saw Martin, assumed he was a criminal acting suspiciously, and perceived that he did not belong in the community. They asserted that Martin was scared and had attempted to run home and that Zimmerman had ignored the dispatcher and confronted Martin, fatally shooting him in the chest. Legal analysts immediately criticized the prosecution for overcharging Zimmerman, saying the evidence did not support a charge of second-degree murder.[39]

Had the prosecutor's office not reacted to the pressure in the community, might they have more carefully charged Zimmerman with a crime that would merit conviction? Did groupthink take over?

Of course, the charges were the start to even more drama regarding the case. More than a year later, after yet another "trial of the century," Zimmerman was found not guilty by a jury of six women, five of them white and one Hispanic.

Rachel Jeantel testified at Zimmerman's trial. One of the jurors, labeled "Juror B37," later told CNN's Anderson Cooper that she did not find Jeantel "credible" because she found her "hard to understand," and she was "using phrases I had never heard before." She also spoke about the protests that took place in Sanford after the shooting as "rioting."[40]

If Jeantel didn't seem so "different," would Juror B37 have reacted differently? Was this a case of value attribution? Anchoring bias? If, for example, Jeantel, an African American, had been white and had spoken in a dialect more familiar to Juror B37, might she, or other jurors, have given Jeantel's testimony more credibility? What if she knew that Jeantel grew up speaking a different language and has an underbite, which affects her speech? Might her response to what she called the "rioting" have affected her sympathies toward Zimmerman, or the way she perceived Martin? If Trayvon Martin were white, would the juror have felt that Zimmerman was plausible in assuming that he was "trying to do something bad in the neighborhood"? Other jurors spoke about impressions they had already formed about the case, as well as their own experiences with crime and law enforcement. Could those have really been completely divorced from their reactions to the witnesses in the trial, or were they examples of confirmation bias?

And so, in the end, the big question that remains is: Was justice done? Is there any way to know the answers to all of these questions and many more?

What happened on the evening of February 26, 2012, is, of course, never to be fully known and is subject to conjecture that will grow more legendary as time passes. Only two people know what happened and one of them is dead. The other has huge reasons to tell the story in a way that exonerates him from blame. I certainly am not going to pretend to know what happened that night.

Yet throughout this entire saga, from the incident to the trial and beyond, there exist dozens of examples of cases where people automatically reacted to what they heard and saw, or thought they heard and saw. They decided who to believe or who not to believe. They jumped to conclusions based on prior existing beliefs, or based on perceived ideological points of view. They made unconscious instant comparisons to circumstances that were reminiscent of circumstances from the past. And they made assumptions based on a limited understanding of what happened, or did not happen.

All of the examples are subject to interpretation. Yet, on another level, what in life isn't subject to interpretation? As I have been saying thus far in this book, this is the way the mind works. Something happens. We see parts of it, because our mind cannot process all of the information in front of us. We then take what we do process, filtered by our previous experience, and evaluate that particular instance based on the biases that we have developed over the course of our lives. To some degree, everything we see and experience is purely based upon interpretation.

We can't even agree on what determinations our assumptions are based upon. After the verdict was handed down, the Pew Research Center for the People and the Press conducted a national poll. When they asked survey participants the question "Are you satisfied or dissatisfied with the Zimmerman verdict?," 39 percent said that they were satisfied and 42 percent were dissatisfied. However, when the results were broken down by race, 49 percent of whites were satisfied and 30 percent were dissatisfied. A total of 25 percent of Hispanics said they were satisfied, with 58 percent expressing dissatisfaction. Among African Americans, 5 percent were satisfied and 86 percent were dissatisfied. When the survey participants were asked, "Is the issue of race getting the correct amount of attention?," the responses were similarly skewed. The overall result was that 52 percent said race was getting "too much" attention and 36 percent the issue was not receiving enough attention. However, when answers to the question were examined by racial group, 60 percent of whites said too much and 28 percent said not enough. A total of 40 percent of Hispanics said too much and 47 percent said not enough. Only 13 percent of blacks said race was receiving too much attention and 78 percent said it was not getting enough attention.[41]

We not only have different interpretations of the facts, but we have different interpretations about how we interpret the facts!

Think about it. How long did it take you to "know" what happened on that rainy night in Sanford, Florida? When you heard the initial news report, did you immediately have an opinion or reaction? What did it remind you of from your past experiences? Whose voice, whose evidence, whose point of view did you have a tendency to believe? How much investigation of all of the facts did you do? How did you interpret what you read, saw, or heard? What did you base those interpretations on? In your mind, who was "guilty" and of what?

We all have our opinions, but how closely related are they to the truth? And, perhaps even more importantly, how do the opinions that we instantly form *influence the "truth" that we end up seeing*?

And how much of all of this reacting did you consciously do? How comfortable were you, or are you still, to share a different point of view from your peer group? Or did groupthink occur in your peer group and one particular point of view became the "right" one?

The Trayvon Martin/George Zimmerman case was tragic. It revealed a dark strain in human unconsciousness, showing our tendency to be driven by biases that we might not even know we have within us. As awful as the loss of a young man might be, it is but one example of how our unconscious minds make choices for us that may have nothing to do with our conscious beliefs or values. Or, in other words, what does or doesn't happen around us.

We can easily see this when we look at the web of automatic assumptions and stereotypes that surrounded the case, because it is a classic case of how complex these webs of biases and assumptions can be, and also of the tragic cost of our own blindness. It is easy to see how certain visual images created a flood of associations and assumptions that resulted in a young man's death. Zimmerman saw a "punk." Martin saw a "creepy-ass cracker." Even if one believes the jury's verdict was justified by poor prosecutorial decisions to charge Zimmerman with the wrong crime, it is hard to look at the evidence and not believe that fear and bias contributed to what happened, how people reacted to what happened, and how the jury ruled on what happened. And that this can happen, *without any of the parties at hand realizing that these forces are motivating them to do what they do.* One does not have to realize the full force of the forces.

Again, we must ask: Was justice served? Is it possible for us to ever know?

The dramatic nature of an event such as the death of Trayvon Martin shines a floodlight on the nature of bias, both conscious and unconscious. The reality is that bias is part of our everyday life. It happens at school, at work, in our communities, and even in our homes. Sometimes it can contribute to quite tragic consequences.

When something like the death of a Trayvon Martin occurs, most people are horrified and see the tragedy of the situation. It is hard to imagine a reasonable person not being deeply saddened at the thought of an innocent teenager dying, no matter the circumstances or justification. Yet, based on their frame of reference, some people might have very different views as to what and who is responsible. For many, it is an obvious case of conscious or unconscious bias. However, some people have said things such as, "Well, this was a tragedy, but there are young people of all races who are seen as potential troublemakers, and how do you know this was about race? Maybe George Zimmerman would have done the same thing if Trayvon had been white." Remember, in the Pew poll I cited earlier in this chapter, a majority of Americans believed too much emphasis had been place on race during the trial.

Thus poses the true challenge in looking at issues of unconscious bias, and one of the reasons unconscious bias is an occurrence that we must deal with every single day. Perhaps it is true that there are people of all races who are seen as potential "troublemakers." And as such, it is "correct" for people to respond to accordingly. People can respond in the way George Zimmerman responded to Trayvon Martin. Or they can think it proper for such "troublemakers" to be stopped and questioned by police. And while it is true that there are "troublemakers" of all races and ages, statistics indicate that blacks and Latinos are stopped far more often by police than are white people.

For example, let's look at the statistics gathered by the New York Civil Liberties Union regarding New York City's controversial decades-old "stop and frisk" law. In 2011, 87 percent of those stopped by the police in the city were African American or Latino. How do such numbers compare to the city's general population? Well, the African American population of New York City is 23.4 percent. In 2011, 53 percent of those stopped by police were African American. The Latino population of the city is 29.3 percent. And in 2011, 33.7 percent of those stopped were Latino. The combined population of whites, Asians, and Native Americans in New York is 47.3 percent, yet only 13.3 percent of those stopped by police were from these groups.

Some might and do say things such as, "It is not bias when you stop more people because more people like them commit crimes!" However, we can just as easily turn that syllogism around. We can suggest that had whites, Asians, and Native Americans been stopped as often as blacks and Latinos, they just might have been found guilty of committing more crimes.

These kinds of statistics are not limited to New York City. In fact, they are more normal than unusual. For instance, in Washington, D.C., a July 2013 study by the Washington Lawyers' Committee for Civil Rights and Urban Affairs found that in a city in which the adult population is 42 percent white and 47.6 percent black, more than eight out of ten arrests were of African Americans, including nine out of ten drug arrests (with six of ten for simple possession). This occurs even though most social scientists believe that actual drug usage numbers are far more equal across race. [42]

I have no doubt that many people who respond to situations like the Trayvon Martin incident do not think race is a factor in their reaction. My guess is that they could pass a lie detector test in that regard. In fact, I'm sure that George Zimmerman probably feels that way as well. But if we understand what the research is telling us about how deeply and pervasively we hold unconscious biases, *the fact that most people are not aware of their bias has almost no bearing on whether or not it is there, or whether or not it motivates our behavior.*

And what is the long-term, functional impact of these biases? What is it that has someone like Trayvon Martin draw the kind of attention that I almost assuredly would never have drawn had I been dressed the same way and done exactly the same things he was doing on that rainy night in Florida? Being able to walk down the street without worrying that I might be seen as a threat is something I and others like me take for granted. Such liberty is actually a privilege that Trayvon Martin and many other young African American and Latino men cannot claim. How does that sense of power and privilege, or lack of it, influence how we operate in life?

Let's take a look.

Chapter Five

Who Has the Power?

If you talk with a harsh, urbanized accent and you use too many profanities that will often get you barred from many arenas, no matter what you're trying to say. On the other hand, polite, formal language is allowed almost anywhere even when all it is communicating is hatred and violence. Power always privileges its own discourse while marginalizing those who would challenge it or that are the victims of its power. —Junot Díaz

Let's now deepen our conversation about stereotyping and the various ways our minds associate certain people with certain qualities. To expand our understanding of situations involving stereotyping, we first must develop a more comprehensive understanding of how power and privilege play out around us because power and privilege are very much involved in any type of stereotyping, whether it's "good" or "bad."

Power is definitely a core factor in all human relationships, one that operates at many different levels. On a personal level, power affects any sense of agency we may feel about our lives. Do we feel confident that we can handle what life throws our way? Do we feel protected from the abuse of power by others? Do we have a sense of control over our own lives? Power is critical to the answers to all of these questions.

Most of the messaging we get about our personal sense of power is subliminal, even as we are receiving the messages. We may see power, but we may not be particularly conscious of it. Messages about power and its uses and abuses can come from our families, our cultures, our religions, and through books, stories, and the mass media. Let's just say I watched television shows and movies when I was younger (and most of us did watch a lot of TV and see a lot of movies when we were growing up). Shows and movies that depicted men as stronger and more powerful than the women they interacted with may cause me, all these years later, and without my realizing it, to fall into those same patterns in my own relationships with women. If I see countless images of male bosses and female subordinates, I may unconsciously slip into a leadership mode when I am working with women, even if they are actually my superiors. The same thing is, of course, true for other distinctions of group dominance.

If somebody from a nondominant group sees people in their group depicted as powerless or subject to the will of others, the perceived lack of a sense of power can be internalized as well. As I discussed earlier, people in nondominant groups may experience *stereotype threat* or *internalized bias* as a result of such power imbalances. These feelings of diminished power are often unconscious, yet they shape people's fundamental view of the world and the people in it.

It also is important to view these dynamics of power in the context of the "us/them" tendencies that I described earlier. When we identify with a particular group as opposed to another (e.g., "men" rather than "women"), it is natural for us to almost immediately begin to experience the power differential that may exist between those groups. Sometimes it is very observable and conscious, but very often these dynamics are just under the surface of our awareness.

In the United States, the list of predominant cultural groups generally includes white people, men, heterosexuals, able-bodied people, Christians, people of higher socioeconomic statuses, those who were native born, and those who are native English speakers, among others. All members of these groups are affected in various ways as a result of their membership in a particular dominant group. Members of nondominant groups (e.g., white women, men and women of color, LGBT people, people with disabilities) are similarly affected by the identities of those in dominant groups. One of the ways this impact plays out is through how much power, privilege, and safety we feel within our day-to-day lives.

Power provides a foundation for our sense of agency in life. Our ability to get things done, to influence outcomes, to exercise authority, and to control our environment has an enormous influence on how secure we feel in our ability to keep ourselves safe, as well as to get what we want and make the kinds of things we want to happen.

There are different ways that this kind of power can play out in organizational and personal life:[1]

- Coercive Power—The ability to use positional force or dominance to get people to comply with your desire. This often comes from positioning someone in the formal structure of an organization. This is an obvious source of power and can manifest in both positive and negative ways. In negative ways, coercive power can motivate people out of fear of the danger that defying an authority figure might bring. In more positive terms, it can motivate people based on the satisfaction that comes with acknowledgment and approval.

- Reward Power—Reward power emerges when one has the ability to give another person things they want (e.g., pay, vacation, job assignments, promotions) or to relieve people of things that they don't want (e.g., telling somebody that they don't have to travel or attend a meeting). Of course, this power is dependent upon the ability of the person in power to continue to provide these kinds of rewards. It also is dependent upon there being alignment between the rewards one has to distribute and the desires of those being rewarded. If, for example, somebody is looking for a promotion but when the offered promotion requires them to move to another city (something they don't believe they are able to do), the reward loses its allure. Rewards can be either personal (e.g., money, material resources, promotions) or more impersonal (e.g., acknowledgments, compliments).
- Relational Power—This form of power comes from a real or perceived connection to some figure or figures of authority. The person with this kind of power may not have any clear titular authority, but may still wield enormous power because of their relationship to someone who does have that power. For instance, some of the most powerful people I have met in corporate life are executive assistants to CEOs. Their titular power is limited, but they control access to the executive's schedule and also often have the ear of the boss. Similarly, people who have personal relationships with a person of power often can open the door to access.
- Resource Control—It is often said that "whoever controls the purse strings," controls the situation. The ability to mobilize or deny the mobilization of organizational, community, or family resources can have a huge influence over behavior and decision making. Even having control over how a budget is organized can be a major area of influence.
- Assumed or Demonstrated Expertise—This kind of power comes with a real or perceived ability to provide expertise that is either limited or nonexistent in a particular situation. So in circumstances relating to health, for instance, a medical doctor may have an enormous amount of authority, regardless of their actual expertise or knowledge in that area of medicine. The perception of expertise can often be more important than the actual level of expertise.
- Informational Power—We all know the expression "knowledge is power." Informational power is based on the access people have to inside information within an organization or a system. This often can be closely tied to hierarchical position, or to relational power. People with informational power can influence through what they know and others don't. They also can adopt reward power by choosing to include or exclude certain people by determining who they will share information with.

- Personality Power—There are some people who generate power and influence simply by the force of their personalities. We sometimes call this "charisma," and even hear of people who can "sell snowballs in Alaska."

When you think of these distinctions in power, in what areas of your life do you feel the most powerful? Where do you sometimes feel powerless?

All of these distinctions of power influence people in various ways and in various combinations. We have our own personal sense of power or powerlessness. This personal sense of power or powerlessness is usually displayed interpersonally, in interactions with others. It can be a function of our way of being with people, the way we behave, or the language we use. These forms of implicit power also can become institutionalized, often without our realization. Various different structures and systems, rules, policies and procedures, and even our language can unwittingly reinforce the dynamics of power. For instance, how many female chair*men* do you run into these days? How often do you see forms that ask for "spouse" in situations where gays or lesbians have not yet been legally allowed to be married, with no alternative designation for a domestic partner? Which holidays are automatic days off in your school or organization? Do the holidays take all religions into account?

It is important to recognize that individual examples may not seem particularly significant in and of themselves. However, webs of circumstances that can run into the dozens can, over time, create a particular power dynamic between people. Often these examples occur in the form of micro-behaviors (micro-advantages or micro-affirmations on the positive side, micro-inequities on the negative side). They are small behaviors that may be slightly bothersome or even insignificant, but they can make a larger impact than we realize, especially when they occur as part of a web of similar behaviors.

The term "micro-inequities" was first coined in 1973 by Mary Rowe, the ombudsperson and adjunct professor of negotiation and conflict management at the MIT Sloan School of Management. She defined micro-inequities as "apparently small events which are often ephemeral and hard-to-prove, events which are covert, often unintentional, frequently unrecognized by the perpetrator, which occur wherever people are perceived to be 'different.'"[2] These may include behaviors such as:

- Constantly having your name mispronounced
- Being interrupted regularly
- Having people avoid making eye contact with you
- Multitasking during face-to-face conversations (e.g., checking emails or texting)
- Calling on members of one group to speak more frequently than others
- Nonverbal signals (facial expressions, eye rolling, etc.)
- Acknowledging some people but not others

- Frequency and dependability of communication
- Events or activities that occur in places that are uncomfortable for members of certain groups

Most of these would be bothersome by themselves, but when they are combined they reinforce a dynamic of power within the culture in which they occur. And they are often also supported by corresponding micro-advantages, including:

- Playing golf or similar activities with the boss
- Attending social events or business lunches
- Having people take your word for it when you give them a reason why something went wrong
- Stopping what you are doing to listen to someone when they are speaking
- Being acknowledged when you enter a room or make a contribution
- Being introduced when meeting someone with a colleague
- Having your ethnicity acknowledged with interest
- Being invited to give your opinion in a conversation
- Always having people accommodate your language

We send dozens of micro-messages to each other in a normal conversation and thousands throughout a normal day. Almost all of them are unconscious. However, depending upon the framework of power that exists in a given relationship, one party or the other might make assumptions about the intent of the deliverer of the message that may be inaccurate, though the impact remains.

These networks of messages create a certain sense of privilege for people in the dominant group. Like the power itself, that privilege generally shows up on the personal, interpersonal, and institutional levels and is characterized in many ways. A privilege is generally a special advantage, immunity, or benefit that is enjoyed by some people but not all. It is often a right that is reserved for a certain group of people who may not be subject to the same rules and sanctions as others. Privileges are often characterized as legitimate or not, depending upon whether they are clearly stipulated and related to clear determinations. However, privilege is often far more subtle, and the roots of it are unclear.

Dominant group identity can often be the source of hidden privilege. However, that privilege may not occur as hurtful behavior. It may simply occur as a presumption of normalcy. It can be so pervasive and so invisible that when we experience its benefits, we often believe we have earned them and, as such, believe that anybody can have access to the same privileges if "they work hard and are smart enough," or employ some similar mental algorithm. To use a baseball analogy, it's somewhat like being born on third base and thinking you hit a triple. The aspects of power and privilege that got them there are so unconscious that the person believes they have achieved things solely by their own merit.

I was once talking to a student who had gone to an excellent college and was back for his first Thanksgiving break. We got into a discussion about the affirmative admissions program that his university had put in place. "I'm just having a hard time making sense of it," the student said. "I believe in equality (and, in fact, I knew this student had very progressive attitudes toward diversity and had even volunteered in neighborhood food banks). But at some point, why should one student get extra points for being of a particular race when somebody else got better grades, SATs, more extracurricular activities, etc.? No matter what race we are, I think we all still need to perform."

Given that I knew the student and had a close relationship with him, I took out a piece of paper and started to ask him some questions. Did he ever feel like he was in any real danger going to or coming home from school? How much time did his parents spend with him on homework? What level of education was available to his parents? How many books did he have in his home? Did he ever worry about his family having the money for extracurricular activities (e.g., sports, music lessons, scouts, martial arts)? Did he have a decent computer at home? Internet service? How old was he when he got the computer? How old was he when he started using it? Was it his, or did he have to share it with other family members? How much access did he have to the computer? Did he have to work to contribute to his family? How many hours? How old was he when he started work? Did he take an SAT preparation class? How many? How many times did he take the SAT so that he could be sure to get the best score possible?

All in all I asked him about thirty or forty questions. After he was finished answering, I asked him to go down the list and check off the ones that he guessed would be true of the average child growing up in the community where the food bank he volunteered in was located. He checked off about 20 percent of the list. "Wow," he said. "I never thought of it that way before."

Most members of dominant groups don't think about things that way, because we don't have to in order to survive. This dynamic is accentuated by the fact that members of dominant groups tend not to see group identity, or to be associated with those identities as clearly or often as people in nondominant groups (as I discussed in chapter 2). That lack of awareness of group identity can easily blind us from seeing the presence of our power and privilege, even when it is so obvious to others around us. This concealing of power and privilege is exacerbated by the fact that we tend to look at bias with an assumption of intent. Because we often think of bias as a function of overt acts of bigotry, we can sometimes remain blind to the invisible structures, systems, and behaviors that bestow and reinforce that power and privilege on a daily basis.

Margaret (Peggy) McIntosh, the associate director of the Wellesley College Center for Women and the founder and codirector of the National SEED Project on Inclusive Curriculum, addressed these phenomena in her well-known 1988 paper "Unpacking the Invisible Knapsack.[3] McIntosh identified fifty different examples of the ways that these privileges, or micro-advantages, occur as "an invisible weightless knapsack of special provisions, maps, passports, codebooks, visas, clothes, tools, and blank checks." Some of them (listed in no specific order) include:

- I can, if I wish, arrange to be in the company of people of my race most of the time.
- I can go shopping alone most of the time, pretty well assured that I will not be followed or harassed.
- I can turn on the television or view the front page of the newspaper and see people of my race widely represented.
- When I am told about our national heritage or about "civilization," I learn that people of my color made that heritage or civilization what it is today.
- I can go into a supermarket and find the staple foods which fit with my cultural traditions. I can go to a hairdresser and find someone who can cut my hair.
- I do not have to educate my children to be aware of systemic racism for their own daily physical protection. I am never asked to speak for my whole racial group.
- I can take a job with an affirmative action employer without having my coworkers suspect I got the job because of my race.
- If I have low credibility as a leader, I can be sure that my race is not the reason for the problem.
- My children are given textbooks and instructed in classrooms which implicitly support my kind of family unit and do not turn them against my choice of domestic partnership.

How does privilege show up in your life? In your organization? Are you aware of the places where you have power and privileges or the places you do not? How does it feel to not have power and privilege?

Many of these kinds of messages are concealed by their obviousness in the world around us. We don't think about them because we don't have to do so. We may be completely unconscious as to how we acquired the messaging that may have led us to experience this power and privilege. This can make it both more difficult to identify the power and privilege and confront it when it is brought to our attention. Here's an illustration. Any U.S. resident who, at this writing, is older than sixteen, probably went to an elementary school where they saw pictures of the presidents of the United States displayed proudly on the wall. As they walked past them each day, did the young, white, Christian boys notice that all of the presidents were members of their "group"? Or were they just "the presidents," and nothing more? And when young girls or people of color walked past those same pictures, did they consciously notice the message that "this is not a club for you," or did that message simply settle into the unconscious mind? One group is left with the unstated communication of "you can be anything you want in life." The other feels that "there are certain things you will never be allowed to do." What impact might such messages make upon our internal sense of self?

And in an attempt to protect us, the people who love us may even inadvertently reinforce the messages. For instance, I can't count how many African American friends and associates of mine have told me that their parents told them "you have to work twice as hard as white people in order to get along in this society." This is clearly a message that is designed to communicate that it was more challenging to have one's talents and skills valued by the dominant culture. Yet, despite its intent, how is that statement understood by those who receive it? One participant in a workshop I conducted stated her understanding in a way that echoes the sentiments I've heard from many others through the years.

> I heard my whole childhood that you have to work twice as hard. And I did. I busted my tail and I made it. I graduated from college. I went to graduate school. I got my Ph.D. But underneath it all I never felt like I was good enough. It wasn't until I was in therapy and trying to figure out why it never felt like enough, that I "cracked the code." When my parents told me that I had to work twice as hard, out of their love for me, they were motivating me to succeed in a challenging world. But as a little child, what I heard was "you're only half as good," and that message has stayed with me my whole life.

This message is strong. Yet, within some of the classic ways that power and privilege have been studied in the diversity field, there is a trap. This is because the study of power and privilege has focused on the particular people (e.g., "white male privilege") rather than the dynamics of power and privilege. The cost of that is that we often create hierarchies of pain, in which one person or group's suffering is not seen to be as important as another's. If we are not careful, this tendency can have people so focused on the aspects of their identities where they do not have power and privilege that they can remain blind to the places where they do. As McIntosh also wrote in her paper:

> After I realized the extent to which men work from a base of unacknowledged privilege, I understood that much of their oppressiveness was unconscious. Then I remembered the frequent charges from women of color that white women whom they encounter are oppressive. I began to understand why we are just seen as oppressive, even when we don't see ourselves that way. I began to count the ways in which I enjoy unearned skin privilege and have

been conditioned into oblivion about its existence. My schooling gave me no training in seeing myself as an oppressor, as an unfairly advantaged person, or as a participant in a damaged culture. I was taught to see myself as an individual whose moral state depended on her individual moral will . . . whites are taught to think of their lives as morally neutral, normative, and average, and also ideal, so that when we work to benefit others, this is seen as work that will allow "them" to be more like "us."

One of the challenges to understanding power and privilege in a more sophisticated way is that we are really talking about two domains of looking at the issue that may at times seem confusing, or even conflicting.

On one level, most people belong to at least one group that affords them privilege. We may be white in a predominantly white culture, or male in a predominantly male environment. We may be Christian, heterosexual, educated, hold a higher than average socioeconomic status, or have basic creature comforts that other people do not possess, such as running water or food security. And despite our power and privilege in some areas, we could be in the nondominant group in others. We may be white and male, but gay, Buddhist, or disabled. We may be introverted in primarily extroverted cultures. So at that level, we may establish some sense of communality with others across our differences.

My dear friend Dr. Johnnetta Betsch Cole, the former president of both Spellman and Bennett Colleges for Women and now the director of the Smithsonian Museum of African Art, shared this example from her own life:

I grew up black, and female in the South, but I did not grow up poor. My great grandfather on my maternal side, Abraham Lincoln Lewis, founded the first insurance company in the state of Florida with six other African American men. He became Florida's first black millionaire. So our family was well known in Jacksonville. It was very important to my mother that we acted normal, and not "full of ourselves." This was, of course, the segregated South, and so many of the business establishments were closed to us. However, because people knew that we had wealth, periodically my mom would get a phone call from the owner of one of the big department stores, who would say, "Mrs. Betsch, we have some great new clothes for the girls, why don't you bring them down to try them on." Of course that didn't mean we were invited during the day. We would have to go after hours. When I was very little I didn't understand exactly what was going on, so it felt kind of special to have the store to ourselves. But at some point, I don't remember how old I was, I realized what was going on. I saw that this wasn't special, it was an insult! And I remember telling my mother that I wouldn't go anymore! That if we couldn't shop there during the day, I definitely was not going to shop in the middle of the night. In the South in those days, race always trumped class.

Most people have some aspects of themselves that allow them to feel privilege and some that do not. Yet on another level, those differences are significant because they are not all equivalent. We still live in social groups, and all social groups have some sense of status determinations that are measured through various criteria: seniority, education level, race, gender, socioeconomic status, religion, organizational status (e.g., leader, manager, employee), geography, native born, or immigrant. In these domains, and potentially others, our experiences are quite different. So how do we reconcile the dissonance between the commonality of our shared experience with lacking privilege, and the differences between the effects of certain privileges over others?

Perhaps it can be helpful to think in terms of a fluid matrix, with power, status, and resources being on the vertical coordinate, and life experience and narrative being on the horizontal one. It's important to know that the sense of fluidity is a critical function of understanding this concept because our sense of power and privilege might change with the situation.

For example, a few years ago I was speaking to an African American man who was a senior vice president with one of my client companies. He was highly educated, very well compensated, and headed a division of more than 250 people. He had an executive office, a designated parking space, and the authority to control hundreds of millions of dollars in resources. He lived in a very large house in a very high-income community. He is a Christian and heterosexual. His commentary to me one day went something like this:

> I know that in most ways I am living the American dream. I've got the doctorate from a top-ranked school, the big job with a big paycheck, fancy car, people to tell what to do . . . in all ways I shouldn't have any concerns. And for the most part, on a daily basis, I don't. But there are some points when it hits me that I am still on the other side of the power and privilege scale. For example, when my two sons got their driver's licenses, I had to sit down and tell them how to very carefully respond if they are ever stopped by a police officer—where to put their hands; what to say or not say; what was the appropriate level of eye contact—enough but not too much. And then, just last month, one of them was coming home driving my car and was stopped in our predominantly white, high-income community, by a white police officer who just wanted to find out "what he was doing there." I know I even think when I am going out for a run, or going to the store, whether the clothes I wear will have people see me as "belonging" in the neighborhood that I have lived in for more than fifteen years! No matter how many of the "brass rings" I've grabbed, it's still there for me. That may be the most frustrating thing of all. There is no way to get away from it.

Power and privilege are all around us, and yet we understand more than ever how unconscious we are to the ways they affect our lives, both in our own self-perception and in the way we behave toward others.

These dynamics play out every day in our communities, schools, and workplaces. For instance, one research study showed that when men and women were observed in leadership situations, female leaders "received more negative effect responses and fewer positive responses than men offering the same suggestions and arguments. Female leaders received more negative than positive responses, in contrast to men, who received at least as many positive as negative responses."[4] In another study, Martha Foschi, a professor of anthropology and sociology at the the University of British Columbia, found that these dynamics lead to double standards which "become a basis for stricter standards for the lower status person" in evaluations of personal characteristics, how rewards are allocated, and sentiments of either like or dislike. They also affect perceptions of beauty, morality, and mental health.[5]

These patterns are often so unconscious that, ironically, the people in nondominant groups who are at the receiving end of this behavior are likely to notice them far more frequently than the people who are exhibiting the behavior. Because people have often assumed motive and reacted accordingly, dominant group members can become very defensive when confronted with behavior that they were not even aware they were engaging in!

Recently, we have developed a better understanding of the way power affects us in very interesting ways. It is easy enough to say, for instance, that people who have power are not as sensitive to others because "they are busy," or have "too much to do." But, as it turns out, there may be other factors involved besides scheduling.

Sukhvinder Singh Obhi, whom I quoted earlier, and his associates took groups of people and randomly stimulated their sense of power by having them reflect on times in their life when they had felt either powerful or powerless. The researchers then had the participants watch a video of a hand squeezing a rubber ball between the index finger and thumb. They then tracked the brain activity to see if there was any difference in the mirror neuron activity when people felt powerful or powerless. It turned out that when people were in a "powerless" mind-set, their mirror system was increased. Their brains reacted more strongly to the mirroring effect of watching the ball. They became more sensitive to the external stimulus, whereas when people were feeling powerful, the mirror neuron activation was lower. Power, it turns out, diminishes our sense of empathy.[6]

Paul Piff and Dacher Keltner, psychologists at the University of California at Berkeley, have tested this hypothesis by focusing on the power and privilege bestowed by social class, one of the most consistent sources of power in most cultures, especially in the United States.[7] Piff and Keltner have conducted a number of studies designed to determine whether income and social status affect people's behavior. What they found was quite dramatic.

In a broad range of research, they discovered that wealth not only seems to correlate with less empathy, but also with increased unethical behavior.

They found that wealthy people were more likely to break the law while driving, including refusing to stop at stop signs when people were waiting to walk across, take things from others, negotiate unethically, break rules to win contests, and generally be more approving of greed. This is not to dismiss all of the generosity that many wealthy people demonstrate through charitable giving, or to say that being wealthy is an intrinsically evil thing. This research was simply aimed at examining everyday occurrences in the lives of people.

It would be easy to take the results of these studies and jump to the conclusion that "poor people are nicer than wealthy people," or to discount the research altogether as "class warfare" (after all, some of the researchers are at the so-called People's Republic of Berkeley). However, it's important to realize that there may be something much more complex within the findings.

We have seen power played out very publicly in all of the sex scandals that powerful people, mostly men, have been engaged in within the past two decades or so. Joris Lammers, an assistant professor of psychology at the University of Cologne in Germany, found that power is more of a factor than gender in this dynamic. Power, among members of both genders, increases the likelihood of sexual infidelity.[8] Lammers found that the most powerful people he observed in his study were 30 percent more likely to have affairs than the least powerful.

Lammers added some interesting observations to this idea in a June 2011 interview with National Public Radio science correspondent Shankar Vedantam. The interview was held in the wake of political sex scandals, including those involving former California Governor Arnold Schwarzenegger and former U.S. Senator John Edwards. In the interview, Lammers suggested that this increased likelihood of sexual infidelity may have to do with the way our brains respond to power. "So you can even see this in brain activation," he said. "If people feel powerful, and you can see that brain structure associated with positive things—with rewards—is just much more activated than the part that is steered toward preventing the bad things from happening."[9]

These findings are consistent with those of Jonathan W. Kunstman and Jon K. Maner, social psychologists at Florida State University.[10] Kunstman and Maner conducted a number of experiments in which they put heterosexual students together in pairs and consciously gave one of the study participants more power than the other. In a short period of time they began to notice a change. The people in the power position became more flirtatious, making more direct eye contact, and touching more. They also were more likely to assume flirtation in the behavior of the other. They seemed to see themselves as more attractive to the other because of their power. Their findings crossed gender, which may in fact mean that the reason so many more men get caught in scandals than women is because more men are in positions of power in our society.

Feeling powerful seems to makes us less oriented toward risk, and more oriented toward rewards. Less oriented toward compassion, and more oriented toward selfishness. Less aware of how we got where we are, and more likely to feel like we earned it ourselves. Does that mean that people with power are not such good people?

What all of this means is that power activates certain aspects of the brain and shuts down others, creating an unconscious tendency to be more or less attentive to the needs of others around us. People in power positions may be unconsciously more susceptible to selfishness and reduced empathy, without ever realizing it. It is not the people who hold the power that are the problem. Rather, it is the impact power makes upon people. This perhaps explains why there are so many historical instances in which people have overturned repressive governments, only to replace them with a new repressive government. It is very much in line with words once spoken by Lord Acton when he said "power tends to corrupt, and absolute power corrupts absolutely."

On the other hand, when people in power come "down from their pedestal" and relate on an equal level with others, their emphathetic responses can increase. Consider that on the tv series "Undercover Boss," the boss always wants to improve employees' working conditions after experiencing them as a peer.

So does that mean we should discourage power, or that we have to regulate people who have it? I would suggest that it means we need to become much more conscious about the places and aspects of our lives in which we have power, either explicit or implicit, so that we can moderate our behavior accordingly. And it means that when we are members of a dominant group in today's diverse society, we have to be especially aware of how social advantages might affect our behavior. In the same sense as any other bias, power can be a blind spot that others see about us, but that we do not see in ourselves.

And all of the dynamics that I have been talking about show up every day. In the next chapter, let's look at a few examples of everyday power that goes beyond the research.

Chapter Six

Like Water for the Fish

Networks of Bias in Everyday Life

There are these two young fish swimming along and they happen to meet an older fish swimming the other way, who nods at them and says, "Morning, boys. How's the water?" And the two young fish swim on for a bit, and then eventually one of them looks over at the other and goes, "What the hell is water?" —David Foster Wallace, Kenyon College Commencement Address, 2005

Over the course of the previous five chapters, I have discussed the way bias manifests in our lives. I have touched on the various ways the mind is designed to process the world we see, how that gives us far more unconscious than conscious forms of perception, and how matters manifest as various forms of bias. However, for the most part, the examples I cited concerned individual choices or circumstances.

When we look at the death of Trayvon Martin, for example, we can see that numerous examples of bias combined to result not only in the death of a young man, but also in the varied reactions of different people, including the media and the investigating police. Then there was the matter of George Zimmerman's court case, the jury's verdict, and the role bias played in those situations.

In fact, these complex networks of bias that surround us every day make a huge impact upon the way we engage in life. And we are, for the most part, unaware of the bias. Culture has a profound influence on our behavior, and it is, for the most part, unconscious. While it may seem relatively easy to correct a single act of unconscious bias, it is almost impossible to notice how deeply we are ensnared in a web of instances in which bias affects our fundamental institutions. In this chapter, I will address this dynamic in three major, powerful cultural systems that profoundly affect our day-to-day life: the legal system, the health-care system, and politics. I won't even begin to cite every example of how bias affects each of these systems, because that would be impossible. I also will not focus on all of the micro-inequities and micro-advantages that occur every day. As I have noted earlier, bias, as well as power, is present in almost every human interaction. However, I do want to identify at least some examples so we can look at how these networks of bias profoundly affect us every single day.

THE LEGAL SYSTEM

Bias starts to affect us from the time we are very young. There are the subtle and not so subtle messages that brand certain people (but not others) as "the criminal element." And people on both sides of the equation of the justice system absorb these messages. It is no secret that the media have contributed to the identification, by a great many people, of African American men as criminals. [1] African Americans and Latinos are portrayed far more (in relation to their population and demographics) as criminals, drug users, sex workers, or generally less functional citizens. Of course, these images are not lost on children of all races who observe these characterizations and internally, as well as externally, absorb the stereotypes and the associated bias. The media contribute to this identification, not simply through fictionalized story lines, but also in the reporting of news. And sometimes those portrayals are particularly startling.

On June 30, 2011, Chicago television station WBBM ran a story about a shooting of two teenagers that had occurred in Chicago's Park Manor neighborhood the previous evening. The incident was the latest in a series of gun violence events that had occurred in the city over the course of several years. During the broadcast, the news reporter interviewed a four-year-old African American boy on the street to get his reaction. Here is a transcript of what was aired that evening:

Boy: "I'm not scared of nothing!"

Reporter: "When you get older are you going to stay away from all of these guns?"

Boy: "No."

Reporter: "No? What are you going to do when you get older?"

Boy: "I'm going to have me a gun!"

It was a chilling interview to watch and hear. And news anchors Steve Bartelstein and Susan Carlson said as much. "That was scary indeed," Bartelstein said. And then Carlson responded that "Hearing that little boy there — wow!"

Were the boy's words proof that young children can become violent based on their exposures? Maybe. But, as it turns out, not quite.

Researchers at the Robert C. Maynard Institute for Journalism Education at Northwestern University obtained the full video of the interview. Somebody on the scene who witnessed the interview but was not a journalist also had recorded it. In the full video, the context of the child's statement was dramatically different:

Reporter: "Boy, you ain't scared of nothing! Damn! When you get older are you going to stay away from all these guns?"

Boy: "No."

Reporter: "No? What are you going to do when you get older?"

Boy: "I'm going to have me a gun!"

Reporter: "You are? Why do you want to do that?"

Boy: "I'm going to be the police!"

Reporter: "Okay, then you can have one."

As I said earlier in this book, context is *everything*. [2]

Bias affects who is drawn into the legal system. Constant images associating crime with African Americans and Latinos result in unconscious links in the minds of everyday citizens, law enforcement officers, lawyers, judges, and juries. Earlier I discussed how this sort of thinking has affected things like the "stop and search" laws in New York City, and the "stand your ground" laws that have been enacted in many states and municipalities, one of which clearly contributed to the death of Trayvon Martin.

Once an accused criminal is in the criminal justice system, they encounter other areas of bias. Who is their attorney? Is it an expensive one that their family can afford? Or is it a low-cost attorney or public defender who, even if they are deeply committed to the case, may not have anywhere near the same resources to provide an adequate defense? In addition, there remains an imbalance in terms of lawyer representation among different racial and ethnic groups. According to the American Bar Association, 75 percent of lawyers are white, 9 percent Asian or Pacific Islander, 7 percent are African American, 6.5 percent Hispanic/Latino, and less than 1 percent are Native

American. And while more than 46 percent of lawyers entering the profession are women, less than 20 percent of women lawyers become partners in firms.[3]

And then, of course, there are the witnesses to crimes real and imagined. It is common knowledge that eyewitnesses have difficulty identifying individuals of another race. These potential errors raise grave concerns and have generated extensive research and commentary. Still, unconscious bias adds still another basis for potential misidentification.

One of the most popularly known studies on implicit bias and eyewitness identification involves a photograph of two men fighting; one man was holding a knife while the other was unarmed. When both men in the photograph were Caucasian, subjects generally correctly remembered which man was holding the knife. When the Caucasian man was armed and the African American man was unarmed, the majority of subjects, both African American and Caucasian, wrongly thought the African American man was holding the knife.[4]

So, knowing that bias is involved, what happens in the interactions between the accused, the lawyer, and the court? How much the lawyer believes and relates to the accused is, obviously, subject to all kinds of biases. And the same is true for the relationship between the judges and the courts. A number of years ago I spent a couple of days observing the proceedings in a Virginia courtroom. It was a lower-level court involving those who had been accused of a variety of infractions, including petty theft, traffic violations, drinking by minors, etc. I watched as defendants were questioned by the prosecuting attorney and the judge.

The defendants who came into the courtroom over the course of those days were extremely diverse. The judge, an older white man, did not seem to (at least on the surface) discriminate against anyone based on their race. However, after a short time, it became apparent to me that some measure of discrimination was being made known to the court by the judge. If any of the defendants had a heavy foreign accent, no matter what type, the judge lost his patience and, appearing visibly frustrated, would send the case quickly to the next level of proceeding. However, with other defendants who spoke with North American accents, the judge more often than not either resolved the case or dismissed it.

Just a few years ago, when I was conducting the research for my book *ReInventing Diversity*, I discovered a study that seemed to explain this behavior. Two University of Chicago researchers, Shiri Lev-Ari and Boaz Keysar, demonstrated that people with nonnative accents were perceived as "less credible" than those with local accents. They found that people were less likely to believe simple information from those with accents that were less familiar.[5] Of course, there can be dozens of similar biases. Race, gender, size, darkness/lightness of skin, and mannerisms all carry their own types of bias. I could continue for quite a while. What is important is to know how the presiding judges react to these biases, with their reaction then sending the accused into different levels of the criminal justice system.

And then there are the potential biases of juries. Of course, much depends on who is serving on the jury. Tufts University psychology professor Sam Sommers and Harvard University Business School professor Michael Norton found that race played a role as to who lawyers chose to allow on a jury, versus who they chose to employ preemptory challenges against to eliminate jurors they did not want. In this study, lawyers more often tended to exclude jurors who were black, even when they had the exact same profile as white ones.[6]

And how do juries decide? Sommers and Norton found that they make better decisions the more diverse they are, especially when the defendants are people of color.

What about how juries process the information they hear in the court? Not surprisingly, bias is involved. Justin Levinson, a professor of law at the University of Hawaii at Manoa, and the founder and director of the Culture and Jury Project, described a fictional incident to prospective jurors. Some were given information which included a picture of "William," and some were given the same information but the photo was of someone named "Tyrone." The pictures were both the same photograph, which had been digitally edited so that William appeared to be white and Tyrone black. The facts of the incident were exactly the same. Levinson found that participants more frequently remembered aggressive details when Tyrone rather than William was the defendant. Levinson concluded that "the race of a civil plaintiff or a criminal defendant can act implicitly to cause people to misremember a case's facts in racially biased ways."[7]

And in yet another study (of which, by the way, there are now hundreds!), Jennifer Eberhardt, a Stanford University psychologist, found that when people are exposed to objects that are described as "crime relevant" (e.g., handguns), they tend to notice black faces more than white faces. When exposed to pictures of the crime relevant objects that have been "degraded," people seem to identify the object more easily when they also are being exposed to a black face as opposed to a white one. The race-crime connection is so strong that it affects what we see.[8] And, as I wrote in *ReInventing Diversity*:

> And it doesn't stop there. It goes right into the courtroom. It is already well documented that murderers of white people are much more likely to be put to death than murderers of black people.[9] Eberhardt and her colleagues also studied the impact of racial stereotyping and unconscious patterns of reaction to the death penalty itself. After collecting the photographs of black defendants who might be eligible for the death penalty in Philadelphia between 1979 and 1999, she presented photographs of two faces of those who had been convicted of killing white people to a group of people, without telling them that the

photos were of convicted murderers. She asked them to rate each face based on how much it appeared to be stereotypically "black." What she found was chilling. While 24 percent of those who were rated as less stereotypically black received a death sentence, 58 percent of those who had been rated as more stereotypically black had received the death sentence. In other words, people were more than twice as likely to be sentenced to death simply because their skin color and features were perceived to be "blacker."[10] And, once again, the people making these decisions do not seem to realize that they are deciding based on racial characteristics. They don't know what they don't know.[11]

Of course, this is not the only example of sentencing disparities. In fact, African American and Latino men are incarcerated more often, given maximum sentences more often, and are slower to be paroled than Caucasians.[12] In a University of Notre Dame study of implicit bias in judges' decisions, Jeffrey Rachlinski and Sheri Lynn Johnson found that white judges especially demonstrated bias in favor of white defendants.[13]

As a final measure of understanding the complexity of this dynamic, we need to realize that bias doesn't stop in the court system. Bias also affects what happens after the prisoner's release. In a study funded by the U.S. Department of Justice, Princeton University professors Devah Pager and Bart Bonikowski and Harvard University professor Bruce Western found there is tremendous employment disparity between white and black ex-convicts. White ex-cons got a substantially higher percentage of job callbacks compared to blacks with identical criminal records. Black men in the study were only one-third as likely to get a positive response as their white counterparts, despite having identical qualifications and drug-related criminal offenses. And, astonishingly, newly released white felons often experience better job hunting success than young black men with no criminal record.[14]

I could continue for quite a long time, because, as I said, there are hundreds of other examples. But the stark reality is that the one constant in the legal system is none other than bias.

THE HEALTH-CARE SYSTEM

There may be no more complex system in our society than the health-care system. As such, it is probably the system where bias makes its greatest impact. At the same time, bias in the health-care system is one of the most perplexing examples of how bias plays out on a daily basis, *despite the conscious intentions of people who are acting in that way*!

The overall data are staggering. In 2002, the Institute of Medicine, a not-for-profit, nongovernmental organization created by Congress under the auspices of the National Academy of Sciences, issued a seminal report on health disparities in America.[15] In the report, the institute noted that racial disparities exist in the treatment of virtually every major disease and, in general, that there are higher incidents of illness manifestation among African Americans, Latinos, and Native Americans. Ten years later, other Institute of Medicine researchers found that progress in addressing the disparities had been slow, to say the least. Among the data presented were: [16]

- Health disparities are not going away. Many study participants agreed that health disparities have persisted over time and across the life course. Furthermore, people of color experience an earlier onset and a greater severity of negative health outcomes.
- Several participants noted that the current economic downturn has had— and will continue to have—serious effects on health, particularly for low-income families and people of color. Living in poverty is a major risk factor for poor health outcomes. And, race/ethnicity and income are inextricably intertwined in the United States.
- Despite a general feeling that the United States is in a "postracial" period, several study participants noted that institutional racism and racial discrimination are very much alive and well. Institutional racism and its effects have well-documented negative effects on health outcomes.
- Many participants discussed the important role of community environmental factors in influencing health outcomes. Residential segregation continues to be a major problem for people of color who live in low-income communities.
- The need to raise awareness of the existence of health disparities in the United States continues to be important; commentary was included regarding the low levels of awareness of health disparities by the general public.

There is tremendous irony within these findings. I have spent a large part of my career working in health care. Before I went into diversity and human resources consulting, I spent several years working for a major hospital. Many of my firm's clients have been health-care providers. My company, Cook Ross, also works closely with the American Association of Medical Colleges on a number of projects. Let me tell you one thing I know for sure: people in health care are among the most dedicated I know. They are deeply committed to healing people, and yet the information contained in the reports cited earlier shows that conscious intent and results are not necessarily aligned. Let's consider some of the factors that cause this to happen. As with the legal system, there is no one simple cause.

Overall, it is important to note that generalized societal bias has been found to affect health. This is not only true in terms of access issues, which I will discuss, but also in the recognition that experiences of discrimination have been found to be "an important type of psychosocial stressor that can lead to adverse changes in health status and altered behavioral patterns that increase health risks."[17] The findings indicate that the daily stress of dealing with negative bias puts a strain on the health of individuals who deal with it. A skeptic might ask whether all of us deal with stress of one kind or another. And, of course, we do. However, this research shows that the systemic nature of prejudice makes a significant impact upon health outcomes. Let's now look at some of the ways this dynamic plays out in the health-care system.

Access

While we predominantly look at the health-care system from the standpoint of treatment, access issues can contribute to creating a predisposition to good or poor health. People in low-income communities suffer from a multitude of areas of access deprivation. And, as the Institute of Medicine study that I just cited indicates, race/ethnicity and income are inextricably interwoven. From the earliest stages, some people may suffer from a lack of access to medical facilities due to patterns of bias that discourage practitioners from establishing offices in certain neighborhoods. The same, of course, is true about many business establishments. Do people in a particular community have access to fresh foods, or do they live in what has been called a "food desert," areas defined by the U.S. Department of Agriculture as "urban neighborhoods and rural towns without ready access to fresh, healthy, and affordable food"?[18] To what degree does socioeconomic status limit people's ability to take time off from work to treat illness, or to take care of their children or elderly family members if they need care? Do they have health insurance? If they do have health insurance, what quality is it? Do their lifestyles allow them to have access to exercise facilities or other wellness activities? (It's hard to find time for your Pilates class when you are working two jobs to support your three children and aging mother!) Is the information people need available in a language they can understand?

All of these issues, and many more that are related, can make a profound impact upon the overall health of a family. And all are dramatically influenced by bias. Now let's look at how this plays out through each step in a typical health-care interaction. We'll start with an ordinary hospital scenario.

At the time of hospital admission, does the admission staff member recognize the biases they have about the patient? How much does the patient's race, gender, sexual orientation, socioeconomic status, or language proficiency play a role in how they are treated, how seriously their concerns are taken, or how they are communicated with by hospital staff? Is it even possible that the admissions staff member can avoid making assumptions or having stereotypes about the patient or the patient's family member? Of course, the patient also may encounter challenges related to their insurance or lack of insurance.

It's crucial to remember that language and interpretation issues are significant in these exchanges.

Once the patient is admitted, they probably interact with a physician or other health professional to determine their situation. There is a whole body of research to indicate that bias plays a role in these kinds of interactions. Earlier in the book I discussed the way patients who are perceived to be obese are treated differently from other patients. This sort of bias also has been found to be true about other identity groups. In a study published in the *New England Journal of Medicine*, Kevin Schulman, a physician and professor of medicine, business administration, and global health at the Duke University School of Medicine, led a large study that found when presented with the same primary symptoms, physicians sent far more white men for cardiac catheterization procedures than either white women or men and women of color.[19] Similar research conducted at the University of Toronto found that women were far less likely to be recommended for knee replacements than men with the same presenting conditions.[20]

Another study found that almost one-third of lesbians, gays, and bisexuals believed medical personnel would treat them differently because of their sexual orientation. That number ballooned to almost 75 percent of transgender individuals. Research also shows that practitioners are more likely to assume that illnesses are sexually related when the patients are LGBT.[21] Further studies have indicated that these kinds of behaviors can be linked directly with how the doctors in question demonstrate implicit bias against a certain group, and researchers have found that unconscious bias plays a bigger role than explicit, conscious bias.[22]

Of course, in addition to bias and stereotypes, differences in culture also play a major role in the treatment of patients. There are hundreds of distinctions in the way cultural medicine plays out, and bias can affect them all. And all of these patient-provider relationships are affected by cultural communication styles or belief systems. When the patient is admitted, how are they and their family members treated? What does "immediate family" mean in their culture, when such a designation by a hospital may restrict visitation? Are people in rooms that bear religious symbols because a religious institution runs the hospital, even if the religion is not that of the patient? Is food available that patients feel comfortable eating?

When the patient is being treated, does the provider know that they may react differently to different medications, or that they commonly use traditional or folk medications? How does the practitioner react to finding that out? Do they disparage the folk medicine?

It also is important to note that all of this is especially true in emergency medical situations, either at the scene of an accident, a home emergency, or within the hospital emergency room itself. At times like this when patients and family members are the most frightened, and practitioners are the most rushed, bias can be especially present.

And, of course, there are numerous other interactions within the health-care continuum: Who gets into medical school? Who conducts research and on whom? How are students treated by faculty members in medical schools and teaching hospitals? How do faculty members interact with each other? How do administrators relate to various faculty members of different races, genders, and the like? And, how do patients interact with each other when they are put into shared spaces?

I could cite more examples, but I believe the point is made. There are literally hundreds of ways that bias plays a role in the health-care system. And it plays a role during times when people are, arguably, at their most vulnerable. And least able to sustain the impact bias may make upon their lives and the lives of their loved ones.

POLITICS

We live in a time when politics in the United States is more fractured than at almost any other point within the past 150 years. The network of contention that exists in our political structure today has created dynamics on both sides of the political spectrum which have greatly polarized people and their political beliefs. As such, it behooves us to ask how thoughtful and conscious we are about choosing our political leaders. Unfortunately, the answer is that most of us are not very thoughtful at all about this important decision.

Imagine you are watching a presidential debate. One candidate answers a question about health care (or for that matter, any other subject). He (maybe someday "she") gives a very thorough, reasonable answer. The other candidate turns to the first and says, "You know, that was a great answer. This is an area you have obviously given a great deal of thought to, and even though I think I am the better overall candidate for president, if I get elected I would really appreciate your input into my health-care plan."

How would you react to such a statement? How might the media react? What would the pundits say? What would the politicos say?

Most of us probably think that a candidate who might say something like that was either weak or intent upon committing career suicide. If his or her base weren't furious, the media would undoubtedly call such a comment nothing less than "a mistake." And yet, by any rational standard, we would, and should, see this kind of open behavior as constructive.

But does rationality have anything to do with politics? In fact, does rational thinking have anything at all to do with our elections today?

As I said earlier, it is no secret that electoral politics in the United States has become as polarized now as any time in our history, except perhaps during the Civil War.

One great example of this polarization was reported by David Wasserman of the Cook Political Report. Wasserman wrote about voters who live near two popular American institutions: Whole Foods Markets and Cracker Barrel restaurants.[23] It turns out that the communities surrounding these two establishments have a dependable historical political constituency. Whole Foods tends to be in liberal communities and Cracker Barrels are in conservative ones. Wasserman followed the 1992, 2000, and 2008 presidential voting patterns of people living near these establishments and found a most interesting trend.

In the 1992 election between President George H. W. Bush and then Governor Bill Clinton, Clinton received 60 percent of the Whole Foods vote and only 40 percent of the Cracker Barrel vote, a 20 percent gap. Eight years later, Vice President Al Gore received 58 percent of the Whole Foods vote and only 26 percent of the Cracker Barrel vote in his contest against then Governor George W. Bush, accounting for a 32 percent gap. And in 2008, then Senator Barack Obama received 81 percent of the Whole Foods vote compared to only 36 percent of the Cracker Barrel vote in his campaign against Senator John McCain, adding up to a significant 45 percent gap!

The tectonic plates of American politics are shifting dramatically, and the crevasses in our national politics seem to grow wider and deeper every day. These crevasses even show up in our choice of supermarkets and restaurants.

The width and depth of these crevasses might make one ask if the issues of the day are any more pressing than in the past. Clearly, we are going through challenging times, and yet, the past fifty years have been full of different, yet equally challenging times.

For example, during the Vietnam War, America was strongly divided on the merits of the war. Despite the division, there were anti-war Republicans like Oregon Senator Mark Hatfield and pro-war Democrats like Washington Senator Henry "Scoop" Jackson. The political parties were not as demanding of "lockstep" behavior as seems to be the case today. In fact, historically, the United States has operated as a bell curve, with a large center where political opinions often crossed party lines. In the second decade of this century, we are confronting more of a "dumbbell" curve in which the partisanship of both parties is paramount and the middle is disappearing and, in many cases, is almost all but gone.

This is a disturbing evolution, and it is one that makes people wonder what it means for the future of our democracy. In a healthy personal relationship, just to make a comparison, we sometimes extricate ourselves from the weeds of our personal "back and forth" in order to look at the relationship itself. We are able to see at those moments how we are stuck in the back and forth of polarizing arguments and know we must reorient ourselves to the overall good of the relationship. In politics, we seem to have lost the ability to do that in almost any way.

It is not a pretty sight.

So, if it's not pretty, then why is this happening? Today's media landscape may provide some answers.

When I was growing up in the 1950s and 1960s, we had much less access to variety in our news. The basic news stations available were ABC, NBC, and CBS, and there was very little political difference between the three networks. In fact, newscasters were intentional about not displaying their political views. In addition, the news was only on each day for a half hour. Editorial comments were occasional and noted, but mostly newscasters were measured on their nonpartisanship. The interpretation of news was left to the viewer, who perhaps also was influenced by occasional newspaper or magazine articles.

Now, of course, we are bombarded by a twenty-four/seven news cycle. Depending upon the news station you watch, you probably get presorted news. A Fox News viewer gets the more conservative side of the story, and an MSNBC viewer usually receives the more liberal. But more importantly, the line between journalism and punditry has virtually disappeared. Very few of today's reporters (especially those on television) seem to be completely objective. In addition, we have masses of talk radio programs, not to mention the explosion of sources such as Twitter, Facebook, Internet blogs, and more. On January 22, 2012, the day after the South Carolina presidential primary, the following narrative was included in a story in the *Washington Post*:

> Once upon a time . . . Dianne Belsom would get up in the morning and read the paper, taking in news stories about candidates and campaigns. Some stuff she agreed with, and some stuff she didn't. This morning, Belsom wakes, makes coffee and settles in at her desktop to fire up Facebook. There on her news feed are more than 100 stories that some of her 460 friends have posted since Belsom went to bed eight hours ago. Over the next three hours, Belsom bops around the web checking out the latest campaign news. Her sources are big and small, from nearby to faraway, but they have one thing in common: With rare exceptions, the news and commentary sites Belsom visits share her worldview.[24]

This is the world we live in today. A self-referential world fueled by a constant flood of information that affirms our already strongly held biases. A world fueled by a media industry that is heavily rewarded for how much it responds to, and inflames, partisan sentiment. Books fill our shelves and digital readers that pour gasoline onto the flames of separation. Some of the more flammable titles from the conservative side include Bill O'Reilly's *Pinheads and Patriots: Where You Stand in the Age of Obama* and Ann

Coulter's *Demonic: How the Liberal Mob Is Endangering America. Liberalism Is a Mental Disorder* is one of the offerings from Michael Savage, a media personality so incendiary he was at one point refused entry into the United Kingdom. Of course, the other side has screeds cut from a not terribly dissimilar cloth. There is Keith Olbermann's "Worst Person in the World" designation for people he deemed deserving of such an "honor." And Senator Al Franken's *Rush Limbaugh Is a Big Fat Idiot* and Ted Rueter's *449 Stupid Things Republicans Have Said* have hardly elevated the political discourse.

In addition to increased polarization, we have seen a "rise of the mob" on both sides of the political spectrum over the past several years. First the Tea Party became a political brand that mobilized voters, candidates, and elections. Then the "Occupy" movements spread like wildfire across the world, appearing in hundreds of cities in a matter of months. These movements also were fueled by our "networked" society. I remember the days of civil rights or antiwar rallies when we would laboriously mimeograph flyers and then fan out all night to staple them to telephone poles or stick them under the windshield wipers of cars. On a good night we would distribute a couple of thousand flyers. Now, one push of the "send" button can call out a message to hundreds of thousands, or even millions, of people.

And what is the impact of all of these media offerings and movements? We might call it "psycho-sclerosis," or a hardening of the attitudes that not only accelerates righteousness, but creates an identification with our points of view that has those who believe otherwise appear to us as "the other," and worse, as "the enemy." As soon as that happens our capacity for reasoning begins to decline. We are, by our nature as humans, already resistant to alternative approaches to our most firmly held beliefs. The great economist John Kenneth Galbraith nailed this when he supposedly once said that most humans, given a strongly held point of view and evidence to the contrary, will quickly go about refuting the evidence!

But why is it that we are so easily swayed to go along with the mob, even when we know a more balanced attitude is healthier for our society and, arguably, for ourselves? As I wrote earlier in this book, we understand more than ever how our desire to "belong" can help create a mob mentality. This is why group behavior is such a profound predictor of individual behavior. Once we identify with a group (Democrat, Republican, Tea Party, Occupy, etc.) our ego structures feel more comfortable when we are going along with that group.

In fact, most decisions like this are not made by our rational mind but instead are deeply influenced by our emotions. We especially see this in the way people relate to LGBT people. In May 2010, when the military's "Don't Ask, Don't Tell" policy was still being debated, CNN and the Opinion Research Corporation conducted a poll in which they asked whether people who are openly gay or lesbian should or should not be allowed to serve in the U.S.

military. The response was 78 percent in favor of not permitting openly gay or lesbian people to serve in the military.[25] Then they asked whether openly homosexual people should or should not be allowed to serve in the military. The answer was only 67 percent positive. In other words, 11 percent of people either don't know what "gay" means or, more likely, the word "homosexual" triggers a more negative emotional reaction than "gay or lesbian." This is not exactly evidence of rational behavior, to say the least!

We interpret the world through a lens that is created by our experience and our identity. Given what I discussed earlier about the polarization of our political identities, people are more likely to have fixed views as their political identities become more fixed. And as soon as we identify strongly as a Democrat or a Republican, the opposite party becomes "the other" and a threat to us. We stop thinking and rely on reaction.

All of this makes perfect sense when we think about how we know our brains work. The amygdala, the brain's fear center, responds to information that threatens us. Our default mechanism is that the "other" is potentially dangerous. The degree of threat that we experience is correlated to the degree to which we identify with our own group. The stronger the identification, the stronger the potential threat of the other. We quickly take those observations, and the limbic system comes in and, in essence, asks us what this reminds us of so we can understand what is happening and react accordingly. We prime ourselves to see that threat coming. So as we approach political conventions, for example, how many people are prepared to carefully listen to the candidates? Not many. Most are prepared to agree with their own candidate and disagree with the other, *even before they know what the candidates are going to say.*

We also have a wide array of biases that play out in our response to political candidates. For instance, in the past one hundred years, the taller candidate has won the presidential election 70 percent of the time! The last man elected president whose height was below average was William McKinley, back in 1896, and he was ridiculed in the press as "a little boy." And yet, have you read anywhere that President Obama is five inches taller than Senator McCain? An actuary would probably say that is pretty compelling data that influenced some people, but it remains concealed in the background.

The mind helps us make meaning of what we see, but it can only do it within the context of what it already knows. Princeton University professors Charles C. Ballew II and Alexander Todorov found that we reflexively choose candidates based on appearance.[26] In fact, we do so in dramatic and quick fashion. Ballew and Todorov showed test subjects pictures of competing candidates for the U.S. Senate and gubernatorial races in 2006 for less than one second and asked the study participants to rate the candidates on competence and trustworthiness. They picked the winners of the gubernatorial elections 68.6 percent of the time and the winners of the Senate races 72 percent of the time. And they did this based on less than one second of exposure! Obviously, this was not thoughtful interpretation. It was emotional reaction.

Our view of politics is dramatically affected by this emotional phenomenon. San Diego State University researchers Thierry Devos and Travis Gaffud and the University of Chicago's Debbie Ma tested the unconscious association that we make between our notions of what an American is and what we think of certain people we encounter.[27] They began by comparing the reactions people had to two actresses: Kate Winslet, the British-born actress best known for films such as *Titanic* and *The Reader*; and Lucy Liu, the Chinese American actress who was born in Queens, New York, and is known for her various television and movie roles, including *Ally McBeal*, *Elementary*, and *Charlie's Angels*. Perhaps, and not surprisingly, more people "automatically" associated the Caucasian, British Winslet with being "more American" than the native-born Liu. The researchers then explored the same dynamic with Hillary Clinton, John McCain, and Barack Obama and found that the same idea held true. In fact, many of the study's participants even thought of former British Prime Minister Tony Blair as more American than President Obama!

There are plenty of other studies that suggest we are influenced by factors we don't understand or are not aware of in full. New York University psychologist Jonathan Haidt has identified five factors that define our political morality.[28] They are: how we feel about causing harm or pain; the sense we have about fairness and equity; our sense of group loyalty; our relationship to hierarchy; and, our sense of purity and sanctity. Liberals, it turns out, tend to place a higher value on the first two, conservatives on the last three. We respond to the needs we inherently and unconsciously feel are important to us. In fact, these feelings definitely affect the way we see the world.

The reality is that liberals and conservatives do see the world in very different ways. University of Nebraska-Lincoln professors Michael Dodd and John Hibbing found this when studying patterns in the way different people looked at photographs.[29] When viewing the photographs, the eyes of those who identified as conservatives unconsciously lingered 15 percent longer on unpleasant images (car crashes, etc.), which Dodd and Hibbing said suggested that conservatives are more attuned than liberals to evaluating potential threats. These findings are not dissimilar to results found by New York University's John Jost, who discovered that conservative students possess more cleaning and organizational items, thus indicating a stronger orientation toward self-discipline and structure, while liberals tend to have more books and travel-related items and focus on less restriction and more novelty seeking. In fact, there are now dozens of peer-reviewed studies that demonstrate that liberals and conservatives don't react differently to the world we are seeing; we each see a different world! [30]

So, the question comes down to this: How conscious are we about things, really?

Though I've chosen to write in this chapter about our legal system, health-care system, and political system, I could have just as easily have talked about our educational systems, the arts, why women continue to struggle in the fields of science, technology, engineering, and mathematics, or almost any other field you can imagine. In fact, wherever you spend your days, decisions are constantly being made, and made unconsciously, in terms of how we hire or fire people, promote them, give them job assignments, and make virtually every talent management decision.

This is how we live our lives, awash in networks and seas of bias. The question is, is there anything we can do about it? There is no question that we will always have biases, and that most will remain unconscious to us. However, in the next chapter, I'll explain how we can work to constructively disengage ourselves, and more effectively navigate the biases we all possess.

Chapter Seven

Shifting to Neutral

How We Can Learn to Disengage from Bias

Until you make the unconscious conscious it will direct your life and you will call it fate. We cannot change anything until we accept it. Condemnation does not liberate, it oppresses! —Carl Jung

If you notice anything, it leads you to notice more and more. —Mary Oliver (award winning American poet)

If you think in any way like I do, all of this research I've cited thus far might seem pretty mind-blowing. As I've read through hundreds of the studies, some of which I have mentioned in this book, I'm often left with a feeling that I can't trust anything I'm seeing in the world around me. To paraphrase the words of one of my firm's clients, I realize that I should no longer believe what I think!

Witty as his statement might be, there is some real truth to it. As the mathematician and philosopher René Descartes famously said (in Latin), "cogito ergo sum" or "I think, therefore I am." For the most part, all of us identify strongly with our thoughts. The notion that our thoughts and feelings may not be "true," but rather are automatically programmed in our minds through our various experiences, and influenced by some of the mental incongruities that I've been discussing, is hard for us to grasp. It is, first of all, hard for us to see the mind in action with any kind of objectivity because we are looking *through* the very mind we are trying to look *at*! We have complicated thinking patterns that are designed to self-justify the very things we are trying to explore. Yet, the question we have to ask is: Can we trust our own perceptions?

It is disquieting to think we cannot trust our own perceptions. Most human beings tend to gravitate toward certainty. It is reassuring to know that the world is as we think it is, and it can be very uncomfortable to accept that things we are not even aware of can influence our thoughts. This is one of the reasons we can feel a sense of insecurity when we realize that we have been manipulated. And yet, lo and behold, all of us are being manipulated all of the time.

Advertising campaigns pull on our emotions by priming our mind with thoughts and images, by using different sounds or colors to make an impact upon our behavior. Political campaigns on both sides of the political spectrum can greatly influence voters by projecting images that call up visceral reactions. In the 1964 presidential campaign, many people were outraged by an advertisement Lyndon Johnson ran against his opponent, Barry Goldwater, which showed a young girl picking at a daisy, followed by an exploding atomic bomb. The message was clearly meant to infer that Goldwater was a warmonger. And in 1988, George H. W. Bush's campaign was accused of dirty tricks when it ran a campaign ad featuring a sinister picture of one Willie Horton, a convict who had committed violent crimes after being released on a prison furlough program supported by Bush's opponent, Massachusetts Governor Michael Dukakis. However, despite the uproar both ads caused, they also were found to have made an enormous impact on the way voters saw the candidates.

Therefore, the question we must ask is this: Is there anything we can do about our unconscious biases? Or, are we destined to simply wander blindly through our lives, biases alive, intact, and operational? What it comes down to is this: Can unconscious bias be eliminated?

The answer is not a simple one, and is not without controversy. Many researchers have long believed that because unconscious or implicit biases develop at very early stages in our lives, and through influences that we are not usually aware of, they may be virtually impossible to change. However, recent research, and knowledge gained from my own experience in working with thousands of people in many different types of organizations and in many different parts of the world, suggest that while it may be difficult to eliminate our biases, we may be able to become aware of some of our biases. We may be able to reframe them, or at least curb their influence on our behavior.

Sometimes, dealing more effectively with unconscious bias involves something as simple as just noticing the bias. One morning I was standing in the kitchen getting ready to leave for work when my wife simply asked me to take out the trash. Now, to be clear, I have no conscious objection to emptying the trash. And yet, at that particular moment, I became annoyed. But in the midst of my annoyance, something interesting happened. As I was tying up the bag, I had a proverbial "aha" moment. My annoyance paused, and I found myself asking myself why I was annoyed by having to take out the trash. On the surface this is, of course, not a profound thought. However, and this is probably because I have spent so much time thinking about the way the mind works, I realized I had moved from my gut emotional reaction to a more thoughtful contemplation. In essence, I had moved from fast brain to slow brain thinking. Why was this simple task eliciting this response? In the next moment I saw it. When I was a little boy, probably seven years old, I used to get into righteous battles with my mom over taking out the trash. And at that moment, in my projection, my wife had become my mother! I chuckled to myself when I noticed it, but more importantly, my whole mood changed. For at least one moment, I was free of the automaticity of my mind. I had confronted my bias.

I don't tell that story to present myself as some paragon of consciousness, but just as a simple example of how our minds can become "liberated" by the awareness of our automaticity.

What happened to me at the moment the resentment occurred was an example of regression. There are times when something triggers a past memory and the feelings associated with that memory. Sometimes it is relatively innocent, as in the case of my reaction to a simple request to take out the trash. Other times, if something triggers a memory of a trauma, the reactions can be much more intense. When we regress to a previous incident like my trash memory, our emotional reactions are often similar to those that we had at the age we were when the original incident happens.

Noticing when we regress in this fashion can be a helpful way to identify the times when we are not reacting to the present moment, but rather are surfacing a patterned reaction or bias of some kind or another. If we pay attention, we can sense that we are reacting from an earlier emotional place. Even if we cannot recall an incident, or know what we are triggering, the very fact of sensing that we are reacting to something from the past can help us "dis-identify" with the reaction and create some freedom to choose a different behavior. By dis-identify, I simply mean that we see the reaction *as a reaction* and not as "the truth"!

We will never be free of all biases. As I've said a number of times, bias is as natural to the human condition as breathing. What we can do to deal with bias is somewhat similar to what we do in a car. We can step on the clutch and shift into neutral. When you step on the clutch, the engine doesn't stop running, but for that moment at least, the engine is not driving the car. The same is true when we bring our awareness to our bias. The bias may still be there, but at that moment we have some ability to manage how much it controls our behavior.

And while we are a culture that moves quickly to "doing," it is important to recognize the importance of being" and awareness as a source of transformation. In the introduction I mentioned a study that was conducted by Justin

Wolfers and Joseph Price that revealed bias among NBA referees. In February 2014 the authors of the original study, along with Devin Pope, from the Booth School of Business at the University of Chicago, found that simply being aware of the issue, even without any conscious action, had created significant change. The authors found that the bias continued during the three years after the initial study, but that after the study received widespread media attention in 2007 the bias virtually disappeared. While the NBA reported no specific actions taken (e.g., no discussions or changes in training or incentives for referees) the awareness and attention to the issue appear to have been enough to create significant change. Simply having it in their span of attention appears to have changed the referees' behavior.

So what we need to ask is whether we can develop practices that can help us more regularly free the mind in that way. I believe we can do so, and I am seeing such behavior occur in countless incidents with people in our workshops and throughout our client organizations. Human beings have an enormous capability for neuroplasticity, which is the capacity of the brain to form new neural connections that allow it to reorganize itself throughout our lives. In some cases, neuroplasticity happens because of disease or injury, when a different part of the brain takes over for the part that has ceased to function. And it also can happen because of a new awareness, new experiences, new norms that develop in our cultures. It can also happen when we develop a new narrative that offers a more positive interpretation of the circumstance that we are confronting. It turns out that the old expression of "you can't teach an old dog new tricks" (which is not true with regard to dogs), also doesn't apply to people.

Neuroplasticity can take place among individuals and can make its presence felt throughout organizations. Consider the cultural dialogue about the rights of gay and lesbian couples to marry. In 2004, the *Washington Post* and ABC News conducted a poll as to whether it should be legal or illegal for gay and lesbian people to marry. The results were strongly anti-marriage equality. A total of 62 percent of the respondents said they thought gay and lesbian marriage should be illegal. Only 32 percent felt it should be legal. In 2013, when the same organizations asked the same question in a new poll, the numbers had practically reversed. In that poll, 58 percent supported marriage equality and only 36 percent opposed it, accounting for a 26 percent shift in only nine years![1]

Any number of factors likely contributed to this overwhelming change in attitude. Still, the important point is that our collective "neural pathways" about marriage equality seem to have been rewired in very short order.

It is challenging to know what standard we use for measuring changes in our unconscious biases. There are some testing mechanisms which have been very effective in giving us feedback as to our positive or negative implicit responses to certain groups. But, as I'll discuss later in this chapter, even they are not without challenge. Anecdotal stories of change are not definitive either, because though they can be powerful and emotionally moving, they are often interpreted through the lens of the very mind possessing open or hidden bias.

The results that people produce are an important metric for sure, but results can be influenced by so many variables that they are hard to attribute to any single behavioral change. They also must be measured over an extended period of time to ensure sustainability.

Even behavior change is not a dependable gauge for determining true transformational change. Think about it. How many areas of your life can you name in which you know exactly what you are supposed to do, and may even go through the motions of changing, but don't deeply embrace the change that is needed? I discussed a personal example earlier in the book when I talked about the fact that I have struggled with my weight for most of my life. I have gained and lost hundreds of pounds. But even when I was heavy, I knew everything there was to know about dieting. It's not that complicated: you eat less and exercise more! I can't tell you how many times I started and stopped, until I realized that the key was not so much knowing what to do, but rather *becoming conscious about why I eat.* It wasn't until I experienced that shift in my way of *being* about eating that I have been able to sustain a healthy diet for an extended time.

I believe we must look at some combination of all of these things (attitude, behavior, and results) to truly create transformation. We have to make sure that people get the information they need to understand what they are dealing with, and then define a clear set of behaviors that can help move us in that direction. We also have to shift our mind-set about how we feel about bias and difference at a fundamental level. We must approach it with a clear awareness of the emotional impact it is making upon us. In my experience, that combination creates the possibility of true transformational change.

Lisa T. Eyler, PhD, Associate Professor of Psychiatry, University of California–San Diego Healthcare System; Clinical Research Psychologist, Veterans Affairs San Diego Mental Illness Research Education and Clinical Center

I have known since my middle school science fair project that, like both my parents, I was destined to be a scientist. There was never a hesitation or question that, as a woman, I was equally qualified to go into this field. I double-majored in biology and psychology, completed a Ph.D. in clinical psychology, and now I'm an associate professor of psychiatry. I have wonderful, accomplished female colleagues and collaborators who inspire me daily. So, when I took the Implicit Association Test, imagine my dismay when the pattern of my responses indicated that I had a moderate preference for associating women with humanities and men with science! How could this be?

Later, I learned that women often have stronger anti-women implicit biases than men, and that women scientists are just as likely to underrate women applicants as men who run science labs. Yet, I still felt dismay that cultural messages contrary to my own identity could be so ingrained in my psyche. I have tried to discover ways in which my own unconscious bias may be influencing my actions and the way I treat the women that I train. At faculty meetings, I now make a point of always taking a seat at the main table, and sometimes I'm the only woman at the table. Before I start to read applications or grants, I bring to mind all the women scientists I admire. When I write letters of recommendation for women trainees, I substitute the name of a male trainee and pay attention to my use of strong adjectives that emphasize competence as opposed to niceness. I try to be a role model to more junior women by embracing a feminine style of relating to others and by not hiding the rewards and challenges of being both a mom and an academic. It's a work in progress, but I feel like I'm at least taking some steps to defy the imprint of society's expectations as I pursue work in the field that I love.

Of course, any movement toward working on identifying and navigating our unconscious biases begins with motivation. We have to see that there is some greater purpose in being more thoughtful and less judgmental, and in learning to not let our automatic assumptions and stereotypes run our lives. This may be easier said than done for some people. This is particularly true when we are part of the dominant group. When we are in the dominant group, we may not be aware of how much our biases affect those within nondominant groups. And, since the biases that we are dealing with generally, at least in the short term, seem to benefit us, our motivation for change can be limited.

Hidden prejudices and biases are surprisingly influential underpinnings to all the decisions we make, affecting our feelings and, consequently, our actions. And there are times when not recognizing this influence on our choices and decision making can do great harm.

Ultimately, there are two major motivators for learning to navigate our unconscious biases. The first comes from a commitment to engaging in healthy interactions between people, equity in our communities and organizations, and justice in society. These are noble reasons and they seem valuable enough to most anyone. But even if you are not inspired by those reasons, it just makes sense for us to make more conscious decisions so we don't hire somebody because he reminds us of a kid we played ball with in fourth grade, or spend more for a car because the salesperson is of a certain race, or buy a bottle of wine simply because of the music that is playing in the background in the store. Making decisions in that way will not only harm others, but doing so also makes us very poor decision makers. And in making such decisions, we will suffer the consequences (which can range from mildly annoying to extremely serious) by hiring the wrong people or buying the wrong product.

At the basic core, it is important for people to have some information or education regarding the topics I've been discussing thus far in this book. Understanding how much the unconscious mind influences us and the basic concepts of how we think opens us to the possibility that there may be things going on that are unknown to us. That doesn't mean that people have to become psychologists or neuroscientists. However, knowing not to believe everything you think is a good start toward managing bias. This is where participating in some kind of unconscious bias education can be helpful.

Social psychologists Gordon Moskowitz of Lehigh University and Jeff Stone from the University of Arizona study the impact of bias on medical decision making, an issue that contributes greatly to the continuing patterns of health disparities that negatively affect African Americans and other blacks, as well as Latinos, Native Americans, women, and LGBT people. "Workshops or other learning modules that help medical professionals learn about non-conscious processes can provide them with skills that reduce bias when they interact with minority group patients," said Moscowitz and Stone. "Examples of such skills in action include automatically activating egalitarian goals, looking for common identities and counter-stereotypical information, and taking the perspective of the minority group patient."[2]

Once we are aware of the dynamics of unconscious bias, we can begin to engage in some practices that seem to make a difference. After decades of work in this area, I have come to believe that there are six major areas of focus that can help us work on our individual patterns of bias. They are:

1. Recognize that bias is a normal part of the human experience.

This first area is by the far the most important. You have bias, yes you do, and so do I. We can't run away from it. Denying we possess it only gives it a greater chance to affect us. As a matter of fact, we can't live without it. Bias is part of our fundamental survival mechanism. All human beings have bias. If we understand that concept, it allows us to bring compassion to others and to ourselves. It means that we need to discard the historic "good person/bad person" paradigm of diversity work and recognize the humanity in us.

If you would like to briefly examine this phenomenon within yourself, take a moment to do this quick exercise. Don't worry about being politically correct in your responses, because nobody will see the answers but you. Take out a piece of paper and write down a list of different identity groups that come to mind (e.g., white people, black people, Latinos, Asians, gays, lesbians, transgender, teenagers, elderly, baby boomers, attorneys, doctors) Make the list as long as you like.

Once you have drawn up the list, look at each item and honestly consider how you feel about people in this group. Look for both biases toward people in the group, and biases against people in the group. Just notice the biases. Check both your thoughts and the emotional feelings. Who do you feel more or less comfortable around? Sometimes it is helpful to look at pictures as well. Obviously, the things we notice will be on a conscious level, but because we are not always present to them, the things we notice often occur as unconscious motivators.

It also is important for us to remember that some groups of people have definitely suffered a great deal more at a societal level because of the institutionalized systems of bias that have negatively affected groups such as people of color, women, LGBT people, people with disabilities, and the like. At the same time, such realization does not stop each of us from having issues we must face and work on. I am Jewish, and I know Jews who rail against anti-Semitism but then make questionable comments about race. I know African Americans who rail against racism but then make questionable comments about sexual orientation. I know LGBT folks who hate homophobia but have questionable attitudes about immigrants.

Do you know anybody who doesn't have some reaction to somebody? If you're honest in your answer, you'll know that everyone has some reaction to everyone else.

When we believe that having bias makes us a bad person, our minds move either to self-recrimination, denial, or self-justification, none of which moves us closer to being fully present to those with whom we interact. Guilt is a pretty dysfunctional emotion. It causes contraction and separation. Think about it. When somebody makes you feel guilty, are you more or less likely to want to be with that person? There is an important difference between feeling guilty and taking responsibility. I once heard that guilt is what you feel because of what you did, but responsibility is what you take because of the kind of person you want to be.

The distinction between guilt and responsibility is not simply a theoretical moral or linguistic distinction. It is a distinction that quite profoundly affects the way we deal with the issue at hand. When we feel guilty we usually feel powerless. We feel violated, either by our own abandonment of our values, or because somebody else "made us feel that way." That's why we often attribute our guilt to others ("Why are you always making me feel guilty?").

Guilt often leads to defensiveness, anxiety, and shame, and because we feel blamed, either by others, or ourselves, it also may lead to retaliation. This is one of the reasons there is such strong white male backlash around diversity and inclusion issues. White men are reacting to being blamed and "made" to feel guilty for things they often don't realize that they're doing, or for privileges they don't realize they have had for longer than any of them have been alive. I want to be clear that I'm not suggesting that there are not a lot of white men who have done things, and do things, that have harmed others. On the contrary. However, for many, these behaviors occur without people ever realizing they are engaging in the behaviors.

On the other hand, when we take responsibility for our actions, we empower ourselves. We can bring compassion to ourselves and to others for our blind spots. We are, by the very nature of the word, "able to respond" to the situation at hand. We can be motivated to grow, to develop, to improve ourselves and transform our ways of being. We have an opportunity to correct our mistakes and move forward and, we hope, improve the situation. In doing so, we can remove the "good person/bad person" stigma, and instead deal with each other as human beings, with all of us trying to figure out how to get along in this world.

Again, I want to be very clear: I am not in any way suggesting we avoid dealing with people who are overtly hostile or biased. We have to establish a zero tolerance policy for that kind of behavior. But the evidence is very clear, and it is that, overwhelmingly, most bias is unconscious. When we treat people who don't know they are demonstrating bias in a way that suggests there is something evil about them, we not only put them on the defensive, but we also lose the ability to influence them because they have no idea what we are focused on.

Once we understand that we have bias, we have to develop a practice to learn to identify our biases. This becomes much easier when we do not see ourselves as bad people for having them. There are a number of ways to begin to identify some of our personal biases. One is by using the IAT discussed earlier in this book. It is a free, computer-based test you can take yourself by going to https://implicit.harvard.edu/implicit/. The website includes a number of different tests that allow you to compare your associations between different groups (e.g., white versus black, male versus female, Christian versus Jewish). It will give you feedback as to which group you associate with in more positive or negative ways.

The IAT is based on a testing model called Stroop testing, which was originally developed by John Ridley Stroop, a psychologist who was one of the pioneers in the study of cognition and interference. The Stroop test is based on the notion that we unconsciously make associations much more quickly than we consciously make associations. In fact, modern technology has since proven Stroop right time and again. For example, the conscious mind takes about three hundred milliseconds to process an image. But when people are observed through functional magnetic resonance imaging (fMRI) machines, we can see that the unconscious reaction in the brain is much faster, about eighty milliseconds. That means that before our conscious mind has noticed something, the unconscious mind may already be in action in response to it.

In the classic Stroop test, participants are shown a series of letter combinations that are simply mixtures of random letters that are printed in different colors. Participants are then asked to quickly state the color they see. They are then shown a second set of words and asked to perform the same task, except this time the letters form the names of colors that are different from the color of the text (e.g., the word "red" in green ink). The inevitable response is a slight hesitancy that makes the second test seem to run slower than the first. The unconscious mind can't help but respond to the word "red," because we have been conditioned to read automatically. The conscious mind hesitates for a moment before realizing it is supposed to say "green."

The IAT shows the participant images of people and related words. The unconscious mind quickly associates the words with the images. Positive words are more quickly associated with the people we feel more positively toward. Negative words are more quickly associated with those about whom we have negative biases. Because the reactions are slightly slower when the words are different than our unconscious biases, the test can identify them by measuring the time it takes to answer each match.

The IAT has been used in hundreds of studies to measure bias, and as such, it has made an enormous contribution to the study of unconscious bias. However, the test is not without its critics. Most of the challenges to the IAT come with the caution that the results may not be as definitive as they suggest. Some researchers have contended that it is not clear what is being measured by the IAT. Other critics maintain that the people who administer it may influence the test. For instance, a participant may respond slightly differently if a white male, or an African American woman, proctors the test. Others have suggested that the test can be influenced by the environmental influences of the time. Negative responses toward Muslims, for example, rose after September 11, 2001, and negative responses toward African Americans diminished immediately after Barack Obama was inaugurated (although they returned to their previous levels shortly afterward). In addition, many people find that when they take the test at different times they get different responses.

My personal experience has been that the test is valuable when used as a directional pointer to explore one's blind spots. In that framework, it has contributed tremendously to our ability to study the impact of unconscious bias. The danger can often be not in the test itself, but in how it is used. For example, I have heard people suggest that potential employees should take the IAT as part of an interviewing process. To me, this would be a very bad idea. I say this because the IAT is a measure of implicit associations, and is not always a measure of behaviors. As I described in an earlier chapter, many people test more positively regarding people in groups other than their own, especially if the groups are nondominant ones that have historically been negatively stereotyped. The key is not to take the IAT result as a "report card on your soul," but rather to see it as a helpful pointer that can give us some insight into our unconscious "programming."

There are a number of other tools that have emerged in more recent years that have brought awareness to our unconscious biases. British psychologist Pete Jones has created a tool, ImplicitlyM, which claims to be the first commercial online test of unconscious bias that reliably measures an individual's risk of exhibiting biased behavior at work. Helen Turnbull, another American psychologist, has created yet another test called "Cognizant," which is similarly claimed to have the ability to measure unconscious biases. Once again, the key in using any of these tests is to use them for exploration and not as a "report card."

Another way to begin to obtain clarity regarding some of your own biases is through the narrative tradition. Each of us has a narrative that makes up our lives, a collection of stories and experiences that have contributed to the way we see and experience the world. Our narrative creates the background filter through which we process what we encounter. This creates a perceptual identity through which we see the world.[3]

Our perceptual identity functions as a lens that is greatly influenced by four major areas. The first is the culture or cultures that we grow up in. We are influenced by culture more than we realize because much of that influence is preverbal. Even as babies we see, feel, smell, hear, and generally sense what is "right" or "wrong" to do. We also are exposed to things that have happened to people like us, so we develop a second lens that is based on our group identity. Women, for example, need not have been victims of rape or sexual violence for them to think about those things when they are walking alone at night, because such things have happened to enough other women. Our natural tendency to associate with those like us (remember our mirror neurons!) causes us to internalize those concerns. We also have gone through hundreds of personal experiences throughout our lives that shape our perceptual lens, as well as the different institutions to which we have belonged in some way or another. All of these things dramatically affect what we see and how we react to what we see.

When we set aside time to reflect on our narrative, we often can find that we have taken certain elements of the past and constructed an entire framework based on those elements. Of course, the challenge for us is that our memories are not nearly as accurate as we think they are, no matter how "vividly" we think we remember things. In fact, we remember things quite selectively and we often make assessments about things based on that limited information.

Identifying where our narratives about different people originate is important. The closer we get to the root of our bias, the more we can create a new narrative that disarms it. The story I mentioned earlier about the African American woman who was told that she "had to be twice as good as white people" is a good example. Once she reframed that narrative, she reported experiencing immense freedom to be herself and appreciate herself.

Timothy Wilson, the Sherrell J. Aston Professor of Psychology at the University of Virginia, has studied this extensively.[4] He has found people can "redirect" their subconscious narrative by being exposed to alternative narratives. For instance, a person who has developed an entrenched negative bias about certain racial groups of people can have that narrative transformed by being exposed to people or stories about people who have lived, worked, and loved together across the divide between their own group and the group against which they harbored the bias. People who are experiencing challenges in their lives can transform their relationship with that challenge when they are exposed to other people who have overcome those challenges.

This method is far more successful than the way we have usually tried to approach changing our narratives through more fear-based methods. Here's a good example. In the 1970s, many juvenile detention programs began to institute "Scared Straight" programs, based on a program that was initially created at Rahway State Prison in New Jersey. The idea was to have young people meet with convicted criminals who would supposedly frighten them back on track by telling them the horrors of prison life. At some level there is logic to this kind of negative deterrent. The only problem is that it hasn't worked.[5] The results indicate that more, not less, of the young people exposed to "Scared Straight" get in trouble. It seems they are stimulated by the strength they see in the anger of the convicts and they, in a somewhat bizarre sense, become unconscious role models to the students. The internal narrative of the students shifts to "maybe I should try that too."

A similar pattern also can be true when people in a dominant group (e.g., white men) are exposed to diversity programs in which they are confronted by the anger of another group (e.g., white women or men and women of color), and told how much they have been hurt, harmed, or abused by the people in the dominant group. This method was a fundamental part of a lot of diversity training programs, and is still used in more subtle forms today. The release of anger may be understandable, and the cathartic impact it makes upon the person releasing it may be very powerful. However, the impact on the member of a dominant group may be regressive in that it leaves them feeling more different from, more afraid of, and less empathetic toward the member of the nondominant group. In fact, studies of approaches to mitigating unconscious bias now demonstrate that this technique is one of the least effective![6]

The key lives in our willingness to explore our own personal narrative. If you are interested in doing this kind of self-exploration, you might want to ask yourself a few simple questions:

- What things did you learn from your culture of origin that affect your values and behaviors today? How are they different from what others may have learned? How do those differences affect your relationships with others?
- Was there a time when you recalled feeling "different" from those around you? How did it make you feel? How did it affect your behavior?
- What institutions were you a part of that influenced your values and behaviors (e.g., religious institutions, Boy/Girl Scouts, schools, clubs)?

When we remove the self-criticism about our biases and take on the task of self-exploration, it can be a very illuminating experience.

Our ego is not permanent. It is constantly shifting and evolving, influenced by the narrative we are in at the moment and the integration of the experiences we are encountering. A lifetime narrative can be rewritten. I will never forget a story I once heard someone tell. It went something like this:

> I was a pretty good baseball player when I was younger. I played all the way through college, but it was an especially important part of my life in high school. I was one of the best players on my team. One of the things that used to really upset me was that my father never came to see me play. He was much older when I was born and was an immigrant, very old world. We never talked about it because he seemed to be always working. He died when I was in college. A number of years later I went back to my fifteenth high school reunion. My old baseball coach, who was a real mentor to me, was still at the school and so, of course, I went over and talked with him for a while. We chatted a bit and then he asked me about my parents. I told him that my father had passed away (my mother was still alive). The coach said, "that's too bad. He was a very nice man." I was a bit stunned. I didn't know that my coach had ever even met my father. I was so nonplussed that I didn't say anything, but the next morning I called my mother and told her what happened. For a moment she was silent. Then she told me something I never knew. It turns out my father was very sensitive about being so "old world" and was afraid my sister and I were embarrassed by him and his ways. He didn't want that to bother me while I was playing. So he would come and watch my games from behind the stands. He apparently almost never missed a game. And then while I was showering, he would sometimes slip in to talk to the coach. I never knew. At first I felt terribly sad, but over time I saw it for what it was: a father's deep love for his son. My whole relationship to my father throughout my life changed. Even though he was dead, we had a whole new relationship!

2. Develop the capacity for self-observation.

To refine our ability to "see ourselves in action," we have to *work to develop the capacity of self-observation*, or, as my friend and colleague Michael Schiesser likes to say, to "turn the flashlight on ourselves." We generally are looking outward at the world, with very little attention to the filter that is interpreting what we are seeing. When we observe ourselves, we are activating our metacognitive ability and activating our prefrontal neocortex. We become more thoughtful. We have the ability to observe ourselves in action.

When we do that, we become less reactive. Our amygdala can begin to "relax" a bit. The more we name what is going on with us, the quieter the amygdala becomes, and we are less likely to be hijacked by the amygdala's automatic reaction. And when we share with others what is going on with us, it softens even more. Scientists who are discovering this are just now catching up to what the Buddha observed almost 2,500 years ago when he said, "that which can be observed, I am not."

So, when we consciously observe ourselves, we have the opportunity to step on the clutch and "shift into neutral" by dis-identifying from the automatic reactions that usually dominate our thinking.

We can learn to observe ourselves at several different levels. For the most part we focus on behavior, what we are saying and doing. I also have been discussing our metacognitive capability, or the capacity to watch what we are thinking. In my experience, one of the most powerful ways to observe ourselves is by learning to observe our somatic responses, or the way our reactions show up in the physical body.

For the most part, our thoughts are not focused on the present moment. They are stimulated by what happens in the present moment, but mostly they quickly then reference either a memory from the past that frames how we interpret what is going on and puts it into a context for us to process, or a fear about what might happen in the future. Our biases clearly engage both aspects of this response. The memory of the past leads us to our beliefs about the person or people we are dealing with, and then informs our concern about our future interactions with those people. How might it be possible to become more aware of these patterns of thinking?

Over the course of the past couple of decades there has been a broad expansion of our awareness of the mind/body connection. Herbert Benson, a cardiologist and founder of the Benson-Henry Mind Body Institute at Massachusetts General Hospital, is one of the people most widely credited with bringing this phenomenon into the mainstream, primarily through his 1975 best-selling book, *The Relaxation Response*.[7] In the book, Benson explained the role that cortisol plays in our stress response.

Cortisol, or hydrocortisone, is a steroid hormone that the human body releases during times of stress. Among other things, cortisol combines with adrenaline to help create memories of shorter-term emotional events. These have been called "flashbulb memories" or snapshots of key moments for which we retain vivid memories. Think about exceptional moments from your past. Where were you when the attack on September 11, 2001, occurred? Or, if you are old enough, when President Kennedy was assassinated? Not hard to remember, is it? And yet, despite our capacity for vivid remembrance, we have a hard time remembering something from just a few days ago.

High cortisol levels also have been shown to be associated with social fear responses, avoidance, and social anxiety disorder, all of which can contribute to the fear-related aspects of bias.[8] Benson has shown that various mindfulness and meditation practices reduce the level of cortisol that is released into the body, quieting the nervous system response.

You can experiment with this yourself. Find a picture of somebody or a group of people who you generally don't feel especially comfortable being around. Look at the picture and then observe where in your body you feel a reaction. Tightness in the abdomen or throat? Increased respiration or heart rate? There is no reason to change whatever sensation you observe, you simply notice it. Then close your eyes for five minutes (you may want to set a timer) and draw your breath a little bit more deeply than usual, focusing into the area of the body that you identified. After the time is up, look again at the picture. Often the visceral reaction to the person or people will be significantly reduced.

Various forms of meditation or other contemplative practices can be very helpful in this regard. Over time they help to quiet the incessant chatter of the mind and bring a sense of deeper calm and reflection that moderates the ability of the amygdala to hijack our perceptions and behaviors and encourages more prefrontal activity. From that quieter place, it is often easier to "see ourselves in action" and adjust our behavior accordingly.

Contemplation and self-observation, like so many other things in life, is a habit that becomes strengthened with practice. Very few people sit down and meditate for the first time and find it to be a simple task. Mostly what we see is how busy our minds are, filled with judgments, self-correction, and seemingly mindless chatter. The more we actively work on developing the capacity to slow down our thinking and watch it, the easier it becomes and the more self-observant we naturally become. Our willingness to be vulnerable to what we see also is important. If we can refrain from judging ourselves too harshly, and instead just work on observing, it is far easier to disengage from the automaticity that our internal narrative creates.

3. Practice constructive uncertainty.

Taking these sorts of breaks in our thinking can disable the stress-bias reaction in our brain and help us be more present to what is going on right now. To do that, we have to develop another practice that is very important in navigating our unconscious bias by creating what I like to refer to as *constructive uncertainty*. I realize that is an odd term—constructive uncertainty—but here's what I mean. We live in a culture that loves certainty. Have you noticed that more often than not it is the person who is the most certain about their point of view (and not afraid to show it!) that wins the argument? We don't have much patience for thoughtfulness. It often seems like we are happier when we quickly get to the wrong answer than we are when we have taken too much time to ruminate over the right one.

Our biases are generally fast, reflexive reactions that emanate from our limbic system. The automaticity of these responses usually puts us in reaction to them without any questioning. To move to a more thoughtful conscious state, to start engaging the prefrontal neocortex in metacognitive thinking, we need to pause. The existentialist psychologist Rollo May once said that "human freedom involves our capacity to pause between the stimulus and response and, in that pause, to choose the one response toward which we wish to throw our weight. The capacity to create ourselves, based upon this freedom, is inseparable from consciousness or self-awareness."[9]

Thus, observing ourselves gives us the opportunity to evaluate the circumstance we are in. We even use the word "PAUSE" as an acronym to remind us to:

- **P**ay attention to what's happening beneath the judgments and assessments.

  - When we slow down and look at what's happening we have an opportunity to distinguish between an event and our interpretation of that event. For example, say somebody shakes your hand softly. Do you have a visceral reaction and association with weakness as many people in the United States do? ("Limp!" "Cold fish!") What happened is that they used less pressure in the handshake than you are used to with most people. The rest is your interpretation, which leads us to the next step.

- **A**cknowledge your own reactions, interpretations, and judgments.

  - This is where you have an opportunity to identify your interpretation *as an interpretation.* You might say something to yourself like, "I can see that when he shook my hand softly, I interpreted that as weakness." As soon as you notice an interpretation as an interpretation, you have moved to a higher level of consciousness. You have given yourself the freedom to which Rollo May referenced. From there you can move to step three.

- Understand the other possible reactions, interpretations, and judgments that may be possible.

  - There may be any number of other reasons for the behavior. In the case of the handshake, the person may come from a different culture (because a significant percentage of people in different parts of the world shake hands more softly than we do in the United States), or may have an injury, or be recovering from an injury. Or they may have arthritis, or—whatever! Looking at all the possibilities reinforces the dis-identification from our initial reaction and opens up the possibility to:

- Search for the most constructive, empowering, or productive way to deal with the situation.

  - What makes the most sense? Should I assume that the person is weak because of my initial reaction to his handshake, or should I get to know him a little better before I make a definitive assessment? What should I say? What is the best way to handle the circumstance? Once you have a plan in place, then you can:

- Execute your action plan.

  - Act consistently with what makes the most sense.

Constructive uncertainty leads to better thinking. We would be far better off if we turned many of our exclamation points about things into questions marks and didn't feel the need to be so sure of ourselves all of the time. In fact, the other benefit of constructive uncertainty is that it makes us far more open to the ideas and perspectives of other people. When you know that you are dealing with an issue or situation in which you find yourself definitively sure of yourself, it can be very helpful to seek out a healthy skeptical point of view. As opposed to cynicism, which can be quite toxic, skepticism can help us see things we may have missed in our certainty. Often when I am working with teams who are excited about a new direction they want to head in, I will ask the team to be consciously skeptical about the plan so that in their enthusiasm they don't miss possible roadblocks that may derail their efforts.

All the same, I do want to be clear that I named this "constructive" uncertainty for a reason. I am not advocating paralysis by analysis, or long, drawn-out navel gazing. I'm simply saying that a pause can help us be more thoughtful and help disengage some of the automaticity of our biases.

4. *Explore awkwardness or discomfort.*

Another way to work on your personal biases is to be open to *exploring those incidents that occur when you feel awkwardness or discomfort around certain kinds of people or certain circumstances.* Putting political correctness aside, there are times when we notice that certain types of people trigger feelings of discomfort within us. Our standard response at times like that is to slip into some kind of "fight or flight" reaction. We either will tend to withdraw or get defensive. Times like this can often be valuable learning opportunities for us. If we are having a strong emotional reaction, some fear is being stimulated, and it is usually another sign that we are reacting from our past. At those moments, when possible, we can learn a lot about ourselves by asking a few questions:

- Am I reacting to what is happening now, or is this person or situation currently threatening to me?
- Is there any immediate action that needs to be taken?
- How do people or situations like this affect my behavior on a regular basis?
- Is there somebody with whom I should talk about the circumstance?

5. *Engage with people in groups you may not know very well, or about whom you harbor biases.*

One of the most effective ways to begin to dis-identify with our biases is through exposure to people and groups we harbor biases against. Gordon Allport is often credited as the "father" of the "contact hypothesis" of race relations. Allport, a Harvard psychologist, postulated that, under the right circumstances, contact between conflicting groups, was an effective way to diminish prejudice and stereotyping. [10]

More recently, a team of researchers led by Calvin Lai and Brian Nosek, social psychologists at the University of Virginia, analyzed eighteen different strategies to see which are the most effective for addressing unconscious bias. [11] They found that some of the traditional strategies for addressing bias have not proven to be all that successful. For instance, exhaustive efforts to get people in the dominant group to understand the plight of people in nondominant groups can often create a greater sense of difference between the groups and, as I noted earlier, reduce the sense of connection and empathy to the "out group."

Lai and Nosek's study did reveal that one of the most effective ways to begin to "reprogram" our biases toward certain groups is to *expose people to counter-stereotypes or exemplars of the particular group in question.* When we are exposed to examples of people who have been successful, or are appealing to us from the group in question, our generalized negative biases toward that group seem to begin to diminish. This may occur through creating an environment in which we are reminded through pictures or other artifacts about the contributions of a particular group. It also is why events such as Black History Month (February), Women's History Month (March), Lesbian, Gay, Bisexual and Transgender Pride Month (June), or National Hispanic Heritage Month (September 15–October 15) can be helpful to expose people to some of these counter-stereotypes. Of course, it is even more helpful when these exemplars are exposed to us on a regular basis every month of the year!

In our own environments, we can begin to expose ourselves through the pictures we have on our walls and computers; by reading stories and learning about people from other groups besides our own; attending cultural festivals; studying another culture's stories and literature, etc. The bottom line is, the more we get to know people for who they are, the less we treat them like what they are (or at least what they appear to us).

6. Get feedback and data.

The final individual intervention I want to point out is *getting feedback and data*. Data can be especially important because information can point us in the direction of concerns to which we may have become unconscious. For example, imagine you are a supervisor who has to write performance evaluations for ten employees, five men and five women. After you finish the reviews you rank them from strongest to weakest and find that four out of the top five scores are women. Does this mean that you have a bias toward women? Not necessarily, but at the very least it should encourage you to explore the question.

Data are also important because all too often we judge the success or failure of our efforts based on how much they "make sense" or on how they feel to the participants, rather than on a real sense of producing empiric results. I recognize that not everything can be measured, but measurement can be helpful to assist us in questioning how successful we are being. One of my clients instituted a mentoring program that was specifically designed to assist female lawyers and young associates of color to successfully adapt to their culture. It was well intended, and the people who participated found it valuable. But the numbers showed that less than 30 percent of the people who were eligible participated, because the rest were concerned that participation was an acknowledgment that they weren't as capable as the white male associates. Only after the communication about the program and its structure were changed did it begin to produce results.

To get these kinds of data and feedback on a regular basis, we have to find ways to create environments around us that allow people to be willing and able to engage in the question. In the next chapter, I will "shift out of neutral" and take a look at the structures we can develop to create more conscious organizational communities.

Chapter Eight

Incubators of Consciousness

Creating More Conscious Organizations

I wanted to make history move ahead in the same way that a child pulls on a plant to make it grow more quickly. I believe we must learn to wait as we learn to create. We have to patiently sow the seeds, assiduously water the earth where they are sown and give the plants the time that is their own. One cannot fool a plant any more than one can fool history. —Vaclav Havel

If the structure does not permit dialogue the structure must be changed. — Paulo Freire

In this section of the book (warning: this is going to be a pretty lengthy section, though I hope you'll find it interesting and useful), I'm going to provide strategies and methods and some good examples of how individuals and groups can work to create genuinely more conscious organizations, even though we know we can never entirely rid ourselves, or our organizations, of unconscious bias. Most biases that we are susceptible to as individuals also can become collective biases within organizations that then easily become "the way we do things around here." There are several forms of bias that occur regularly in organizations that are particularly important to watch out for in the course of our work.

One big problem that gets in the way of organizations becoming more conscious is a dependence on doing things "the way we've always done them in the past." I call this "status quo bias." Doing things the same way through the years, again and again, can be a good thing in many areas, such as in not changing a recipe for the world's best mashed potatoes. But such "stability" is usually not advisable for organizations that wish to become not only more conscious, but much more inclusive, as well as productive. How does it

121

happen? It's not like we usually start out with an intention to create mindless agreement within our organizations. It evolves over time.

I'm sure that anybody reading this has had the experience of seeing groups function in this way. In the 1950s and 1960s there were a rash of experiments conducted by social psychologists that demonstrated group conforming behavior and consistently demonstrated our willingness to "go along to get along." For most of us, it is simply easier, and more socially acceptable, to go along with the group. That is not to say there aren't exceptions. For example, some people are noticeable outliers in most of the groups to which they belong. It also doesn't mean that every individual doesn't have moments of uniqueness and the courage to express their uniqueness. But as a rule, group conformity is a powerful influence, even when we let go of a better solution and go with the familiar or popular one.

A great example of such nonuseful stability might be seen within the world's most prestigious orchestras. As late as 1970 (a few years into the ascent of the women's movement), the symphony orchestras considered the best in the United States, including the Boston Symphony Orchestra, the Cleveland Orchestra, the Philadelphia Orchestra, the New York Philharmonic, and the Chicago Symphony Orchestra were overwhelmingly male in their musician composition. I mean really overwhelming, as only about 5 percent of the musicians in those orchestras at the time were women. The numbers were similar in major orchestras in San Francisco, Detroit, Los Angeles, as well as Pittsburgh. Even a decade later, in 1980, after the women's movement greatly accelerated awareness of gender discrimination, no American orchestra was more than 12 percent female.

It not only was common practice to have mostly male orchestras, but the male factor wasn't even very well concealed. For example, the legendary Zubin Mehta, the former conductor of the Los Angeles Philharmonic, the New York Philharmonic, the Teatro del Maggio Musicale in Florence, the Bavarian State Opera in Munich, and the music director (for life!) of the Israel Philharmonic Orchestra, once said "I just don't think women should be in an orchestra."[1] And, judging from the numbers, his view was borne out by orchestras all over.

The good news is that status quo bias can be reprogrammed. Since 1980, the numbers of female musicians in major orchestras have risen dramatically. In Boston and Chicago, 35 percent of musician hires made since 1980 have been women. In New York, that number has been 50 percent. Overall there has been a 30 percent increase in new female hires and a 25 percent increase in the overall female participation in orchestras. As of 2009, the top five orchestras in the United States averaged almost 37 percent female in their musician numbers.[2]

What happened? Was this an organic change brought on by the women's movement of the 1960s and 1970s? The women's movement certainly provided inspiration but the real change was driven and influenced by specific actions. What happened was that orchestras began to change what had been "normal" cultural practices as to how musicians were selected and managed.

Before the 1970s, music directors of orchestras generally chose all of an orchestra's musicians, with occasional input from the conductor. Of course, virtually all of the people doing the selecting were men. Musicians were generally chosen based on personal exposure, recommendations from others, or other similar connections.

However, in those activist 1970s and 1980s, a number of things started to change. First, orchestras started expanding the auditions beyond invitation. Advertisements were placed in musician union communications and other similar publications. The number of people who auditioned jumped from an average of twenty per orchestra to more than one hundred. In addition, the "audience" for the auditions was expanded. Many of the audition audiences now included members of the orchestra or, in some cases, a broader range of administrative staff.

And orchestras did one other thing. They began to shield the auditioning musician from the evaluators by using some kind of screen that allowed the audience to hear the music but not see the musician. The musicians were given numbers instead of being introduced by name. And, in some cases, they even had the musicians walk out on carpet so that the sound of shoes on the stage would not reveal anything. In other words, the evaluators were now being asked to evaluate the music rather than the physical appearance of the person making it.

Two economists, Claudia Goldin, the Henry Lee Professor of Economics at Harvard University, and Cecilia Rouse, dean of the Woodrow Wilson School of Public and International Affairs at Princeton University, studied this transition extensively to see if they could determine what factors contributed the most toward increasing the number of female musicians. They concluded that "the switch to blind auditions can explain 30 percent of the increase in the proportion female among new hires and possibly 25 percent of the increase in the percentage female in the orchestras."[3]

Of course, gender barriers remain in place in most of the world's orchestras. There are very few female symphony conductors in major symphonies around the world. And old attitudes have not completely gone away. As recently as September 2013, the principal conductor of the National Youth Orchestra of Great Britain and the Royal Liverpool Philharmonic, Vasily Petrenko, said that orchestras "react better when they have a man in front of them" because "a cute girl on a podium means that musicians think about other things." He went on to say that "musicians have less sexual energy and can focus more on the music" and "when women have families, it becomes difficult to be as dedicated as is demanded in the business."[4]

Such startling attitudes aside, there is no question that significant progress has been made on behalf of female musicians. And there wasn't one single decision or policy that created this change. It was a change that was generated by transforming several different patterns of behavior that had been in place for generations. The combination of more open auditions, greater inclusion in the evaluator pool, the removal of auditioning musician names, "blind" auditions, the carpeted floors, and so on, were part of a web of activity that changed the landscape of the gender composition of orchestras.

As I discussed at length earlier in this book, we are social creatures. And many of us like music, which is why I chose to make an example of the unconscious bias issues concerning gender that have affected the world's top orchestras. It is very difficult to change our behavior, and especially our unconscious belief systems, unless we have some interaction that can provide a "mirror" through which we can more clearly observe our own behavior. We live and work in communities which have value systems and behavioral norms that affect all of us all of the time. And those communities also send us constant subliminal messages about what is "normal," right or wrong, or appropriate. Left to our own devices, we often can self-justify our beliefs and behaviors. When we have to interact regularly with others, we have the opportunity to create communities of consciousness that can potentially help us live to a higher standard.

I say potentially, because as I also discussed earlier, the power of community influence can go in both directions. History has shown us all too many examples of the horrors that group consciousness can create when it is negative.

Nonetheless, the organizations we work in, study in, pray with, or join with in any other sense of community also can be the most powerful places for us to change and sustain new behavior. Having the support of a group can help us continue to engage in new behavior, even as the inclination to slip into old patterns arises. That is one of the reasons why people who maintain contact with 12 Step communities tend to fall back less frequently into addictive behavior. The support of the community helps to keep us focused on where we want to be, both now and in the future.

However, within our communities, we need to be careful about two other forms of bias. Primacy bias can create a sense of disproportionality in some of the ways we relate to people and circumstances around us. For instance, people are often presumed to be smarter when they are doing more important tasks, *even when the person assigned to the less important task does a better job.* Often, this can create poor decision making. Recency bias occurs when we are drawn to deal with the most recent challenge, rather than focusing on the big picture. On a societal scale, the media can contribute to this bias. The latest story dictates our passions and actions. But true cultural change occurs through long-term planning and sustainable action.

Let's now talk about the place where most of us spend the greatest percentage of our nonsleeping life: work. And in our workplaces, we also are far more likely to encounter a broad, diverse set of people than almost anywhere else in life. As a result, workplaces (and symphony orchestras definitely are workplaces) are some of the best laboratories for exploring ways to diminish our unconscious biases, especially in the various ways we manage talent. Keep in mind that the activities I am going to discuss also can be easily adapted to support any organization in creating a greater sense of consciousness about bias, as well as a greater ability to navigate it in a way that mitigates the impact of bias.

Talent management is essential to any organization. The way we identify the people we are going to recruit, choose the people we are going to hire, bring people into the organization, make job assignments, evaluate talent, determine promotions, and decide who to terminate are all decision paths that are potentially career making or limiting. And all are rife with opportunities for unconscious bias to play a role.

In my experience, I have seen there are a number of organizational activities that can especially help reduce the impact of bias and encourage more conscious decision making. I'll discuss many of them at length later in this section. However, to have these activities not simply become the next "diet" that people don't follow, it is important to shift the context of how the organization sees these activities.

Paul Cornillon, Senior Vice President of Research and Development, Arla Strategic Innovation Centre

Arla is on a change journey from a Northern European-based company to a globally operating one including employees and customers from many different cultures. As such, Arla has a very engaging and challenging vision that requires top performing professionals who will deliver growth. Our diversity and inclusion training and awareness program enlightens leaders in their ability to trigger performance through appropriate selection, empowerment, and engagement of their employees during work. Not only does it allow people to make a difference in their day-to-day operations, but it also secures the future of the company for the next twenty years to come by developing the workforce and having the most efficient team at all the hierarchical levels.

All too often we have stumbled in our efforts to create inclusive organizations, or limited our ability to create the results we have been looking for by engaging in well-meaning efforts that have produced unintended consequences. In an attempt to reduce offensive behavior, for example, we have developed a practice of "political correctness," or discouraging people from saying or doing the "wrong" things, especially those regarding race. The challenge is that political correctness, while well intentioned, has served to suffocate the open discussion of issues. Because we have demonized bias and failed to recognize its normalcy, the mere mention of someone's bias can result in public humiliation or organizational retribution. As a result, the very things we should discuss are forced ever more deeply into the underground.

To prepare an organization to begin doing more comprehensive work on uncovering its patterns of bias and developing new, more inclusive behaviors, it is essential to communicate clearly what you are going to be doing and why you are going to do it. How will reducing the impact of bias not only create a greater sense of equity within the organization, but also forward the organization's ability to accomplish its purpose? How is this different from things we have done in the past? And, why is this not simply a "gotcha game" that will end up getting people in more trouble for what they react to, or believe in?

After the intention of the effort has been clearly communicated, it is important to provide education to help people become aware of and understand patterns of unconscious bias, including areas where bias might be prevalent, the impact of bias upon performance, and ways to mitigate bias and its impact on work-related decisions. This kind of education is important because it helps shift the paradigm from which you or your team are viewing the situation. It helps people feel more comfortable with looking at their own biases and creates a new context for understanding bias.

Awareness is an interesting thing, because it is hard to measure and calibrate. Still, it may be the most fundamental stage in the evolution toward consciousness. Think about awareness in simple terms. Almost all of us can probably remember a time when we had a hard day at work or at school. The day was finally finished and, feeling exhausted, frustrated, or whatever, you headed home. You got to the front door and walked in to find your young son or daughter, or perhaps your spouse or partner waiting for you. Normally you would be glad to see them, but, because you are feeling irritable, maybe you snap, even just a little. Your child or spouse sulks to the other room, their feelings hurt. After you settle in you stop and have a moment of awareness and realize that you took out your grouchiness from your bad day on your innocent family member.

Sound familiar? Maybe you don't have children, and for you it is your spouse or partner, roommate, or even dog, but my guess is that almost everybody reading this knows exactly what I mean. It is not unusual for this to happen. In fact, it is completely normal. When our reserves are low, our "fast brain" can take over. We can react without thinking.

But then, if we are lucky, something happens. We have a moment when we stop and say to ourselves, "Wait! What am I doing? It's not their fault that

I had a bad day!" At that moment, we have moved into a greater level of awareness. We become conscious of the way we are reacting. And, for many of us, another thing tends to happen. We go and find our family member and apologize. We sit with the child and reconnect from our more conscious, less reactive self. We pet the dog. We may even say: "I'm really sorry. I had a hard day at work. I didn't mean to take it out on you." Such awareness gives us a new ability to consider our actions and modify them in more appropriate ways.

Unconscious bias education does not completely shift people's awareness, but it can be a powerful beginning for the process of shifting awareness. Most importantly, it can help people begin to shift their mind-set about how they are approaching their behavior within the system. All of the strategies in the world won't make any difference if you have not created a shift in mind-set.

Once people have a fundamental understanding of bias, they can begin to expand their awareness by doing continued personal exploration, looking at the ways they and their teams are functioning and installing some of the new organizational structures and systems that can help reduce bias in the everyday process. You also can explore how you represent and bring yourself to the outside world (e.g., customers, vendors, marketing, or public relations), and then create some metrics and measurements that can help you track your progress.

Of course, one of the most important shifts in mind-set is in understanding that bias makes an impact upon every organizational decision. And instead of wondering "if" bias affects organizations, we should begin to wonder "where" bias makes its mark. That may seem negative at first blush, but remember, bias is everywhere; the only question is whether we are willing to look for it. This requires a willingness to honestly assess the way we operate. This means reviewing every aspect of the employment life cycle for hidden bias. And this includes examining job postings and advertisements, the way we screen résumés, conduct interviews, and handle onboarding. It means looking at how we handle job assignments, mentoring and sponsorship, performance reviews, as well as how we identify high performers and decide how people are promoted and terminated, etc.

In the same sense that our own individual systems of behavior are dominated by unconscious, "fast brain" reactions, our organizations also are dominated by normative behaviors, or memes, that we have been engaging in for so long they have become concealed by their obviousness. In other words, they have become so "normal" to us that we don't even question them in any way. Therefore, we must pause to see ourselves and our organizations in action. When we do, what we often find is that some of the things we have been doing, all with the best of intentions, can have unintended negative consequences.

A fine illustrative example of good intentions bringing forth negative consequences is the mentoring program I described in the previous chapter. The effort had the best of intentions, but after six months, the firm's partners realized something was not right. One of the partners told me "we were surprised that less than a third of the new associates who were available for the program signed up for it." Why would people not sign up for a program that was designed to support them in being successful?

Similarly, a flextime arrangement that was designed to allow lawyers with young children to work at 75 percent of the normal schedule so they could continue to progress in the firm and also manage their family obligations went virtually unused. Why? Because the female attorneys, who were the primary target audience for the program, encountered embedded biases in the system that assumed that if they were not working a 100 percent schedule, they weren't "serious about their career." And male attorneys who took advantage of the program were teased with subtle or not so subtle messages (e.g., "Oh, now you're Mr. Mom?") that they too weren't serious about their career.

Even the best program ideas, behaviors, or activities will fail if they are introduced into a context which trivializes them or has them perceived as a threat to the established order, especially when the dominant culture of an organization doesn't understand that there is a problem in the first place. To be successful, we have to find out how the organizational unconscious functions.

To discover some of the concealed patterns of behavior that sustain the organizational unconscious, it can be very helpful to conduct an organizational mapping process using employee surveys, interviews, focus groups, and data review and search for patterns that indicate bias by gender, age, race, sexual orientation, national origin, and other demographic characteristics. In addition, you might conduct customer, client, or patient satisfaction surveys and break out results by key demographic groups. You might want to initiate studies within your department, company, or industry, to determine where there are patterns of bias (e.g., determine whether résumés with equivalent education and experience are rated equally when the names are gender, racially, or culturally distinct).

Sometimes it also can be helpful to conduct anonymous surveys with former employees to understand the issues they faced, what steps could be taken for them to consider coming back (if you want them back!), whether they are likely to encourage or discourage prospective employees from applying for positions at your company, and whether they encourage or discourage prospective clients from hiring you.

Once you have an understanding of some of the patterns of bias that occur in your organization, it is important for people throughout the organization to understand how these behaviors are affecting the results the organization is trying to produce. How are they inhibiting you from hiring and retaining the best talent? Do they create a culture within the organization that does not permit the organization to function at its highest potential level? Are they affecting your ability to be successful in the marketplace?

Once there is a general organizational understanding about why it is necessary to bring more awareness to our conscious decision-making processes, there are many things you can do to begin to alter the practices that lead to them and to structure processes, systems, and metrics that can help you keep them on your radar screen so that you can make decisions in a more conscious way. Some of these may require restructuring certain ways of doing things, but many are small measures that can make a big impact because they are strategically selected and highly leveraged.

The brilliant futurist and inventor R. Buckminster Fuller called these kinds of restructuring activities "trim tabs." A trim tab is the small flap that is often on the edge of the rudder of a large ship (or airplane). Because the ship's rudders are so large and cause enormous drag in the water, they are very difficult to "steer." However, the trim tab is much smaller and can be moved with less effort. When the trim tab moves, it then moves the larger rudder, which moves the ship. It requires less effort, but produces a big result.

There are hundreds of ways that bias affects our day-to-day lives. As I've said before, some of the most important (which also affect the most people) are the various stages of the talent management process. The decisions that leaders in organizations make about their employees can make or break a job, a career, or a livelihood.

At every stage of the talent management process, it is valuable to discuss the importance of remembering that our unconscious tendencies might be very different from our conscious ones. Our ability to observe them increases when we slow down and look out for them with some measure of care. It is especially important to watch for structural biases. Or, in other words, are there any things about the talent management process that benefit one person versus another?

For instance, many organizations consider social and "extracurricular" activities to be part of the culture of the organization. But even when these activities are considered open to anybody who wants to participate in them, the nature of the activities can be exclusionary. Watching sporting events, participating on company or office intramural teams, or even getting together on weekends to volunteer can unconsciously exclude people who either don't enjoy those events or who have competing family commitments.

One of my clients was a fast-growing, very successful company. Every Friday afternoon, almost from the time the company was started, the employees went to a local restaurant and bar within a few blocks of the office for a "happy hour" to end the week. It was an important informal part of the organization's culture. The bar had a Western theme and even had a bull-riding machine. Nobody was "officially required" to attend the happy hours, but the chief executive officer was always there and the "real team players" never missed it. Of course, not everybody was so keen on going. Some employees had small children and wanted to get home to get their weekend started. Some of the women didn't feel comfortable with the environment in the bar. One person, a recovering alcoholic, felt it was unhealthy for him to be in a bar. Another was a very religious person who didn't feel it was right to be in that kind of environment. A gay employee thought the cowboy atmosphere was quite homophobic. And one of the African American employees said the bar reminded him too much of a *de facto* segregated bar in his hometown where blacks were not welcome.

There was nothing in the invitation that was exclusionary. Yet so many people felt excluded.

I'm not suggesting that we have to operate from the "lowest common denominator" and only engage in activities that everybody likes. But how carefully do we think about the formal and informal activities that make up our organizational community? Do we try to balance the kinds of activities that may unconsciously include some and exclude others?

On the other hand, bringing groups together to work on tasks that require interdependency can be a great way to mitigate the impact of concealed biases. I'm sure all of us have heard stories of people put together in unusual circumstances that required them to work together and in doing so, softened some of the group biases they may have previously felt. Soldiers in warfare; members of sports teams; or, business people faced with crucial deadlines. When the task is larger than we can do by ourselves, we must learn to rely on others, and that often creates the opportunity for a new way of looking.

In 1971, Elliott Aronson discovered this in his creation of the "Jigsaw Classroom."[5] Working in the newly desegregated schools of Austin, Texas, Aronson found children with strongly entrenched racial attitudes. He gave groups of children tasks that required interdependency for the children to be successful (e.g., some had parts of the jigsaw puzzle and others had different parts; they couldn't complete the jigsaw without working together). Faced with circumstances that require us to focus on something larger than ourselves, it appears that our egoistic survival needs begin to include others. This can happen at times of community trauma, including something like a huge snowstorm that gets neighbors to work together.

Enacting the jigsaw puzzle theory or a snowstorm community work crew can work to break down barriers between groups in organizations. Creating project teams that require people to work together can sometimes inspire a relaxing of native biases and open people up to seeing the value in each other's contribution.

If you assume that bias exists within your system (because as long as human beings are there, it does!), then you should be regularly asking yourself and your team questions about how you go about your decision making.

EIGHT GREAT QUESTIONS TO ASK WHILE MAKING GROUP DECISIONS

The encouraging news is that, as we found with our individual decision making in the previous chapter, there are things we can do to help us become more conscious about our group decision making as well. I've identified eight questions we should ask on a regular basis. Building these questions into your decision-making processes can do a lot toward helping you make more conscious decisions, whether they are talent management decisions or any others. I've also included some recommendations as to actions you can take in response to the answers you get! The questions are:

1. Are there patterns of privilege or exclusion that are visible in your team or organization (e.g., tall leaders, men in certain positions, people from certain countries, certain names)?

It is more common than not to see organizations in which one group or another is over- or underrepresented, either in general, or in certain job classifications or levels of the organization. It also is very common for there to be a "perfectly logical explanation" for these results that lives within the narrative of the organization. "People just don't apply." "There aren't many like them in our profession." Or "we have done everything we can!"

It is easy to hear the implicit guilt that is present in these kinds of denials. However, if we admit that bias is present, what does it mean about us as an organization? Once we remove the guilt (albeit, not an easy thing to do) we have a task in front of us. Are we looking to find the real cause? Perhaps the explanation is something out of your control, but unless you are willing to explore all of the possible reasons, rather than approaching the exploration from the point of view that "we're not guilty!," it will be hard to discover the leverage points that may be contributing to the result you are seeing. You then may want to ask the question: "What are the unconscious biases in our organization that may be contributing to the results we are producing?"

2. Is there any reason to suspect that the team making the recommendation might have bias that is motivated by self-interest?

Teams and organizations are made up of individuals. And each of us develops unconscious patterns that are self-protective and self-justifying in various areas of our lives. Three State University of New York at Buffalo psychologists, Brett W. Pelham, Matthew C. Mirenberg, and John T. Jones, described this as "implicit egotism" and found it creates an interesting mix of irrational behaviors.[6]

Pelham and his colleagues conducted ten studies that evaluated the choices people make about where they live and what they do for a living, all of which point to the ways our choices are consciously and unconsciously influenced by our own sense of self. Five of the studies showed that people are disproportionately likely to live in places with names similar to their own (e.g., St. Louis has a lot of folks named Louis). Another showed that this same phenomenon applied to the numbers of their birthdays and the names of cities (e.g., Two Harbors, Minnesota, has a disproportionate number of residents born on the second day of a month). The other three studies showed that people tend to disproportionately choose careers that sound like their names (so there is "Dennis or Denise the Dentist").

Are we clear about what is motivating our decisions?

3. Have we explored the broadest range of possibilities regarding the situation we are dealing with at that moment?

Often, especially in haste, we jump to the first or second solution to a challenge that is in front of us. As soon as somebody says something that seems possible, we swing into action. That may make for the fastest decision making, but it probably does not lead to the best decisions. We encourage our clients to conduct a *conversation for possibility* to fully explore all the options before choosing the next path. To do this effectively, there are a number of key components that must be considered:

- Designate a specific amount of time during which you will search for all possible solutions. Use a brainstorming-type format which allows all ideas to be welcomed and not judged or dismissed. Some of the best ideas in history were considered stupid at first. Consider these real quotes:
- "Who the hell wants to hear actors talk?"—Harry M. Warner, Warner Brothers Pictures, 1927
- "Sensible and responsible women do not want to vote."—President Grover Cleveland, 1905
- "There is no likelihood man can ever tap the power of the atom."—Robert Millikan, Nobel Prize in Physics, 1923
- "Heavier than air flying machines are impossible."—Lord Kelvin, president, Royal Society of Science, 1895
- "Babe Ruth made a big mistake when he gave up pitching."—Tris Speaker, Hall of Fame outfielder, 1921
- And, my personal favorite, "A guitar's all right, John, but you'll never earn your living by it!"—John Lennon's Aunt Mimi

History is filled with examples of things that made no sense at all—until they did!

- Do not assume that the person who suggests an option is necessarily the one who will be responsible for implementing it! One of the greatest deterrents to innovation is the fear that "If I come up with an idea, I'll have to be the one to do it!"
- Be careful not to have your decisions dominated by status quo bias, primacy bias, or recency bias.
- Request additional options from outside of the group. Do not make a decision about which option to act on until the conversation for possibility has come to completion.

Once the conversation for possibility is complete, you can then choose the action plan that makes the most sense. It also is valuable to do some scenario planning. What unintended consequences might come from hiring or promoting this person? What might happen if we don't? If you consider all of these options, your chances of success will be much, much greater!

4. Check for groupthink: Were there dissenting opinions within the team and were they adequately explored?

Groupthink is one of the greatest deterrents to true diversity of thought. We also know there is an established link between diversity of identity and diversity of thought.[7] Often groupthink is a function of accepted patterns of bias that have become part of the organizational culture, "the way we do things around here." At other times, we may have come to a group determination that certain biases are agreed to and even codified. Remember, in chapter 1, I said we call these biases "qualifications."

Full inclusion or exclusion in conversations also can be a function of organizational power (e.g., once "the boss" weighs in, nobody challenges it!). Sometimes this power manifests as a sense of confidence or inherent privilege on the part of certain people who are more likely to believe that people are interested in what they have to say. There also can be cultural or gender norms that may have some people feeling more comfortable than others about sharing their ideas, especially conflicting ones. And there can be any other number of identity dynamics.

To avoid groupthink, it is important to create standards all agree to that invite differences of opinion. This may involve directly "polling" the group to solicit a broad range of opinions. Offer discreet ways for people to posit their thoughts. Consider asking for opinions from outside of the group. Remember, at times when groupthink is particularly strong, it also may be helpful to ask somebody to play the role of "skeptic" for the group and ask a question such as, "If there were some reasons that this might not be a good idea, what might they be?"

5. Are the people who are making the recommendation inordinately enamored with it, or are people who are opposed to it surprisingly strongly opposed to it?

We would like to think we are rational, but we often find ourselves in circumstances in which strong emotions can dominate our decision making. This has been called an "affect heuristic," a kind of quick decision-making process that is often dominated by our immediate fears or concerns, or a desire for immediate gratification. In organizations, this can be driven by the classic WIFM response (What's in it for me?). What is making us so attached to the decision? It can be hard to spot in us because our minds often justify the decision as "making sense." This is another place where the feedback from others can be very valuable to us.

6. Is it possible that a similar person or experience from the past is unduly influencing your perception of the current person or situation?

A strong sense of attachment or aversion to a potential talent choice, or a new idea, is usually a good sign that an individual, or sometimes an entire group, has a strong emotional reaction to the situation at hand. It is often easy to spot these kinds of situations because people can become emotionally "triggered," resulting in an emotional response that occurs when somebody is reacting to the present circumstance because of a past memory or fear that they are unconsciously reminded of at that moment. One of my clients told me this illuminating story:

> We were interviewing somebody for a supervisory position and he seemed to have all of the right qualifications. All of the others really liked him, but something about him was getting under my skin. He just seemed smug and arrogant to me. I didn't notice it until later that night when I was talking to my wife about it. I knew that he reminded me of somebody. And then it hit me like a lightning bolt. It was my big brother! My big brother was always bossing me around and telling me what to do. He always thought he had all of the answers. And this guy was triggering that same emotional response in me as my brother! I started laughing as soon as I realized it!

Checking for these kinds of aversions and attachments can be very valuable, both in you and in others. When we see them in ourselves, it is important to ask if such is relevant to the situation. When we see it in others, it is important to avoid being accusatory so that you don't trigger defensiveness as a response.

Make sure to identify past situations that are affecting the decision and look carefully at how relevant they are to the current one. Check for the "halo/horn" effect. In other words, are we either overly positive or negative in our "memory" of that past event or person? Remember that memory can be very selective. The "good old days" might not have been so good at the time, and that person we now can't stand may have been our friend or even lover at another time.

It is often worthwhile to consider how you would make the decision if you were in a completely new environment with no history. Think about it.

7. Do you have all of the information you need to make the best decision?

Our haste in making decisions often can permit our biases to take over. For example, the job we must fill, or the promotion that has to be decided upon, can often rush our process and fuel biases. When we "trust our gut" in situations like this, we are almost always relying on unconscious, emotional information. Sometimes, such circumstances are unavoidable. In those cases, it is helpful to stop and use the PAUSE model I described in the previous chapter.

Checklists also can be very important to be sure that all of the right information was checked out. You might ask yourself, "If we had to make this decision again in the future, what information would we want?" and then see if you can get more of that information.

8. Do you know where the information you are using came from? Are you clear that it was from a dependable source? Are you clear about what it is proving?

Some of our most problematic biased decisions come from a reliance on information that is sketchy at best. And this is often the case not because of our own biases but because of the biases of the person who is giving us the information. We rely on written or oral recommendations, for instance, that might be shaded by the bias of the person making the recommendation. Or perhaps the reference we are speaking to is somewhat quiet or understated in their delivery. Do we take that to mean less enthusiasm on their part than another person's extroverted and effusive reference? Is culture a factor in how we interpret information?

Some of our greatest blind spots regarding various types of circumstance can come from the people we trust the most. When somebody we know and trust gives us feedback about a potential talent move, we are far less likely to consider that his biases might be at play. Or, perhaps, they saw the employee in question in a circumstance that influenced their view of the employee.

One of my clients in a professional services firm told me this story (the names are changed to protect the innocent!):

We had this first year summer associate named Maggie. The first day she arrived, she was assigned to Larry, one of our more senior associates. It turned out that he was on a tight time crunch to write a proposal and needed some research done so, practically before she knew where the bathrooms were, Maggie was doing research for Larry. Now, she was brand new to the company so she wasn't an expert, but she did the best she could, given the situation. Larry took her work and it was "okay." He went back and completed it to his standard. The next day one of our other senior associates, Bill, asked him how Maggie had done. "Okay," was all that Larry said in reply. Not exactly a stirring endorsement. Then one of the other consultants asked Bill if he knew anything about Maggie. Bill, of course, said that he heard that she was "just okay." In a week or two it seemed as if everyone at the company thought Maggie was mediocre, and all because she was put in an unfair circumstance that then became a story about her being just "okay"!

So, as hard as it is to spot our own biases, we have to watch out for how the biases of others influence us. As such, it's important to be careful to check the source of your information to ensure that bias was not part of their analysis. Whenever possible, try to include data from multiple sources.

None of these eight questions are foolproof, and it is difficult to use all of them all of the time, but even using some of them some of the time can help you to remember to bring consciousness into your group decision making. By doing so, you not only increase your ability to recognize and navigate your biases, but you also are far more likely to make better decisions!

There are many ways that we can begin to build structures in organizations that allow us to make more conscious decisions. In the appendix I offer a whole range of ways that you can create a more conscious organization. For now, let's look at an example of an organization that has taken that on.

FINDING SUCCESS BY CHANGING SYSTEMS AT BAE SYSTEMS

Unconscious bias training, even when done incrementally, can bring about many positive changes. Consider this testimony from another client of ours, Andrea Lewis, the chief diversity officer for BAE Systems:

Our investment in unconscious bias training has served to raise awareness across our leadership population as to how unconscious bias affects our decision-making processes, especially regarding talent decisions. It also shows up in the realm of other business-related decisions, such as what types of business to pursue, and how we develop relationships with our customers. There is a heightened awareness of the need to "level the playing field," and to have more buy-in for our diversity efforts, especially those regarding the diversification of our leadership cadre. The term "unconscious bias" is becoming part of our language, lending legitimacy to people's experiences, and giving them permission to openly discuss their bias and its impacts.

Lewis says BAE is working to incorporate the management of bias more formally into their talent processes. They are crafting dialogue questions to be embedded in three key processes:

- Meetings to calibrate who is "high potential" (with an annual rating process)
- Succession planning calibrations (an annual process to populate the plans)
- Selection processes for participants in key leadership development programs

The BAE people are starting with these processes because they involve facilitated meetings where leadership can guide and influence this approach. The questions they will ask participants in the meetings will help identify criteria they informally tend to use, what some of their common biases are, and how they can look outside of their individual lenses to consider other points of view.

Another result is that the leadership at BAE is starting to see more diversity in the leadership ranks. They are tracking the representation of women and people of color, and overall the trend is upward. There are many efforts they have put into place to achieve this result. Unconscious bias training is one of many such efforts, although Lewis believes the training has been extremely important to the company for a great many reasons. Such training has created greater commitment among BAE's leaders to the need to seek more diversity, to the need to reach outside of comfort zones and seek a greater diversity of staff. It has made the introduction of other efforts (for instance, diverse slates and diverse interview panels) easier to implement. Lewis believes that the interaction of these efforts will, in the longer run, help BAE achieve the parity and inclusion they are looking to create.

As well, BAE's overall effort has produced many champions of diversity and managing unconscious bias. People are questioning the role of bias during meetings, and they report thinking differently about the candidates and qualifications they are seeking and about the teams they are putting together. One BAE leader said "we've been able to evaluate, in hindsight, when we've hired the wrong people, and when we've overlooked someone who might have been a great employee." All of these informal actions are working together with the more formal strategies described earlier to embed this into the culture. Of course, real diversity and inclusion take time. Lewis says that "We at BAE are on a journey that starts with awareness and education, which we have achieved, continues with capitalizing on that awareness with augmented processes, and moves toward a transformation supported by many other efforts."

And what is being done at BAE Systems can be done at organizations anywhere and everywhere. We all just need to not think so much about continuing to do things the way we've always done them in the past. Except maybe when it comes to that favorite recipe for mashed potatoes.

Conclusion

A Brave New World, A Grand New Journey

This being human is a guest house. Every morning a new arrival.
A joy, a depression, a meanness, some momentary awareness comes as an
unexpected visitor.
Welcome and entertain them all! Even if they are a crowd of sorrows, who
violently sweep your house empty of its furniture, still, treat each guest honor-
ably. He may be clearing you out for some new delight.
The dark thought, the shame, the malice. Meet them at the door laughing and
invite them in.
Be grateful for whatever comes. Because each has been sent as a guide from
beyond. —Jelaluddin Rumi, translation by Coleman Barks

People often ask me whether people are less biased today than they might
have been in the past. The answer is not an easy one. In some ways, we
certainly have made inroads into various aspects of personal bias. Overt
expressions of race and gender bias, or homophobic remarks, are not accepted as readily as they were not all that many years ago. In fact, such
expressions now often draw strong negative reactions. The news is full of
stories about public figures held accountable for offensive remarks. Yet,
there remain many who criticize criticisms of expressions of bias, likening
them to "political correctness." I believe they do this because they do not
understand that such expressions are not as acceptable as they once were
because they represent forceful signs that the morality of our culture concerning difference is changing.

Young people who now grow up in schools with greater diversity have a
different sense of the world than those of us who grew up in formally or
informally segregated schools. We see change all around us as more and

more states allow lesbian and gay couples to have the same rights to marriage as heterosexual couples. And yes, we now have had an African American president as well as viable female candidates for the presidency. On the surface, things are evolving.

Things are evolving and yet, our human tendency toward bias is still very much a part of our day-to-day life. It may not be focused as much on the same identities as it once was, but that doesn't mean that bias is not still alive and well in our personal and collective views of the world. When I was younger, hardly anyone talked about Islam, but today, Islamophobia is rampant. In the United States, being a "Republican" or "Democrat" used to be a distinction that indicated a particular angle on the world. Now such distinctions have become hardened tribal identities. Here in the United States, but also in European countries that have traditionally celebrated their social liberalism and openness, there is a resurgence of nationalism stimulated by the perceived threat from the presence of immigrants who look and act differently from the majority population. Global businesses are struggling to learn how to effectively operate across borders and time zones. And every day, in every way, our lives are being changed by a sense of communications connectivity that defies anything imaginable by people just a generation or two ago.

Against the backdrop of ever-shifting communication norms, new research frontiers are giving us the opportunity to learn more about the human brain, the mind, and consciousness than we have ever known before. As I have tried to demonstrate in this book, what we are learning is that bias is with us every day, and in every way; bias is with us, not just in areas related to people and diversity, but also in every decision we face in life. Bias is, in fact, one of the fundamental ways in which we navigate our lives. How do we deal with the reality that very few of the decisions we make are made with full consciousness? It is an uncomfortable reality, especially for those of us who like to think of ourselves as being "free thinkers," capable of exercising "free will." As we sit in the nether zone between those two points, we must question the future that beckons us.

Personally, I find myself looking with great optimism toward that future, because it will take place in an ever-expanding context of human interaction and cooperation. I know that sometimes it doesn't feel that way, because the massive access we have to information lets us hear about every incident or misstatement, however guilty or innocent. But the facts are undeniable. A greater percentage of people are exposed to education on the planet today than ever before, and not just in their local schools. Younger and younger children are receiving their education (for better or for worse) through online schools. And through programs such as Nicholas Negroponte's One Laptop Per Child program (http://one.laptop.org), children in villages all around the world are connected to each other through the Internet. New ways to treat illnesses are discovered all the time, resulting in improved health care for people worldwide. We also know that fewer people, per capita, are dying due to warfare on this globe today than ever before in human history. As Dr. Martin Luther King Jr. once so aptly said: "The arc of the moral universe is long, but it bends toward justice."

All of this progress notwithstanding, this is no time for complacency. Alongside these discoveries, we carry old mind-sets that threaten to pull us backward from every step forward we take. Even as the topic of unconscious bias has proliferated in the community of people who are working to address diversity and inclusion issues, I see the new information being put into the same old paradigms of thinking. "You may not be biased," the diversity facilitator says, "but you are *unconsciously biased!*," as if the accusation reveals hidden evil in the one "accused" by the facilitator. In fact, research undeniably shows that *all people have bias, and that overwhelmingly, we have no idea that we possess bias.* Being accusatory or trying to make some-body feel guilty for possessing something everyone has shuts people down and makes them less likely to consider change!

The same tools that give us a new ability to function in the world also can create new challenges. Cyber connection permits communication with our entire community of people throughout the world. But such connection also allows the possibility of cyberbullying. Mass communication begets mass miscommunication, with all of it happening faster and more expansively than ever before.

The real question for us is this: How do we respond to this change? The shift to a new way of thinking and being can happen quite quickly, very much like the shift in our experience of the Dallenbach cow in chapter 2. Once the mind organizes itself around the view of the cow, it is almost impossible not to see it, even though it was, for all intent and purposes, invisible less than a minute before. The shift in paradigm occurs spontane-ously and almost intuitively. It doesn't have to be planned for, organized, or strategized about for the shift to occur. However, to grasp what these new understandings of the mind and the brain are teaching us, and fully compre-hend the depth with which they can potentially change our view of the world, we require a deeper commitment to a new way of thinking and being. In fact, it is that commitment to transforming the way we see things that is even more primary than the plans we make or the things we choose to do. That commit-ment to see the world differently begins when we turn our view from its focus on others and the outside world to a better understanding of our own inner world and ourselves.

In his landmark treatise on paradigm shifts in science, *The Structure of Scientific Revolutions*, Thomas Kuhn wrote, "Rather than being an interpret-er, the scientist who embraces a new paradigm is like the man wearing inverted lenses." Contradictions or challenges, he goes on to say, "are terminated, not by deliberation and interpretation, but by a relatively sudden and unstructured event like the gestalt switch." In that sense, adopting a new paradigm or a new way of thinking is not *just* like seeing Dallenbach's cow for the first time: rather, it demands commitment, and the acceptance that there are new ways *beyond what feels "normal" or "comfortable."* In fact, accepting a new paradigm or a new way or thinking gives us an entirely new view of the world that exists all around us.

I believe that the possibility of a brave new world lies in our ability to develop human consciousness. In this book, I have mostly focused on the ways that the unconscious mind affects our ability to deal with people who are different from us. The unconscious mind requires us to deeply engage in the question of who we are as human beings. What motivates us? How do we learn to see ourselves, and our behavior, with enough clarity to navigate through life with others in a constructive way?

At the deepest core, our ability to expand our consciousness relies directly on our ability to be conscious to the way that fear affects us. In so many ways, our lives are less protected than ever before. We are more exposed to more people, and a wider variety of people. Public and private lives intersect through social media. The same "foe" versus "friend" mechanism of the mind is waiting right there to influence us. And the antagonistic outliers, who in the past would stay hidden in the corners, now find each other by the hundreds over the Internet. A cereal commercial that first aired in 2013 (depicting a mixed-race family) engenders thousands of negative comments. Many people respond in a similarly negative fashion to an Indian American woman being named Miss America 2014. Politicians are compared to Hitler or Satan. So much fear is always lurking, just beneath the surface. Given all that swirls and lurks around us, for better or for worse, how do we react to that inherent fear of "the other"?

At the core, this book has a single message and it is this: To the extent that you can see that you are your unconscious biases and then can see how much they manage your life, you no longer have to be imprisoned by those biases. Even when you notice that the bias is present, you now have the capacity to see yourself as something other than the bias. You no longer have to feel compelled to act as a result of it, nor do you have to be compelled to drive it away through guilt or shame. At that point, you have the capacity to simply watch your bias and see it for what it is . . . a learned thought pattern your mind has adopted as "truth." The power of biases comes when we identify with them; the way to learn not to be dominated by them is by dis-identifying with those biases. We can permit them to lose their power by realizing that we are not them; since you can see them, they are not you. From that place, we can see that, as long as we find a way not to act on them, our biases need not be a matter of grave circumstance or seriousness, but rather a loop that is running through our mind that we can choose to act on or not, rather than having to fight with, or struggle to subdue. Being able to simply witness those biases, to put that proverbial flashlight on them, gives us the ability to transcend them.

But to do so effectively requires self-compassion. It requires a willingness to forgive ourselves and to understand that we have a deeper self inside of us that can be the core of our morality and our way of being, *if we choose to do the work necessary to make it so*. It is a self that is not nearly as separated from others as we may think. That is hard for us to understand, because so much of how we see the world is given by the "them versus us" paradigm that we have been taught is so essential to our survival. Our very language, either speaking or in thought, is designed to have us see the world that way. And since we see, speak, and hear the world in that way, we can become more deeply stuck in protecting and defending ourselves from the "other." The more we fear the "other," the greater the threat they pose to us. In that sense, most of our challenges in life derive from the fact that we see ourselves as separate and apart from each other.

Yet, perhaps, there is another way beyond our addiction to dualism, or seeing things with two opposite parts or principles. In fact, perhaps that very addiction is an illusion. When we can learn to develop compassion for our own biases, we possess fewer defenses against them, we can see them more clearly, and we are better able to learn to dis-identify from those biases. And when we develop that capacity for self-compassion another remarkable thing happens: We naturally become more compassionate toward others. As we see ourselves more truly for who we are, we see the same in others.

Many of us have seen the magnificent forests full of aspen trees that grow in large "stands" throughout the northern areas of North America. The trees are extraordinary, ramrod straight, and often standing nearly one hundred feet tall. There can be thousands of them in just one stand. Still, we look at each of these trees and see it in its solitary magnificence.

But there is something interesting under the surface of these forests. These trees are not at all separate. Underneath the soil, they are connected by a common root system, and that makes each of these clusters of trees among the largest organisms on Earth. A new tree grows because the root sends out a runner that then grows into another tree. The largest of these is called "Pando" (Latin for "I spread"), and is located in the Fishlake National Forest in south-central Utah. Pando covers more than 106 acres and has been estimated to collectively weigh almost seven thousand tons, making it the heaviest organism in the world. It also is thought to be more than eighty thousand years old, making it one of the world's oldest known living organisms.

And yet we see it as a lot of single trees.

The trees bring us to a perfect metaphor for we who are as human beings. We look at the "other" as if he or she is separate from us. We see the other group as a threat. And yet, we are all deeply connected. We share a common destiny on this planet. We all seek pleasure and do our best to avoid pain. We want what is best for our children and grandchildren. All of us are the products of that which we have seen before. And we are all (for the most part) unconscious about the "programming" that runs our thoughts and our lives.

We can transcend. We can, through discipline, practice, and awareness, find a new way to relate that honors our differences, *yet also builds upon our similarities*. While the potential for mass destruction looms broadly in the world and our global community expands, we are more and more invited to recognize, as R. Buckminster Fuller said, that "we are not going to be able to operate our Spaceship Earth successfully, nor for much longer unless we see it as a whole spaceship and our fate as common. It has to be everybody or nobody."

That is the path before us. It is indeed the "road less traveled" when we look at our common history. But it is a road that is worth paving clear.

What could be a greater journey?

Appendix

A TOP TEN LIST OF WAYS TO IDENTIFY AND NAVIGATE BIAS
IN TALENT MANAGEMENT

Probably the most important way that bias affects organizations is in the way we manage talent. Let's look at ten aspects of the talent management system where we have discovered ways to identify and navigate our biases, understanding that many of these practices can apply to several aspects of the talent management process. Remember, in any aspect of the talent management process there are biases on both sides: the rater biases of the people who are doing the evaluating or hiring, and the self-rater bias of the person who is being evaluated.

Recruitment

Organizations are often blind to many aspects of their recruiting practices because they occur outside of the day-to-day structure and even the organization's physical environment. Yet, where we find the best people can make a huge impact on how we develop as an organization. Consider the following aspects of your recruitment process:

- Evaluate your job descriptions and announcements for bias.
- Does the way the job description is written demonstrate an imbalance of gender or cultural patterns (e.g., male versus female pronouns or adjectives that might be culturally influenced like "high-powered," or "relationship oriented")?
- Are the job criteria clearly listed, and is it clear what is required to do the job effectively, versus what is merely preferred?

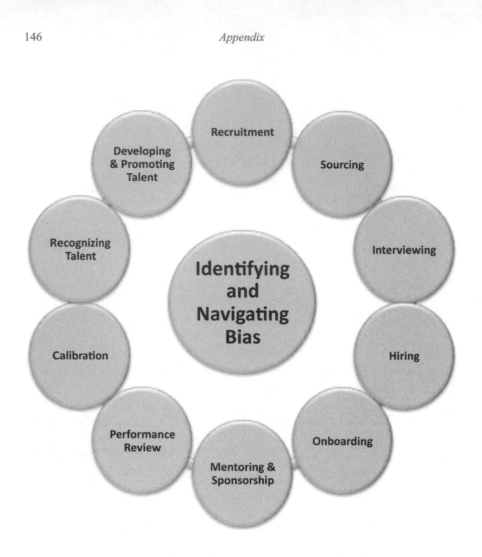

- Does the way the job or the personal qualities are described limit interest to some people rather than others? For example, describing a quality as "outgoing" might discourage an introvert. Is the possibility left open for a variety of leadership or employee styles that can work just as well?
- Are there additional criteria that might be included that could encourage a broader range of candidates?
- Does the organization's benefit package encourage a particular kind of hire?
- Do you include clear criteria for cultural competency and inclusion in your hiring statement? (One of my clients put a sign up in their human resources department, where people filled out job applications, that read,

"At our organization we value diversity and inclusion. If you don't, please don't waste your time or ours by filling out an application.")

- Try to ensure that there is as much consistency as possible in interpersonal interactions. For instance, if you are meeting two candidates, and you meet one in the office but another over lunch, you have created two very distinct environmental influences. For many people, eating together increases a sense of social connection. For others, it may make it harder to be focused. If you meet and interview one candidate in person, another through video call, and a third on the telephone, you may similarly be creating an unintentionally uneven playing field.
- Ensure that all of your recruiters, interviewers, hiring managers, and supervisors have exposure to the key concepts of unconscious bias and that they regularly review them before engaging with potential employees. This can assist them in being more aware of their biases.
- Include a diversity of people in the recruiting process. One way to do this is by taking advantage of your organization's affinity groups or employee resource groups (ERGs).
- Watch out for unchallenged patterns of judgments in the qualities you are looking for in candidates. For instance, many organizations recruit only from certain schools. Such recruiting gives an enormous advantage to people based on socioeconomic status, legacy status, or other advantages that helped them get into schools that others might not possess. It also does not take into account that talented people may have unusual résumés. In other cases, people may put a heavy emphasis on the extracurricular activities that students have engaged in, without realizing that the ability to do this may be influenced by their family situation, socioeconomic status, or even their physical abilities or disabilities. A student who has to work to put him or herself through school or help support the family may be limited in their ability to participate in extracurricular activities.
- Notice the biases you might have embedded into the "standards" or "qualifications" you have established for the recruits. Remember, in most cases standards and qualifications are simply biases all of us have agreed to enforce.
- Be careful of arbitrary standards that represent preferences rather than work-related competencies.
- Be very conscious of your first impressions of people. It is important to ask yourself, "Why do I immediately like or dislike this person?" If you have an instant like or dislike of somebody it is almost always because they are reminding you of somebody from your past. Otherwise, how would you know to like or dislike them after just a few seconds? Is that relevant to how well they might do their job? It is fine to listen to your "gut," but don't trust it without question!
- Track recruitment data to identify patterns that may reveal hidden biases.

- Learn how to respond to recruits who ask about representation in the organization. For example, if a young, talented recruit of color asks how many people of color are in the organization's leadership group, and you know you don't have enough, don't try to hide the truth or polish it up. Even if you convince them to come, they will find out soon enough that they have been deceived. Look them directly in the eye and say that you don't have enough. Tell them what you are doing about the issue. Tell them you have formed a diversity council and that you are conducting diversity training programs and teaching people about unconscious bias throughout the system, for example. Most importantly, tell them that "we need talented young people like you to join us and help us become the inclusive organization we want to be!"

Sourcing

Where do you find talent you are trying to recruit? Many people don't even realize some of the great sources of talent they are missing. You may be able to reduce the bias in your sourcing system by doing things such as:

- Sponsor in-house topic-centric discussion sessions for prospective recruits, where they can discuss their goals and accomplishments, and the organization can provide an overview of available opportunities.
- Host alumni events where former high-performing employees are invited back for an evening of networking. This provides an opportunity to recapture talented people from the target group who, given their new external experiences, may be able to add great value to the organization.
- Create relationships with organizations that support certain special needs groups (e.g., people with disabilities) who may be able to lead you to sources of talent that might not make their way into "mainstream" channels, and also may be able to help your organization learn how to accommodate these talented individuals if you decide to recruit them and bring them on as employees.
- Examine current "go-to" institutions for recruitment. Do they provide candidates who are diverse in identity and economic factors? If not, expand your resources.
- If you use executive search firms and other similar resources, be sure to monitor their practices. One of the most challenging aspects of working with resources like this is that they may have a particular kind of "ideal" candidate that they search for and promote, and their own internal biases can eliminate talent before you ever get a chance to see it yourself. They may also not be subject to many fair hiring laws and guidelines.

Interviewing

The interview process is often the first time we have an opportunity to engage deeply with the candidate in question. Many of the practices listed previously also may be appropriate to consider in the interviewing process. Here are a few more:

- Pre-issue interview questions to candidates before an interview. Having the questions beforehand removes barriers to both introverts and people from other cultures. While it may reduce the benefit of "quick thinkers," "good thinking" is better than "quick thinking" any day!
- Avoid distractions when you are interviewing recruits. By setting up an environment in which you are giving the candidate your full attention, you avoid the multitude of distractions that can have you treat candidates differently from each other. Set aside undisturbed time. Turn off your email, texting, and phones, or go into a different room. If you have something weighing heavily on your mind, try to get it resolved at least to the point that you can focus on the interview before you start. You are far better off asking the candidate to wait for a few minutes while you get something handled than you are to jump right in while you are distracted.
- Are there certain triggers you have developed to eliminate people? Does a soft handshake disqualify a candidate in your eyes? As I noted earlier in the book (and I use it again because it's a particularly good example), Henry Ford supposedly wouldn't hire anybody who salted their food without tasting it when he took them to dinner. Using these kinds of singular disqualifiers is almost guaranteed to engage bias. How do you know that the person doesn't have a hand injury or a disability, or come from a culture in which shaking hands more softly (what you think is a "limp fish") is normal? Be careful not to confuse your triggers with having anything to do with the potential competence of a recruit.
- Remove as many identifiers as possible in the early stages of the recruitment process. Studies have shown that people can be strongly influenced by various identifiers. To test this theory, economists Marianne Bertrand and Sendhil Mullainathan put white-sounding names (Greg Baker and Emily Walsh) or black-sounding names (Lakisha Washington and Jamal Jones) on the same résumé and found that even among companies with affirmative hiring practices, the exact same résumé prompted 50 percent more callbacks for interviews when the names on it sounded "white."[1]
- Include a diversity of people in the interviewing process. It's often true that different people can pick up subtleties that others might miss. Does the candidate relate differently to different kinds of people? Might they feel more comfortable in an initial interview with somebody from a different identity group or personality type?

- Pay attention to the informal interactions with others on your team that occur when the candidate is in your space. How do they treat administrative or support staff? Do they have one "manner" with you but a different one entirely with others?
- Try to maintain some consistency in the location and format of interviews. If, for example, you interview some people in the office and some over lunch, the environment may unconsciously impact the interview.

Create decision-making tools to use before the interview takes place. It is difficult (and inadvisable) in our litigious society to sit down openly with a group and ask, "When you look at this résumé, do you notice if you have any biases?" However, it is completely appropriate, and indeed, it can be very helpful to ask people to take a few minutes on their own to answer the following questions before looking at the résumé or conducting an interview:

- Does anything about this person remind you of anybody? Is that a positive or negative association?
- Are there any things on the résumé that you react strongly to, in particular?
- What similarities or differences does the candidate have to your own experience (e.g., going to the same school or a rival school; playing a sport; being a musician; coming from a particular place; or, speaking a language)? How does such affect you, positively or negatively? An old friend and colleague of mine once worked as one of a group of admissions officers for a well-known university. At one point the university brought in a consultant to study the way each of them had selected students for the freshman class. In every case there was a discernible pattern. One liked music and a candidate who was a musician did better with that admissions officer. Another had been an athlete, and she liked athlete candidates. Each had a "type" to which they were drawn. What's your type?
- Make yourself available, both logistically and personally, to the person you are interviewing. The more authentic you are, the more likely they will be as well and both your biases and theirs will be easier to spot.
- Be aware of your own personal biases concerning career expectations and accomplishments. For example, how do you relate to the candidate's ambitiousness? Are they too ambitious? Not ambitious enough? How does their level of ambition relate to your own?
- Attempt to gain a deeper understanding of the candidate's background and the unique path they took to get where they are now. One of our greatest myths is the myth of "meritocracy." We act as if all data sets are the same when they decidedly are not. What did the person need to overcome in order to accomplish what they accomplished? Is somebody who is a relatively new immigrant to the United States, for example, and for whom

English is a second language, less of a talent because their grades are slightly lower than somebody who lived their whole life in a high-income family with all of the support you can imagine? Who will have the greater "upside" in the long run?

- Ensure adequate time for interviews to surpass first impressions. Many of the professional services organizations we have worked with, especially law firms, run potential associates through a sort of "speed dating" process in which they meet with six to eight partners for fifteen minutes. These kinds of conversations with potential recruits are tremendously advantageous to members of dominant groups who are used to the general culture with which they are dealing. Longer interviews tend to be great equalizers of this potential disparity.

Hiring

We have now reached the stage of the ultimate question. And that is: Will you hire the person? Before you do so, consider these factors:

- In reviewing résumés, be careful to watch for patterns of bias before the résumé even reaches you. Studies have shown that reference letters for women tend to be shorter, place less emphasis on research and more on teaching. They also tend to contain fewer superlatives such as "brilliant" or "superb."[2] Reviews of publications also can be skewed by bias. Peer reviewers have been found to give women lower scores than men who displayed the same level of scientific productivity.[3] Additionally, the very fact that people were able to do research or not may be the result of bias. A 2005 RAND Corporation study found that women were only 63 percent as likely to receive federal government grant funding as men.[4] How might a candidate's past salary structures affect the offer you make or your willingness to hire that person? Are they "overqualified" in your eyes?
- Be careful to watch for biases in your reaction to the person or people who recommended a candidate or provided references. I'm not suggesting that they be ignored. However, if we are not careful, these can be places where the bias of another individual influences our own decision.
- Work with the people in your organization who are responsible for hiring and train them to be aware of the values and behaviors that especially trigger biases. At Cook Ross, we created a simulation exercise to use with talent managers that we call The Big Decision™. In the exercise, we give group members four to eight different résumés with an accompanying narrative about the individual that might come from their references, and so on. They each have different pictures, names, and pronouns, but, unbeknownst to the participants, the content of the résumé and narrative is identical, word for word. We ask the participants to determine, on a scale

of 0 to 100 percent, how likely they would be to hire the individual. It is not uncommon to have a 50, 60, or even 70 percent spread among the results. We don't see the world as it is; we see it as we are!

- Use diverse panels for hiring, but be sure that the panels do not slip into groupthink, or become dominated by a particular individual or individuals.
- Collect demographic data on your patterns of hiring and review it regularly. The fact that a pattern emerges does not necessarily indicate bias in your process, but it should be a red flag for you to investigate.
- Pay attention to any patterns in who accepts or declines offers to see if there are any messages there about unconscious "vibes" you are sending out during your interviewing process. You also may want to conduct follow-up interviews with people who declined your offer to see if you can ascertain any patterns in their reasons for declining.

Onboarding

How we bring people into an organization is often undervalued and misunderstood. Many studies have shown that, especially in today's workforce, most people decide within the first three to four months whether they see this as a short- or long-term position for themselves. Yet, in many organizations we have consulted with, people don't even start paying attention to newer employees until they have been around for more than three to four months. What kinds of things can we do to create an onboarding process that gives the new hire the highest probability of getting a fair chance to succeed?

- Emphasize the importance of the first few months of the employee's tenure and develop a structured onboarding process that everybody participates in.
- Assume that the more "different" people are from the dominant environment, the more specialized attention you may need to pay to observe how they are integrating into the culture. Avoid making premature assumptions about the person's performance. People who are familiar with a culture like the one in your organization may get up to speed faster but still not be the best long-term employee.
- Provide cultural as well as logistical orientation. Most organizations have so many "unwritten" rules that some people may find out about them and some may not learn about any at all. Make unwritten or unspoken cultural "rules" as clear as possible.
- Be systematic rather than intuitive when giving initial assignments and job opportunities. Often a new hire gets to show off their abilities early simply because of circumstances or because somebody takes a liking to the person. This can leave another potential talent waiting for the chance to show

what they can do. If you are tracking the work projects that people are put on, you can monitor this behavior.

- Watch for initial impressions about personality ("warmth"), competence, and "fit." When people are described as "not a good fit," it often can be a personal, superficial judgment, and can diminish or even eliminate somebody whose different take on things is exactly what the organization needs!
- As I mentioned earlier, be careful not to let the behaviors or biases of others affect your opinion too strongly. Sometimes they are built on circumstances that are suspect.
- One way to help new employees be successful is to assign coaches or "ambassadors" for them, by teaming them up with existing successful employees. The existing employee often can do a lot toward easing the new employee's transition into the organization by showing the new person the ropes.
- Make a point to get to know new employees personally so that you have a better chance to understand their needs. There also is then a far greater chance that they will come to you if they are experiencing any difficulties during their transition.
- Finally, develop a tracking system across the board for new hires to watch comparative integration processes. How are they doing compared to their peers? Have they had the same opportunities to be successful? Have they had the same access to leadership? By following the relative experience of different people, you have a far greater chance of fairly assessing their performance and identifying where biases have contributed to their success or failure.

Mentoring and Sponsorship

Another effective way to support the development of people within your organization is to create mentoring and sponsorship opportunities. Mentoring can provide an organized way to ensure that employees have guidance in learning how to be successful within the organization, and also to have somebody whose job it is to keep an eye on subtle biases that might inhibit their success. Sponsors can be sure that everybody has somebody to advocate for them within the organizational system and can prevent the unconscious advantage of some over others. Now, obviously, no system is immune from failure, and certain mentors or sponsors might be more influential than others. But at least if there is somebody looking out for the new employee, that person has a better chance of getting a fair shot. Some of the most important things to keep in mind when making mentors and sponsors successful include:

- Be sure to communicate clearly the purpose of mentoring and its structure.
- Consider creating a uniform mentoring process across the board instead of specialized mentoring for certain groups (e.g., mentoring programs for women or people of color). Specialized mentoring programs are well intended, but my experience with them has often been that they may inadvertently reinforce negative stereotypes and biases. Remember the story I told earlier in this section about the law firm that asked Cook Ross to evaluate such a program? By creating a uniform structure, they could compare the relative opportunities that each gets and correct accordingly if there are imbalances.
- Invest in training mentors, especially as they might assist in understanding ways that culture can affect the mentoring relationship. Often mentors are assigned because they are higher-level people in the organization, but nobody makes the effort to be sure they know how to mentor. In addition, they may not understand how the experience of their protégé might be very different if they come from a different identity group.
- Address both formal and informal mentoring practices. Especially watch where informal mentoring creates unintended inequity or privilege among some people or groups of people.
- Monitor mentoring to track effectiveness and to spot patterns of bias. If you are regularly checking on how the mentoring process is working, you should be able to see patterns and prevent some people from "falling through the cracks."
- Watch for patterns of job assignments and stretch assignments between both individuals and groups. Research has shown that one way biases can unconsciously play out in organizations is through the opportunities that employees get to show what they can do. If one employee gets one or two chances to perform and another gets five or six, the latter one will clearly have more opportunities to prove their value. More often than not, young white male employees get more stretch assignments than either white women or men and women of color. White men are often rewarded for potential, whereas others are rewarded for performance. This kind of inequity can increase the disparity of development.
- Mentoring banks also can assist employees in taking responsibility for their own development. For instance, ask several high-performing employees to donate a certain number of hours per month to the mentoring "bank." You can structure a way to identify what particular competencies each can deliver on. The protégé can then go to the bank and contact one of the employees for some time to support them in developing one of the designated competencies. So Meghan might contact Matthew and ask if she can get two hours of mentoring on writing proposals, while David might ask Angela for an hour of mentoring on business development.

Performance Review/Employee Assessment

The performance review process is one of the areas where unconscious biases can proliferate. Most of us remember being in school and having teachers who were harder or easier on grades. It might have been easier to get an A from one professor than a B from another. The same is true for performance reviews. There are a number of ways to enhance the performance review process so that biases are mitigated and employees get the feedback they need to be successful:

- Give feedback regularly and consistently. The feedback session should simply be a time to review those things that are always being discussed and to help the employee plan for ways to improve their performance
- Ensure that employees have clear criteria and skills established for their position so that they know what they have to do to be successful.
- Check established metrics to balance "gut" reactions. Be sure that what gets measured is indicative of performance. Imagine, for example, that a sales team is being held accountable for only their financial results. How can you know that one person didn't benefit from an easy opportunity that came to the company, while another did an incredible job to almost get a different sale, but it didn't work out? This can be an area where primacy bias and recency bias can often play major roles.
- Review the conversation about unconscious bias before the review process begins. While you are doing performance reviews, create an observer or "shadow" role for somebody so that the process is being observed for biases.
- Explore alternatives to rated assessments. Any rated assessment, whether it is a numerical assessment (e.g., 1–5) or a named rating (e.g., outstanding, adequate, poor) is begging for bias to occur because of the different ways that supervisors relate to those ratings. Consider using narrative or conversational assessments on a regular basis in which employees are told what they should stop doing, start doing, and continue to do.
- Use decision aids prior to performance review sessions to identify and navigate biases related to work styles, interpersonal traits, personal relationships, assumptions about feelings, lifestyle, teamwork, or personal goals, and who has influenced your interpretation.
- Be careful to observe rater biases relating to current projects or clients. It is easy to slip into evaluating employees more or less positively because they happen to be working on a project or with a client or customer that is very important to the leader. The rater should ask themselves questions such as Is my own agenda influencing my behavior in evaluating this employee? Are there past experiences of mine that are influencing factors? Does this employee remind me of anybody, positively or negatively? Are

differences in work style or approach a factor? What strategies can I use to navigate these biases?

- Watch out for bias in pattern recognition responses. Does one person benefit because they do things "the way we do it around here," rather than because it is the most innovative, productive, and effective way?
- Create ways for people to bring attention to their projections about the employee being evaluated.
- Watch for overall employee engagement. Are they "in the loop" or out of it? Does their particular work situation (geography, family status, children, maternity/paternity leave, flextime, telecommuting, etc.) affect their level of inclusion?
- Watch for places where you might be measuring against personal standards as opposed to measuring against success.
- Get broad input. If a broad range of people are involved in a process in which their voices are genuinely included, the deferential impact of personal biases can be minimized. Of course, this assumes that the group functions on a high level and doesn't fall subject to groupthink.
- Explore contrary viewpoints.
- Look for patterns of assessment among different groups. For example, are women in general rated differently than men?

Calibration

It has been said that everything that is important can be measured. In general, I don't agree with the universality of that statement. There are many critical areas of life (e.g., love, trust, and teamwork) that are difficult, if not impossible, to measure. But I do think there are certain aspects of the talent management system that are important to calibrate so you can more easily keep track of the results your system is producing. Biases in calibration can be mitigated when you

- Begin calibration meetings with a stated commitment to equity and inclusion and create meeting structures and processes that ensure inclusion of all participants in the meeting.
- Ensure a shared understanding of the relative weight of various metrics that are being calibrated.
- Challenge organizational cultural patterns that weight one area over another.
- Question expectations that seem to favor dominant over nondominant behaviors—for example, masculine over feminine leadership styles.

Recognizing Talent

Recognizing the talent you have in the system is critical to the long-term growth and development of both the employee and the organization. Should somebody be in the promotional pipeline? Are there high potential employees who should be especially developed? You may want to:

- Note the clarity with which an employee communicates their career goals and aspirations. The perceived enthusiasm that they demonstrate may affect your reaction.
- Note patterns as to which people are more or less willing to take challenging assignments.
- Notice who has had access to coaching or mentoring, formally or informally.
- Explore talent beyond the "usual suspects." Are there people hidden in certain functions who get very little exposure?
- Watch how the work styles of people are evaluated relative to the dominant work style of the organization.
- Watch how culture or personality may affect how employees engage in "face-time" opportunities. A few years ago, we conducted a development program for the top women leaders in a global organization. The women spent a year together in the program and during the last session a group of senior leaders, all men, came to interact with the program participants. Each of the male leaders sat with five or six of the women and discussed the state of the company. I was observing one of the groups and noticed that one of the women, who was Korean, wasn't saying anything. After quite a while I finally asked her if she had anything to add. She then launched into a series of statements and questions that were probably the sharpest anyone had offered. But had she not been invited into the conversation, she may never have had the chance to offer those observations.
- Watch for expectations to have the employee follow your career path. Listen for their desired path and don't assume that your path is their right path.
- Look for talent that can provide something new to the organization and not only at people who are talented at doing what you are already doing.

Developing and Promoting Talent

- Build a career development structure that monitors how all employees are developing and creates an opportunity to move employees to the next level. Remember, while we may not be able to eliminate all aspects of unconscious bias, structured processes tend to build more equity than unstructured processes. Consider job assignments, clear performance objectives, regular feedback opportunities, and ongoing growth opportunities.

- Look for patterns of awareness about employees. Which employees are "known" by the organization's leadership? Which are unknown? Are there patterns of group identity present in this (e.g., are more men known than women)?
- Make sure there is a written development plan for every employee and routinely evaluate and compare those plans for patterns of differential treatment.
- Watch trends in self-assessment. Do people tend to overrate or underrate themselves consistently? Personal and cultural patterns greatly influence comfort and facility with self-promotion. I once had a client who asked employees to regularly rate themselves, their performance, and their potential. One of the employees was a Vietnamese woman who came from a culture where self-promotion was frowned upon. She worked closely with an American man of European origin who had no such cultural restrictions. The cultural differences showed in their self-assessments. The woman's were relatively understated; the man's were the opposite. They shared their observations with each other. Later, the woman told me that "if I ever bragged about myself that way, my grandfather would turn in his grave." Keep this in mind when evaluating how employees present themselves.
- Monitor what educational experiences people are exposed to, such as conferences, in-house educational programs, or tuition reimbursement.
- Check for specific training needs within the organization that might make an impact upon people's ability to observe their biases (e.g., sexual harassment training, training around issues relating to sexual orientation, disability, or generational issues).
- Watch for subtle differentiators. For example, one of my clients, Tinna Nielsen, the chief diversity officer for the Danish dairy company Arla Foods, told me about this experience:

> Extensive organizational and external research was conducted (including focus groups, leader interviews, review of international mobility processes, etc.) to reveal potential for gender bias. Results showed that the first trigger for an international assignment rested with the employee herself or himself, as revealed by their own answer to one question in their online Talent Profile. The question concerned whether or not they would take an international assignment. Research showed that women tended to answer the question with a "no" due to their reflection of that current moment, with thoughts of home and life demands on her right then ("How will I ever get everything arranged? So much is depending on me to be here and available."). Whereas men tended to answer the question with a "yes" ("I'll sort it out when the time comes. There's no firm offer right now."). The system inclusion "nudge" that we put in place

was to change the question to read: *Will you consider an international assign-*
ment at some point in the future?

• Encourage the employees to share their professional aspirations and not
only what they think the leader wants to hear. Encourage them to take
responsibility for their own development.

Track how the employees experiences inclusion:

• How has their mentoring gone?
• Do they feel included in their team?
• Do they feel like they are developing the relationships they need to
progress within the system?
• Do they feel like they are being sponsored?

Monitor how stretch assignments, career development opportunities, learning
opportunities, and promotions are distributed.

• Are there "go-to people" who get more opportunities?
• How diverse and inclusive is the group?
• How much like the leader are the people in the group?
• Evaluate trends in your own and the organization's positioning of people?
Do certain kinds of people tend to get more opportunities than others?
• Challenge yourself to increase your bandwidth for styles that are different
from the "mainstream."

Overall, it's helpful to train people in third-party complaint functions
(human resources, legal department, unions, and ombudspeople) to be aware
of unconscious attitudes and behaviors and to respond in affirmative ways
with things such as education and counseling rather than with immediate
uses of legal threats or punishment.

You also may want to create "hidden" client, customer, and patient interactions where anecdotal patterns of bias can be identified for use in training
and development.

Finally, where possible, conduct customer, client, or patient outcome
analyses of results of different groups by or toward key demographic groups.
We often don't notice what we are missing because we are not asking the
right questions. We once worked with a hospital that had relatively high
patient satisfaction scores, but they never looked at the scores broken down
by race, gender, or other identity groups. When they finally started to look at
the separated group data, it became apparent that the patients of color had a
far less positive experience than the white patients. If we are going to get the
right answers, we have to ask the right questions!

Remember, one way to lessen the chances that bias will be making decisions for you is to routinely question yourself and your team about the way you are making decisions. I know that this list of questions may seem very daunting. However, keep in mind that it is not necessary, or even advisable, to do and ask all of these things at once. Find those places where you can begin to "install" little changes that can make a big difference to your organization and the people in it!

Bibliography

Abrams, Lindsay. "Study Proves That Politics and Math Are Incompatible." *Salon*, September 5, 2013, http://www.salon.com/2013/09/05/study_proves_that_politics_and_math_are_incompatible/.

Alcindor, Yamiche, and Marisol Bello. "Zimmerman Passed Lie Detector Test." *USA Today*, June 27, 2012.

Allport, Gordon. *The Nature of Prejudice*. Cambridge, MA: Perseus Books, 1954.

Ames, Daniel L., and Susan T. Fiske. "Intentional Harms Are Worse, Even When They're Not." *Psychological Science* 24, no. 9 (2013): 1755.

Anderson Cooper 360. "Juror B37: Rachel Jeantel Wasn't a Good Witness." CNN, July 16, 2013, http://ac360.blogs.cnn.com/2013/07/16/juror-b37-rachel-jeantel-wasnt-a-good-witness/.

Areni, Charles S., and David Kim. "The Influence of Background Music on Shopping Behavior: Classical Versus Top 40 Music in a Wine Store." *Advances in Consumer Research* 20 (1993): 336–40.

Ariens, Chris. "Another Misleading Edit Costs Another NBC News Employee Her Job." TVNewser.com, May 2, 2012, http://www.mediabistro.com/tvnewser/lilia-luciano-fired-misleading-edit_b125484.

Aronson, Elliott. *The Jigsaw Classroom*. New York: Sage, 1978.

Audio transcript of George Zimmerman call to Sanford police, YouTube, February 26, 2012, http://www.youtube.com/watch?v=zFRP545ZhP8.

Ballew, Charles C. II, and Alexander Todorov. "Predicting Political Elections from Rapid and Unreflective Face Judgments." *Proceedings of the National Academy of Sciences of the United States of America* 104, no. 46 (November 13, 2007): 17948–53.

Banks, R. Richard, and Richard Thompson Ford. "(How) Does Unconscious Bias Matter?: Law, Politics, and Racial Inequality." *Emory Law Journal* 58, no. 5 (2005): 1053–122.

Beckett, Katherine, and Theodore Sasson. *The Politics of Injustice: Crime and Punishment in America*. Thousand Oaks, CA: Sage, 2003.

Bennett, William J. "Rush to Judgment in Trayvon Martin Case." CNN, March 30, 2012.

Benson, Herbert. *The Relaxation Response*. New York: HarperCollins, 1975.

Bertrand, Marianne, and Sendhil Mullainathan. "Are Emily and Greg More Employable Than Lakisha and Jamal?" National Bureau of Economic Research, NBER Working Paper no. 9873, July 2003.

Bleich, Sara N., Wendy L. Bennett, Kimberly A. Gudzune, et al. "Impact of Physician BMI on Obesity Care and Beliefs." *Obesity* 20, no. 5 (2012): 999–1005.

Boyle, Matthew. "Cain: 'Swirling Rhetoric,' 'War of Words' in Trayvon Case Must Stop, Facts Are Needed before Rushing to Judgment." *The Daily Caller*, March 26, 2012.

Brown, David. "Motor Vehicle Crashes: A Little-Known Risk to Returning Veterans of Iraq and Afghanistan." *Washington Post*, May 5, 2013.

Busse, Meghan R., Ayelet Israeli, and Florian Zettelmeyer. "Repairing the Damage: The Effect of Price Expectations on Auto-Repair Price Quotes." National Bureau of Economic Research, NBER Working Paper no. 19154, June 2013.

Butler, Bob. "TV Station Takes Four-Year-Old Child's Quote out of Context." Maynard Institute, July 27, 2011, http://mije.org/health/tv-station-takes-four-year-old-childs-quote-on-context.

Butler, Doré, and Florence L. Geis. "Nonverbal Affect Responses to Male and Female Leaders: Implications for Leadership Evaluations." *Journal of Personality and Social Psychology* 58, no. 1 (January 1990): 48–59.

CNN. "Spike Lee Apologizes for Re-tweeting Wrong Zimmerman Address." March 28, 2012.

CNN. "CNN Poll: Nearly Eight in Ten Favor Gays in the Military." May 25, 2010, http://politicalticker.blogs.cnn.com/2010/05/25/cnn-poll-nearly-8-in-10-favor-gays-in-the-military/.

Casasanto, Daniel, and Kyle Jasmin. "Good and Bad in the Hands of Politicians: Spontaneous Gestures during Positive and Negative Speech." PLoS ONE 5(7): e11805. doi:10.1371/journal.pone.0011805 (2010), http://www.plosone.org/article/info%3Adoi%2F10.1371%2Fjournal.pone.0011805.

Castellanos, Dallina. "Geraldo Rivera: Hoodie Responsible for Trayvon Martin's Death." *Los Angeles Times*, March 23, 2012.

Chabris, Christopher F., Adam Weinberger, Matthew Fontaine, et al. "You Do Not Talk about Fight Club If You Don't Notice Fight Club: Inattentional Blindness for a Simulated Real-World Assault." *i-Perception* 2 (2011): 150–53.

Cikara, Mina, Emile G. Bruneau, and Rebecca R. Saxe. "Us and Them: Intergroup Failures of Empathy." *Current Directions in Psychological Research* 20, no. 3 (June 2011): 149–53.

Cohen, Richard. "Racism vs. Reality." *Washington Post*, July 15, 2013.

Crugnale, James. "Anderson Cooper Interviews Witnesses to Trayvon Martin Shooting." Mediaite, March 20, 2012, http://www.mediaite.com/tv/anderson-cooper-interviews-witnesses-to-trayvon-martin-shooting/.

Cuddy, Amy J. C., Susan T. Fiske, and Peter Glick. "Warmth and Competence as Universal Dimensions of Social Perception: The Stereotype Content Model and the BIAS Map." *Advances in Experimental Social Psychology* 40 (2008): 61–149.

Damasio, Antonio. *Descartes' Error: Emotion, Reason and the Human Brain*. New York: G. P. Putnam's Sons, 1994.

Dias, Elizabeth, and Madison Gray. "Trayvon Martin Case: Why the Grand Jury Decision Doesn't Change Much." *Time* (newsfeed), April 9, 2012, http://newsfeed.time.com/2012/04/09/trayvon-martin-case-why-the-grand-jury-decision-doesnt-change-much/.

Dodd, Michael, Amanda Balzer, Carly M. Jacobs, et al. "The Political Left Rolls with the Good and the Political Right Confronts the Bad: Connecting Physiology and Cognition to Preferences." *Philosophical Transactions of the Royal Society* 367 (2012): 640–49.

Dodgson, Philip G., and Joanne V. Wood. "Self-esteem and the Cognitive Accessibility of Strengths and Weaknesses after Failure." *Journal of Personality and Social Psychology* 75, no. 1 (July 1998): 178–97.

Drew, Trafton, Melissa L. H. Vö, and Jeremy M. Wolfe. "The Invisible Gorilla Strikes Again: Sustained Inattentional Blindness in Expert Observers." *Psychological Science* 24, no. 9 (September 2013): 1848–53.

Eack, Shaun M., Amber L. Bahorik, Christina E. Newhill, et al. "Interviewer-Perceived Honesty as a Mediator of Racial Disparities in the Diagnosis of Schizophrenia." *Psychiatric Services* 63, no. 9 (September 1, 2012): 875–80.

Eberhardt, Jennifer L., Phillip Atiba Goff, Valerie J. Purdie, et al. "Seeing Black: Race, Crime, and Visual Processing." *Journal of Personality and Social Psychology* 87, no. 6 (December 2004): 876–93.

Eberhardt, Jennifer L., Paul G. Davies, Valerie J. Purdie-Vaughns, et al. "Looking Deathworthy: Perceived Stereotypicality of Black Defendants Predicts Capital Sentencing Outcomes." *Psychological Science* 17, no. 5 (2006): 383–86.

Eisenberger, Naomi I., Matthew D. Lieberman, and Kipling D. Williams. "Does Rejection Hurt? An fMRI Study of Social Exclusion." *Science* 302, no. 5643 (October 10, 2003): 290–92.

Escobar, Javier I. "Diagnostic Bias: Racial and Cultural Issues." *Psychiatric Services* 63, no. 9 (September 1, 2012): 847.

Fisher, Marc. "Polarized News Market Has Altered the Political Process in South Carolina Primary." *Washington Post*, January 20, 2012.

Florida Office of the Attorney General. "Attorney General Pam Bondi's Statement on the Shooting of Trayvon Martin." news release, April 9, 2012, http://www.myfloridalegal.com/newsrel.nsf/newsreleases/D4A1D38C2D7F679E852579C70076D745.

Fortuna, Robert. "Kids' Race May Play a Role in ER Treatment for Pain." *Pediatrics* (September 23, 2013).

Foschi, Martha. "Double Standards for Competence: Theory and Research." *Annual Review of Sociology* 26 (August 2000): 21–42.

Francescani, Chris. "George Zimmerman: Prelude to a Shooting." Reuters, April 25, 2012.

Gibson, Dave. "Witness: Trayvon Martin Was Punching Zimmerman 'MMA Style,'" *The Examiner*, May 19, 2012, http://www.examiner.com/article/witness-trayvon-martin-was-punching-zimmerman-mma-style.

Goldin, Claudia, and Cecilia Rouse. "Orchestrating Impartiality: The Impact of 'Blind' Auditions on Female Musicians." *American Economic Review* 9, no. 4 (September 2000): 738.

Gray, Madison. "New Evidence: Trayvon Martin Had Drugs in His System." Time (newsfeed), May 17, 2012, http://newsfeed.time.com/2012/05/17/new-evidence-trayvon-martin-had-drugs-in-his-system/.

Green, Alexander R., Dana R. Carney, Daniel J. Pallin, et al. "Implicit Bias among Physicians and Its Prediction of Thrombolysis Decisions for Black and White Patients." *Journal of General Internal Medicine* 22, no. 9 (September 2007): 1231–38.

Guttman, Matt, and Seni Tienabeso. "Zimmerman Medical Report Shows Broken Nose, Lacerations after Trayvon Martin Shooting." ABC News, May 15, 2012, http://abcnews.go.com/US/george-zimmerman-medical-report-sheds-light-injuries-trayvon/story?id=16353532.

Hawkins, Jeff, and Sandra Blakeslee. *On Intelligence: How a New Understanding of the Brain Will Lead to the Creation of Truly Intelligent Machines.* New York: Times Books, 2004.

Hodzic, Amra, Lars Muckli, Wolf Singer, et al. "Cortical Responses to Self and Others." *Human Brain Mapping* 30, no. 3 (March 2009): 951–62.

Hosek, Susan D., Amy G. Cox, Bonnie Ghosh-Dastidar, et al. "Gender Differences in Major Federal External Grant Programs." RAND Corporation Technical Report 37, 2005.

Institute of Medicine of the National Academies. "How Far Have We Come in Reducing Health Disparities? Progress since 2000," 2012.

Johns Hopkins University Bloomberg School of Public Health. "Physician's Weight May Influence Obesity Diagnosis and Care," news release, January 26, 2012, http://www.jhsph.edu/news/news-releases/2012/bleich-physician-weight.html.

Jones, Jeffrey M. "Same-Sex Marriage Support Solidifies above 50 Percent in U.S." *Gallup Politics*, May 13, 2013.

Jost, John T., Dana R. Carney, Samuel D. Gosling, et al. "The Secret Lives of Liberals and Conservatives: Personality Profiles, Interaction Styles, and the Things They Leave Behind." *Political Psychology* 29, no. 6 (2008).

Kahan, Dan. M., Ellen Peters, Erica Cantrell Dawson, et al. "Motivated Numeracy and Enlightened Self-Government." *Social Science Research Network*, September 3, 2013.

Kahneman, Daniel, and Amos Tversky. "Judgment under Uncertainty: Heuristics and Biases." *Science* 185, no. 147 (September 27, 1974): 1124–31.

Kaplan, Marty. "Scientists' Depressing New Discovery about the Brain." *Salon*, September 17, 2013, http://www.salon.com/2013/09/17/the_most_depressing_discovery_about_the_brain_ever_partner/.

Kelley, Harold. "The Warm Cold Variable in First Impressions of People." *Journal of Personality* 18 (1950): 431–39.

Kelly, David J., Alan Gibson, Michael Smith, et al. "Three-Month-Olds, but Not Newborns, Prefer Own-Race Faces." *Developmental Science* 8, no. 6 (May 2005): 31–36.

Kelly, David J., Paul C. Quinn, Alan M. Slater, et al. "The Other Race Effect Develops during Infancy." *Psychological Science* 18, no. 12 (December 2007): 1084–89.

Kennedy, Helen. "Trayvon Martin Shooter Lie Detector Test, Police Interview Tapes Released by George Zimmerman's Attorney." *New York Daily News*, June 21, 2012.

Kovaleski, Serge. "Trayvon Martin's Friend Tells What She Heard on Phone." *New York Times*, May 18, 2012.

Kristof, Nicholas D. "What? Me Biased?" *New York Times*, October 29, 2008.

Kunstman, Jonathan W., and Jon K. Maner. "Sexual Overperception: Power, Mating Motives, and Biases in Social Judgment." *Journal of Personality and Social Psychology* 100, no. 2 (February 2011): 282–94.

Lai, Calvin K., Maddalena Marini, Carlo Cerruti, et al. "Reducing Implicit Racial Preferences: I. A Comparative Investigation of Eighteen Interventions." *Social Science Research Network*, October 2, 2012, http://papers.ssrn.com/sol3/papers.cfm?abstract_id=2155175.

Lambda Legal. "When Health Care Isn't Caring: Lambda Legal's Survey on Discrimination against LGBT People and People Living with HIV," http://data.lambdalegal.org/publications/downloads/whcic-report_when-health-care-isnt-caring.pdf.

Lammers, Joris, Janka I. Stoker, Jennifer Jordan, et al. "Power Increases Infidelity among Men and Women." *Psychological Science* (July 19, 2011).

Langer, Gary. "Poll Tracks Dramatic Rise in Support for Gay Marriage." ABC News, March 18, 2013, http://abcnews.go.com/blogs/politics/2013/03/poll-tracks-dramatic-rise-in-support-for-gay-marriage/.

Leddy, Chuck. "Scaling Boston's Blue Wall of Silence." *Boston Globe*, July 21, 2009.

LeDoux, Joseph. *The Emotional Brain: The Mysterious Underpinnings of Emotional Life.* New York: Simon & Schuster, 1998.

Lev-Ari, Shiri, and Boaz Keysar. "Why Don't We Believe Non-Native Speakers? The Influence of Accent on Credibility." *Journal of Experimental Social Psychology* 46, no. 3 (2010).

Levinson, Justin. "Forgotten Racial Equality: Implicit Bias, Decision Making, and Misremembering." *Duke Law Journal* 57, no. 2 (2007).

Luscombe, Richard. "Trayvon Martin Killing: Witness Says He Saw Zimmerman Walk Away Uninjured." *The Guardian*, March 29, 2012.

Maslow, Abraham H. "A Theory of Human Motivation." *Psychological Review* 50 (1943): 370–96.

May, Rollo. *The Courage to Create.* New York: W. W. Norton, 1975.

McIntosh, Margaret. "White Privilege and Male Privilege: A Personal Account of Coming to See Correspondences through Work in Women's Studies." 1988. Wellesley College Center for Research on Women, Working Paper 189.

McNary, Dave. "Over One-third of Respondents Report 'Disrespectful' Treatment." *Variety*, September 27, 2013.

McNerny, Samuel. "Jonathan Haidt and the Moral Matrix: Breaking out of Our Righteous Minds." *Scientific American* (blog), December 8, 2011, http://blogs.scientificamerican.com/guest-blog/2011/12/08/jonathan-haidt-the-moral-matrix-breaking-out-of-our-righteous-minds/.

Moss-Racusin, Corinne A., John F. Dovido, Victoria L. Brescoll, et al. "Science Faculty's Subtle Gender Biases Favor Male Students." *Proceedings of the National Academy of Sciences of the United States of America* 109, no. 41 (2012): 16474–79.

Nelson, Robert L. "State of the Profession: Trends in Legal Diversity: Selected Findings from the Research Group on Legal Diversity." September 2012. Presentation before the Leadership Council in Legal Diversity, Washington, D.C.

Nelson, Steven. "Jesse Jackson Says Trayvon 'Murdered and Martyred,'" *The Daily Caller*, March 26, 2012.

North, Adrian C., David J. Hargreaves, and Jennifer McKendrick. "In-Store Music Affects Product Choice." *Nature* 390 (1997): 132.

———. "The Influence of In-Store Music on Wine Selections." *Journal of Applied Psychology* 84 (1999): 271–76.

North, Adrian C., Amber Shilcock, and David J. Hargreaves. "The Effect of Musical Style on Restaurant Customer Spending." *Environment and Behavior* 35 (2003): 712–18.

Obhi Singh, Sukhvinder, Jeremy Hogeveen, and Michael Inzlicht. "Power Changes How the Brain Responds to Others." *Journal of Experimental Psychology General* (July 1, 2013), doi:10.1037/a0033477, http://www.researchgate.net/publication/244479763_Power_Changes_How_the_Brain_Responds_to_Others.

Osborne, William, and Abbie Conant. "The Representation of Women in European and American Orchestras." Update 2009, http://www.osborne-conant.org/orch2009.htm.

Page, Scott E. *The Difference: How the Power of Diversity Creates Better Groups, Firms, Schools and Societies.* Princeton, NJ: Princeton University Press, 2008.

Pager, Devah, Bruce Western, and Bart Bonikowski. "Discrimination in a Low-Wage Labor Market: A Field Experiment." *American Sociological Review* 74 (October 2009): 777–99.

Pelham, Brett, and Hart Blanton. *Conducting Research in Psychology: Measuring the Weight of Smoke.* Independence, KY: Cengage Learning, 2012.

Pelham, Brett W., Matthew C. Mirenberg, and John T. Jones. "Why Susie Sells Seashells by the Seashore: Implicit Egotism and Major Life Decisions." *Journal of Personality and Social Psychology* 82, no. 4 (2002): 469–87.

Pew Research Center for the People and the Press. "Big Racial Divide over Zimmerman Verdict: Whites Say Too Much Emphasis on Race, Blacks Disagree." July 22, 2013, http://www.people-press.org/2013/07/22/big-racial-divide-over-zimmerman-verdict/.

Piff, Paul K., Daniel M. Stancato, Stéphane Côté, et al. "Higher Social Class Predicts Increased Unethical Behavior." *Proceedings of the National Academy of Sciences of the United States of America* 109, no. 11 (March 13, 2012): 4086–91.

Politics Nation, MSNBC, Al Sharpton Statement on Trayvon Martin. April 11, 2012, http://www.nbcnews.com/id/45755884/vp/47023022#47023022.

Price, Paul C. "Are You as Good a Teacher as You Think?" *Thought and Action* (Fall 2006): 7–14.

Rachlinski, Jeffrey J., Sheri Lynn Johnson, Andrew J. Wistrich, et al. "Does Unconscious Racial Bias Affect Trial Judges?" *Notre Dame Law Review* 84, no. 3 (2009).

Ramachandran, V. S. *The Tell-Tale Brain: A Neuroscientist's Quest for What Makes Us Human.* New York: W. W. Norton, 2011.

Redelmeier, Donald A., and Simon D. Baxter. "Rainy Weather and Medical School Admission Interviews." *Canadian Medical Association Journal* 181, no. 12 (December 8, 2009): 933.

Robles, Frances. "Shooter of Trayvon Martin a Habitual Caller to Cops." *Miami Herald,* March 19, 2012.

———. "A Look at What Happened the Night Trayvon Martin Died," *Miami Herald,* March 26, 2012.

———. "Detective in Martin Case Says He Was Pressured to File Charges." *Miami Herald,* July 12, 2012.

Ross, Howard J. *ReInventing Diversity: Transforming Organizational Community to Strengthen People, Purpose, and Performance.* Lanham, MD: Rowman & Littlefield, 2011.

Rowe, Mary. "Saturn's Rings: A Study of the Minutiae of Sexism Which Maintain Discrimination and Inhibit Affirmative Action Results in Corporations and Nonprofit Institutions." May 1974. Paper presented at the Graduate and Professional Education of Women conference of the American Association of University Women.

Schulman, Kevin A., Jesse A. Berlin, William Harless, et al. "The Effect of Race and Sex on Physicians' Recommendations for Cardiac Catheterization." *New England Journal of Medicine* 340 (February 25, 1999): 618–26.

Schwartz, Alan. "Study of NBA Sees Racial Bias in Calling Fouls." *New York Times,* May 2, 2007.

Seltzer, George. *Music Matters: The Performer and the AFM.* London: Scarecrow Press, 1989.

Sheffield, Matthew. "NBC News President: Network Should 'Probably' Apologize On-Air for Repeatedly Running Fake Zimmerman Clip." Newsbusters.org, http://newsbusters.org/blogs/matthew-sheffield/2012/04/23/nbc-news-president-network-should-probably-apologize-air-repeated.

Simons, Daniel J., and Christopher F. Chabris. "Gorillas in Our Midst: Sustained Inattentional Blindness for Dynamic Events." *Perception* 28, no. 9 (1999): 1059–74.

Smedley, Brian D., Adrienne Y. Stith, and Alan R. Nelson, eds. "Unequal Treatment: Confronting Racial and Ethnic Disparities in Healthcare," Committee on Understanding and Eliminating Racial and Ethnic Disparities in Healthcare, Institute of Medicine of the National Academies, March 2002.

Sommers, Samuel R., and Michael I. Norton. "Race-Based Judgments, Race-Neutral Justifications: Experimental Examination of Peremptory Use and the Batson Challenge Procedure." *Law and Human Behavior* 31, no. 3 (June 2007): 261–73.

Sowell, Thomas. "Who Is 'Racist'?" Real Clear Politics, April 24, 2012, http://www.realclearpolitics.com/articles/2012/04/24/who_is_racist_113933.html.

Steele, Shelby. "The Exploitation of Trayvon Martin." *Wall Street Journal*, April 6, 2012.

Stone, Jeff, and Gordon Moskowitz. "Non-Conscious Bias in Medical Decision-Making: What Can Be Done to Reduce It?" *Medical Education* 45, no. 8 (2011): 768–76.

Stutzman, Rene. "Zimmerman Lawyers Depose 13-Year-Old Witness Who Heard Screams, Cries for Help." *Orlando Sentinel*, March 1, 2012.

Stutzman, Rene, and Bianca Prieto. "Trayvon Martin Shooting: Screams, Shots Heard on 911 Call." *Orlando Sentinel*, March 17, 2012.

Stutzman, Rene, and Amy Pavuk. "Lawyer for Trayvon's Family: Wolfinger and Police Chief Met the Night Teen Was Killed." *Orlando Sentinel*, April 2, 2012.

Tau, Bryon. "Obama: 'If I Had a Son, He Would Look Like Trayvon,'" *Politico*, March 23, 2012, http://www.politico.com/politico44/2012/03/obama-i-had-a-son-hed-look-like-trayvon-118439.html.

Trix, Frances, and Carolyn Psenka. "Exploring the Color of Glass: Letters of Recommendation for Female and Male Medical Faculty." *Discourse and Society* 24, no. 6 (November 2013).

Tronick, Edward, Lauren Adamson, H. Als, et al. "Infant Reactions in Normal and Perturbated Interactions." April 1975. Paper presented at the biennial meeting of the Society for Research in Child Development, Denver, CO.

Turley, Jonathan. "New Witness Reportedly Comes Forth in Support of Zimmerman's Account of Martin Shooting." JonathanTurley.org, March 26, 2012, http://jonathanturley.org/2012/03/26/witness-martin-was-on-top-of-zimmerman-before-fatal-shot/.

United States Department of Agriculture. Agricultural Marketing Service, http://apps.ams.usda.gov/fooddeserts/foodDeserts.aspx.

Vamburkar, Meenal. "NBC News Admits 'Error' in Editing George Zimmerman's 911 Call, Apologizes." Mediaite, April 3, 2012, http://www.mediaite.com/online/nbc-news-admits-error-in-editing-george-zimmermans-911-call-apologizes/.

van Peer, Jacobien, Philip Spinhoven, and Karin Roelofs. "Psychophysiological Evidence for Cortisol-Induced Reduction in Early Bias for Implicit Social Threat in Social Phobia." *Psychoneuroendocrinology* 35, no. 1 (January 2010): 21–32.

Vedantam, Shankar. "Power May Increase Promiscuity." National Public Radio, June 10, 2011, http://www.npr.org/2011/06/10/137112887/some-suggest-power-increases-promiscuity.

Walker, Samuel, Cassia Spohn, and Miriam DeLone. *The Color of Justice: Race, Ethnicity and Crime in America*. Independence, KY: Cengage Learning, 2011.

Washington Lawyers' Committee for Civil Rights and Urban Affairs. "Racial Disparities in Arrests in the District of Columbia, 2009–2011: Implications for Civil Rights and Criminal Justice in the Nation's Capital." July 2013, http://www.washlaw.org/pdf/wlc_report_racial_disparities.pdf.

Wasserman, David. "Will the 2012 Election Be a Contest of Whole Foods versus Cracker Barrel Shoppers?" *Washington Post*, December 9, 2011.

Weingarten, Gene. "Pearls before Breakfast: Can One of the Nation's Great Musicians Cut through the Fog of a D.C. Rush Hour? Let's Find Out." *Washington Post*, April 8, 2007.

Welch, Kelly. "Black Criminal Stereotypes and Racial Profiling." *Journal of Contemporary Criminal Justice* 23, no. 3 (August 2007): 276–88.

Welch, William M., Yamiche Alcindor, and Donna Leinwand Leger. "Police Report: Trayvon Martin's Shooting Was 'Avoidable.'" *USA Today*, May 18, 2012.

Wemple, Erik. "Why Did the *New York Times* Call Zimmerman 'White Hispanic'? *Washington Post*, March 28, 2012.

————. "NBC to Do 'Internal Investigation' on Zimmerman Segment." *Washington Post*, March 31, 2012.

Wennerås, Christine, and Agnes Wold. "Nepotism and Sexism in Peer Review." *Nature* 387 (May 22, 1997): 341–43.

William, David R., and Selina A. Mohammed. "Racism and Health: Pathways and Scientific Evidence." *American Behavioral Scientist* 57, no. 8 (August 2013): 1152–73.

Williams, Mary Elizabeth. "Conductor: 'A Cute Girl on a Podium Means That Musicians Think about Other Things,'" *Salon*, September 3, 2013, http://www.salon.com/2013/09/03/conductor_a_cute_girl_on_a_podium_means_that_musicians_think_about_other_things/.

Wilson, Greg. "Dershowitz: Prosecutor in Trayvon Martin Case Overreached with Murder Charge." Fox News, April 25, 2012.

Wilson, Timothy D. *Redirect: The Surprising New Science of Psychological Change*. Boston: Little, Brown, 2011.

Wimmer, G. Elliott, and Daphna Shohamy. "Preference by Association: How Memory Mechanisms in the Hippocampus Bias Decision." *Science* 338, no. 6104 (October 2012): 270–73.

Wright, James G., Cornelia M. Borkhoff, Gillian A. Hawker, et al. "The Effect of Patients' Sex on Physicians' Recommendations for Total Knee Arthroplasty." *Canadian Medical Association Journal* 178 (March 11, 2008): 653–55.

Wynn, Karen, and Neha Mahajan. "Origins of 'Us' versus 'Them': Prelinguistic Infants Prefer Similar Others." *Cognition* 75, no. 1 (August 2012): 227–33.

Xu, Xiaojing, Xiangyu Zuo, Xiaoying Wang, et al. "Do You Feel My Pain? Racial Group Membership Modulates Empathetic Neural Responses." *Journal of Neuroscience* 29, no. 26 (July 1, 2009): 8525–29.

Notes

INTRODUCTION

1. Adrian C. North, David J. Hargreaves and Jennifer McKendrick, "In-Store Music Affects Product Choice," *Nature* 390 (1997), 132. Adrian C. North, David J. Hargreaves, and Jennifer McKendrick, "The Influence of In Store Music on Wine Selections," *Journal of Applied Psychology* 84 (1999): 271–76.

2. Charles S. Areni and David Kim, "The Influence of Background Music on Shopping Behavior: Classical Versus Top 40 Music in a Wine Store," *Advances in Consumer Research* 20 (1993): 336–40.

3. Adrian C. North, Amber Shilcock, and David J. Hargreaves, "The Effect of Musical Style on Restaurant Customer Spending," *Environment and Behavior* 35 (2003): 712–18.

4. Alan Schwartz, "Study of NBA Sees Racial Bias in Calling Fouls," *New York Times*, May 2, 2007.

5. Corinne A. Moss-Racusin, John F. Dovido, Victoria L. Brescoll, et al., "Science Faculty's Subtle Gender Biases Favor Male Students," *Proceedings of the National Academy of Sciences of the United States of America* 109, no. 41 (2012): 16474–79.

6. Consumer.healthday.com, Friday, May 24, 2013, "Many Medical Students have Anti fat Bias, Study Finds."

7. Sara N. Bleich, Wendy L. Bennett, Kimberly A. Gudzune, et al., "Impact of Physician BMI on Obesity Care and Beliefs," *Obesity* 20, no. 5 (2012): 999–1005.

8. Johns Hopkins University Bloomberg School of Public Health, "Physician's Weight May Influence Obesity Diagnosis and Care," news release, January 26, 2012, http://www.jhsph.edu/news/news-releases/2012/bleich-physician-weight.html.

9. Howard J. Ross, *ReInventing Diversity: Transforming Organizational Community to Strengthen People, Purpose, and Performance* (Lanham, MD: Rowman & Littlefield, 2011).

10. R. Richard Banks and Richard Thompson Ford, "(How) Does Unconscious Bias Matter?: Law, Politics, and Racial Inequality," *Emory Law Journal* 58, no. 5 (2005): 1053–1122.

11. Daniel L. Ames and Susan T. Fiske, "Intentional Harms Are Worse, Even When They're Not," *Psychological Science* 24, no. 9 (2013): 1755.

1. IF YOU ARE HUMAN, YOU ARE BIASED

1. Donald A. Redelmeier and Simon D. Baxter, "Rainy Weather and Medical School Admission Interviews," *Canadian Medical Association Journal* 181, no. 12 (December 8, 2009): 933.

2. Jeffrey M. Jones, "Same-Sex Marriage Support Solidifies above 50 Percent in U.S.," *Gallup Politics*, May 13, 2013.

3. Dave McNary, "Over One-third of Respondents Report 'Disrespectful' Treatment," *Variety*, September 27, 2013.

4. FreeDictionary.com: http://www.thefreedictionary.com/bias.

5. Joseph LeDoux, *The Emotional Brain: The Mysterious Underpinnings of Emotional Life* (New York: Simon and Schuster, 1998).

6. Wikipedia: http://en.wikipedia.org/wiki/William_Graham_Sumner.

7. Brett Pelham and Hart Blanton, *Conducting Research in Psychology: Measuring the Weight of Smoke* (Independence, KY: Cengage Learning, 2012).

8. Daniel Casasanto and Kyle Jasmin, "Good and Bad in the Hands of Politicians: Spontaneous Gestures during Positive and Negative Speech," PLoS ONE 5(7): e11805. doi:10.1371/journal.pone.0011805   (2010),   http://www.plosone.org/article/info%3Adoi%2F10.1371%2Fjournal.pone.0011805.

9. David Brown, "Motor Vehicle Crashes: A Little-Known Risk to Returning Veterans of Iraq and Afghanistan," *Washington Post*, May 5, 2013.

10. Amy J. C. Cuddy, Susan T. Fiske, and Peter Glick, "Warmth and Competence as Universal Dimensions of Social Perception: The Stereotype Content Model and the BIAS Map," *Advances in Experimental Social Psychology* 40 (2008): 61–149.

11. Cuddy, Fiske, Glick, "Warmth and Competence as Universal Dimensions," 65.

12. Cuddy, Fiske, Glick, "Warmth and Competence as Universal Dimensions," 65.

13. Cuddy, Fiske, Glick, "Warmth and Competence as Universal Dimensions," 71.

14. Cuddy, Fiske, Glick, "Warmth and Competence as Universal Dimensions," 72.

15. Cuddy, Fiske, Glick, "Warmth and Competence as Universal Dimensions," 73.

16. Dan M. Kahan, Ellen Peters, Erica Cantrell Dawson, et al., "Motivated Numeracy and Enlightened Self-Government," *Social Science Research Network*, September 3, 2013.

17. Lindsay Abrams, "Study Proves That Politics and Math Are Incompatible," *Salon*, September 5, 2013, http://www.salon.com/2013/09/05/study_proves_that_politics_and_math_are_incompatible (emphasis added).

18. Marty Kaplan, "Scientists' Depressing New Discovery about the Brain," *Salon*, September 17, 2013, http://www.salon.com/2013/09/17/the_most_depressing_discovery_about_the_brain_ever_partner/.

19. Antonio Damasio, *Descartes' Error: Emotion, Reason and the Human Brain* (New York: G. P. Putnam's Sons, 1994).

20. Philip G. Dodgson and Joanne V. Wood, "Self-esteem and the Cognitive Accessibility of Strengths and Weaknesses after Failure," *Journal of Personality and Social Psychology* 75, no. 1 (July 1998): 178–97.

2. THINKING ABOUT THINKING

1. Karen Wynn and Neha Mahajan, "Origins of 'Us' versus 'Them': Prelinguistic Infants Prefer Similar Others," *Cognition* 75, no. 1 (August 2012): 227–33.

2. David J. Kelly, Alan Gibson, Michael Smith, et al., "Three-Month-Olds, but Not Newborns, Prefer Own-Race Faces," *Developmental Science* 8, no. 6 (May 2005): 31–36. David J. Kelly, Paul C. Quinn, Alan M. Slater, et al., "The Other Race Effect Develops during Infancy," *Psychological Science* 18, no. 12 (December 2007): 1084–89.

3. V. S. Ramachandran, *The Tell-Tale Brain: A Neuroscientist's Quest for What Makes Us Human* (New York: W. W. Norton, 2011).

4. Xiaojing Xu, Xiangyu Zuo, Xiaoying Wang, et al., "Do You Feel My Pain? Racial Group Membership Modulates Empathetic Neural Responses," *Journal of Neuroscience* 29, no. 26 (July 1, 2009): 8525–29.

5. Mina Cikara, Emile G. Bruneau, and Rebecca R. Saxe, "Us and Them: Intergroup Failures of Empathy," *Current Directions in Psychological Research* 20, no. 3 (June 2011): 149–53.

6. Abraham H. Maslow, "A Theory of Human Motivation," *Psychological Review* 50 (1943): 370–96.

7. Naomi I. Eisenberger, Matthew D. Lieberman, and Kipling D. Williams, "Does Rejection Hurt? An fMRI Study of Social Exclusion," *Science* 302, no. 5643 (October 10, 2003): 290–92.

8. Edward Tronick, Lauren Adamson, H. Als, et al., "Infant Reactions in Normal and Perturbated Interactions," April 1975. Paper presented at the biennial meeting of the Society for Research in Child Development, Denver, CO.

9. G. Elliott Wimmer and Daphna Shohamy, "Preference by Association: How Memory Mechanisms in the Hippocampus Bias Decision," *Science* 338, no. 6104 (October 2012): 270–73.

10. Wimmer and Shohamy, "Preference by Association," abstract.

11. Amra Hodzic, Lars Muckli, Wolf Singer, et al., "Cortical Responses to Self and Others," *Human Brain Mapping* 30, no. 3 (March 2009): 951–62.

12. Jeff Hawkins and Sandra Blakeslee, *On Intelligence: How a New Understanding of the Brain Will Lead to the Creation of Truly Intelligent Machines* (New York: Times Books, 2004).

3. THE MANY FACES OF BIAS

1. Daniel J. Simon, and Christopher F. Chabris, "Gorillas in Our Midst: Sustained Inattentional Blindness for Dynamic Events," *Perception* 28, no. 9 (1999): 1059–74.

2. Trafton Drew, Melissa L. H. Vö, and Jeremy M. Wolfe, "The Invisible Gorilla Strikes Again: Sustained Inattentional Blindness in Expert Observers," *Psychological Science* 24, no. 9 (September 2013): 1848–53.

3. Drew, Vö, and Wolfe, "The Invisible Gorilla Strikes Again."

4. Chuck Leddy, "Scaling Boston's Blue Wall of Silence," *Boston Globe*, July 21, 2009.

5. Christopher F. Chabris, Adam Weinberger, Matthew Fontaine, et al., "You Do Not Talk about Fight Club If You Don't Notice Fight Club: Inattentional Blindness for a Simulated Real-World Assault," *i-Perception* 2 (2011): 150–53.

6. Howard J. Ross, *ReInventing Diversity: Transforming Organizational Community to Strengthen People, Purpose, and Performance* (Lanham, MD: Rowman & Littlefield, 2011), 142.

7. Charles C. Ballew II and Alexander Todorov, "Predicting Political Elections from Rapid and Unreflective Face Judgments," *Proceedings of the National Academy of Sciences of the United States of America* 104, no. 46 (November 13, 2007): 17948–53.

8. Shaun M. Eack, Amber L. Bahorik, Christina E. Newhill, et al., "Interviewer-Perceived Honesty as a Mediator of Racial Disparities in the Diagnosis of Schizophrenia," *Psychiatric Services* 63, no. 9 (September 1, 2012): 875–80.

9. Javier I. Escobar, "Diagnostic Bias: Racial and Cultural Issues," *Psychiatric Services* 63, no. 9 (September 1, 2012): 847.

10. Harold Kelley, "The Warm Cold Variable in First Impressions of People," *Journal of Personality* 18 (1950): 431–39.

11. Robert Fortuna, "Kids' Race May Play a Role in ER Treatment for Pain," *Pediatrics* (September 23, 2013).

12. Wikipedia: http://en.wikipedia.org/wiki/Checker_shadow_illusion.

13. Gene Weingarten, "Pearls before Breakfast: Can One of the Nation's Great Musicians Cut through the Fog of a D.C. Rush Hour? Let's Find Out," *Washington Post*, April 8, 2007.

14. Paul C. Price, "Are You as Good a Teacher as You Think?" *Thought and Action* (Fall 2006): 7–14.

15. Daniel Kahneman and Amos Tversky, "Judgment under Uncertainty: Heuristics and Biases," *Science* 185, no. 147 (September 27, 1974): 1124–31.

16. Meghan R. Busse, Ayelet Israeli, and Florian Zettelmeyer, "Repairing the Damage: The Effect of Price Expectations on Auto-Repair Price Quotes," National Bureau of Economic Research, NBER Working Paper No. 19154, June 2013.

4. LIFE, DEATH, AND UNCONSCIOUS BIAS ON A RAINY NIGHT

1. Frances Robles, "Shooter of Trayvon Martin a Habitual Caller to Cops," *Miami Herald*, March 19, 2012.

2. Chris Francescani, "George Zimmerman: Prelude to a Shooting," Reuters, April 25, 2012.

3. Audio transcript of George Zimmerman call to Sanford police, YouTube, February 26, 2012, http://www.youtube.com/watch?v=zFRP545ZhP8.

4. Frances Robles, "A Look at What Happened the Night Trayvon Martin Died," *Miami Herald*, March 26, 2012.

5. Yamiche Alcindor and Marisol Bello, "Zimmerman Passed Lie Detector Test," *USA Today*, June 27, 2012.

6. Robles, "Shooter of Trayvon Martin a Habitual Caller to Cops."

7. Rene Stutzman and Bianca Prieto, "Trayvon Martin Shooting: Screams, Shots Heard On 911 Call," *Orlando Sentinel*, March 17, 2012.

8. William M. Welch, Yamiche Alcindor, and Donna Leinwand Leger, "Police Report: Trayvon Martin's Shooting Was 'Avoidable,'" *USA Today*, May 18, 2012.

9. Rene Stutzman and Amy Pavuk, "Lawyer for Trayvon's Family: Wolfinger and Police Chief Met the Night Teen Was Killed," *Orlando Sentinel*, April 2, 2012.

10. Al Sharpton statement on Trayvon Martin, *Politics Nation*, MSNBC, April 11, 2012, http://www.nbcnews.com/id/45755884/vp/47023022#47023022.

11. Steven Nelson, "Jesse Jackson Says Trayvon 'Murdered and Martyred,'" *The Daily Caller*, March 26, 2012.

12. Bryon Tau, "Obama: 'If I Had a Son, He Would Look Like Trayvon,'" *Politico*, March 23, 2012, http://www.politico.com/politico44/2012/03/obama-i-had-a-son-hed-look-like-trayvon-118439.html.

13. "Spike Lee Apologizes for Re-tweeting Wrong Zimmerman Address," CNN, March 28, 2012.

14. Dallina Castellanos, "Geraldo Rivera: Hoodie Responsible for Trayvon Martin's Death," *Los Angeles Times*, March 23, 2012.

15. Richard Cohen, "Racism vs. Reality," *Washington Post*, July 15, 2013.

16. William J. Bennett, "Rush to Judgment in Trayvon Martin Case," CNN, March 30, 2012.

17. Shelby Steele, "The Exploitation of Trayvon Martin," *Wall Street Journal*, April 6, 2012.

18. Thomas Sowell, "Who Is 'Racist'?" Real Clear Politics, April 24, 2012, http://www.realclearpolitics.com/articles/2012/04/24/who_is_racist_113933.html.

19. Matthew Boyle, "Cain: 'Swirling Rhetoric,' 'War of Words' in Trayvon Case Must Stop, Facts Are Needed before Rushing to Judgment," *The Daily Caller*, March 26, 2012.

20. Erik Wemple, "Why Did the *New York Times* Call Zimmerman 'White Hispanic'?" *Washington Post*, March 28, 2012.

21. Matthew Sheffield, "NBC News President: Network Should 'Probably' Apologize On-Air for Repeatedly Running Fake Zimmerman Clip," Newsbusters.org, http://newsbusters.org/

blogs/matthew-sheffield/2012/04/23/nbc-news-president-network-should-probably-apologize-air-repeated.

22. Chris Ariens, "Another Misleading Edit Costs Another NBC News Employee Her Job," TVNewser.com, May 2, 2012, http://www.mediabistro.com/tvnewser/lilia-luciano-fired-misleading-edit_b125484.

23. Ariens, "Another Misleading Edit Costs Another NBC News Employee Her Job."

24. Meenal Vamburkar, "NBC News Admits 'Error' in Editing George Zimmerman's 911 Call, Apologizes," Mediaite, April 3, 2012, http://www.mediaite.com/online/nbc-news-admits-error-in-editing-george-zimmermans-911-call-apologizes/.

25. Erik Wemple, "NBC to Do 'Internal Investigation' on Zimmerman Segment," *Washington Post*, March 31, 2012.

26. Elizabeth Dias and Madison Gray, "Trayvon Martin Case: Why the Grand Jury Decision Doesn't Change Much," *Time* (newsfeed), April 9, 2012, http://newsfeed.time.com/2012/04/09/trayvon-martin-case-why-the-grand-jury-decision-doesnt-change-much/.

27. Florida Office of the Attorney General, "Attorney General Pam Bondi's Statement on the Shooting of Trayvon Martin," news release, April 9, 2012, http://www.myfloridalegal.com/newsrel.nsf/newsreleases/D4A1D38C2D7F679E852579C70076D745.

28. Frances Robles, "Detective in Martin Case Says He Was Pressured to File Charges," *Miami Herald*, July 12, 2012.

29. Jonathan Turley, "New Witness Reportedly Comes Forth in Support of Zimmerman's Account of Martin Shooting," JonathanTurley.org, March 26, 2012, http://jonathanturley.org/2012/03/26/witness-martin-was-on-top-of-zimmerman-before-fatal-shot/.

30. Rene Stutzman, "Zimmerman Lawyers Depose 13-Year-Old Witness Who Heard Screams, Cries for Help," *Orlando Sentinel*, March 1, 2012.

31. Madison Gray, "New Evidence: Trayvon Martin Had Drugs in His System," Time (newsfeed), May 17, 2012, http://newsfeed.time.com/2012/05/17/new-evidence-trayvon-martin-had-drugs-in-his-system/.

32. James Crugnale, "Anderson Cooper Interviews Witnesses to Trayvon Martin Shooting," Mediaite, March 20, 2012, http://www.mediaite.com/tv/anderson-cooper-interviews-witnesses-to-trayvon-martin-shooting/.

33. Richard Luscombe, "Trayvon Martin Killing: Witness Says He Saw Zimmerman Walk Away Uninjured," *The Guardian*, March 29, 2012.

34. Dave Gibson, "Witness: Trayvon Martin Was Punching Zimmerman 'MMA Style,'" *The Examiner*, May 19, 2012, http://www.examiner.com/article/witness-trayvon-martin-was-punching-zimmerman-mma-style.

35. Serge Kovaleski, "Trayvon Martin's Friend Tells What She Heard on Phone," *New York Times*, May 18, 2012.

36. Kovaleski, "Trayvon Martin's Friend Tells What She Heard on Phone."

37. Helen Kennedy, "Trayvon Martin Shooter Lie Detector Test, Police Interview Tapes Released by George Zimmerman's Attorney," *New York Daily News*, June 21, 2012.

38. Matt Guttman and Seni Tienabeso, "Zimmerman Medical Report Shows Broken Nose, Lacerations after Trayvon Martin Shooting," ABC News, May 15, 2012, http://abcnews.go.com/US/george-zimmerman-medical-report-sheds-light-injuries-trayvon/story?id=16353532.

39. Greg Wilson, "Dershowitz: Prosecutor in Trayvon Martin Case Overreached with Murder Charge," Fox News, April 25, 2012.

40. "Juror B37: Rachel Jeantel Wasn't a Good Witness," *Anderson Cooper 360*, CNN, July 16, 2013, http://ac360.blogs.cnn.com/2013/07/16/juror-b37-rachel-jeantel-wasnt-a-good-witness/.

41. "Big Racial Divide over Zimmerman Verdict: Whites Say Too Much Emphasis on Race, Blacks Disagree," Pew Research Center for the People and the Press, July 22, 2013, http://www.people-press.org/2013/07/22/big-racial-divide-over-zimmerman-verdict/.

42. "Racial Disparities in Arrests in the District of Columbia, 2009–2011: Implications for Civil Rights and Criminal Justice in the Nation's Capital," Washington Lawyers' Committee for Civil Rights and Urban Affairs, July 2013, http://www.washlaw.org/pdf/wlc_report_racial_disparities.pdf.

5. WHO HAS THE POWER?

1. With appreciation to John R. P. French (the late professor emeritus of psychology at the University of Michigan) and Bertram Raven (professor emeritus of psychology at UCLA) for their important work regarding power's role in human relationships.

2. Mary Rowe, "Saturn's Rings: A Study of the Minutiae of Sexism Which Maintain Discrimination and Inhibit Affirmative Action Results in Corporations and Nonprofit Institutions," May 1974. Paper presented at the Graduate and Professional Education of Women conference of the American Association of University Women.

3. Margaret McIntosh, "White Privilege and Male Privilege: A Personal Account of Coming to See Correspondences through Work in Women's Studies," 1988. Wellesley College Center for Research on Women, Working Paper 189.

4. Doré Butler and Florence L. Geis, "Nonverbal Affect Responses to Male and Female Leaders: Implications for Leadership Evaluations," *Journal of Personality and Social Psychology* 58, no. 1 (January 1990): 48–59.

5. Martha Foschi, "Double Standards for Competence: Theory and Research," *Annual Review of Sociology* 26 (August 2000): 21–42.

6. Sukhvinder Singh Obhi, Jeremy Hogeveen, and Michael Inzlicht, "Power Changes How the Brain Responds to Others," *Journal of Experimental Psychology General* (July 1, 2013), (ePub ahead of print), doi:10.1037/a0033477: http://www.researchgate.net/publication/244479763_Power_Changes_How_the_Brain_Responds_to_Others.

7. Paul K. Piff, Daniel M. Stancato, Stéphane Côté, et al., "Higher Social Class Predicts Increased Unethical Behavior," *Proceedings of the National Academy of Sciences of the United States of America* 109, no. 11 (March 13, 2012): 4086–91.

8. Joris Lammers, Janka I. Stoker, Jennifer Jordan, et al., "Power Increases Infidelity among Men and Women," *Psychological Science* (July 19, 2011).

9. Shankar Vedantam, "Power May Increase Promiscuity," National Public Radio, June 10, 2011, http://www.npr.org/2011/06/10/137112887/some-suggest-power-increases-promiscuity.

10. Jonathan W. Kunstman and Jon K. Maner, "Sexual Overperception: Power, Mating Motives, and Biases in Social Judgment," *Journal of Personality and Social Psychology* 100, no. 2 (February 2011): 282–94.

6. LIKE WATER FOR THE FISH

1. Kelly Welch, "Black Criminal Stereotypes and Racial Profiling," *Journal of Contemporary Criminal Justice* 23, no. 3 (August 2007): 276–88.

2. Bob Butler, "TV Station Takes Four-Year-Old Child's Quote Out of Context," Maynard Institute, July 27, 2011, http://mije.org/health/tv-station-takes-four-year-old-childs-quote-context.

3. Robert L. Nelson, "State of the Profession: Trends in Legal Diversity: Selected Findings from the Research Group on Legal Diversity," September 2012. Presentation before the Leadership Council in Legal Diversity. Washington, D.C.

4. Gordon Allport, *The Nature of Prejudice* (Cambridge, MA: Perseus Books, 1954).

5. Shiri Lev-Ari and Boaz Keysar, "Why Don't We Believe Non-Native Speakers? The Influence of Accent on Credibility," *Journal of Experimental Social Psychology* 46, no. 3 (2010).

6. Samuel R. Sommers and Michael I. Norton, "Race-Based Judgments, Race-Neutral Justifications: Experimental Examination of Peremptory Use and the Batson Challenge Procedure," *Law and Human Behavior* 31, no. 3 (June 2007): 261–73.

7. Justin Levinson, "Forgotten Racial Equality: Implicit Bias, Decision Making, and Misremembering," *Duke Law Journal* 57, no. 2 (2007).

8. Katherine Beckett and Theodore Sasson, *The Politics of Injustice: Crime and Punishment in America* (Thousand Oaks, CA: Sage, 2003), 173.

9. Beckett and Sasson, *The Politics of Injustice: Crime and Punishment in America*, 173.

10. Jennifer L. Eberhardt, Paul G. Davies, Valerie J. Purdie-Vaughns, et al., "Looking Deathworthy: Perceived Stereotypicality of Black Defendants Predicts Capital Sentencing Outcomes," *Psychological Science* 17, no. 5 (2006): 383–86.

11. Howard J. Ross, *ReInventing Diversity: Transforming Organizational Community to Strengthen People, Purpose, and Performance* (Lanham, MD: Rowman & Littlefield, 2011), 138–39.

12. Samuel Walker, Cassia Spohn, and Miriam DeLone, *The Color of Justice: Race, Ethnicity and Crime in America* (Independence, KY: Cengage Learning, 2011).

13. Jeffrey J. Rachlinski, Sheri Lynn Johnson, Andrew J. Wistrich, et al., "Does Unconscious Racial Bias Affect Trial Judges?" *Notre Dame Law Review* 84, no. 3 (2009).

14. Devah Pager, Bruce Western, and Bart Bonikowski, "Discrimination in a Low-Wage Labor Market: A Field Experiment," *American Sociological Review* 74 (October 2009): 777–99.

15. Brian D. Smedley, Adrienne Y. Stith, and Alan R. Nelson, eds., "Unequal Treatment: Confronting Racial and Ethnic Disparities in Healthcare," Committee on Understanding and Eliminating Racial and Ethnic Disparities in Healthcare, Institute of Medicine of the National Academies, March 2002.

16. "How Far Have We Come in Reducing Health Disparities? Progress since 2000," Institute of Medicine of the National Academies, 2012.

17. David R. William and Selina A. Mohammed, "Racism and Health: Pathways and Scientific Evidence," *American Behavioral Scientist* 57, no. 8 (August 2013): 1152–73.

18. United States Department of Agriculture, Agricultural Marketing Service, http://apps.ams.usda.gov/fooddeserts/foodDeserts.aspx.

19. Kevin A. Schulman, Jesse A. Berlin, William Harless, et al., "The Effect of Race and Sex on Physicians' Recommendations for Cardiac Catheterization," *New England Journal of Medicine* 340 (February 25, 1999): 618–26.

20. James G. Wright, Cornelia M. Borkhoff, Gillian A. Hawker, et al., "The Effect of Patients' Sex on Physicians' Recommendations for Total Knee Arthroplasty," *Canadian Medical Association Journal* 178 (March 11, 2008): 653–55.

21. "When Health Care Isn't Caring: Lambda Legal's Survey on Discrimination against LGBT People and People Living with HIV," Lambda Legal, http://data.lambdalegal.org/publications/downloads/whcic-report_when-health-care-isnt-caring.pdf.

22. Alexander R. Green, Dana R. Carney, Daniel J. Pallin, et al., "Implicit Bias among Physicians and Its Prediction of Thrombolysis Decisions for Black and White Patients," *Journal of General Internal Medicine* 22, no. 9 (September 2007): 1231–38.

23. David Wasserman, "Will the 2012 Election Be a Contest of Whole Foods versus Cracker Barrel Shoppers?" *Washington Post*, December 9, 2011.

24. Marc Fisher, "Polarized News Market Has Altered the Political Process in South Carolina Primary," *Washington Post*, January 20, 2012.

25. "CNN Poll: Nearly Eight in Ten Favor Gays in the Military," CNN, May 25, 2010, http://politicalticker.blogs.cnn.com/2010/05/25/cnn-poll-nearly-8-in-10-favor-gays-in-the-military/.

26. Charles C. Ballew II and Alexander Todorov, "Predicting Political Elections from Rapid and Unreflective Face Judgments," *Proceedings of the National Academy of Sciences of the United States of America* 104, no. 46 (June 2007): 17948–53.

27. Nicholas D. Kristof, "What? Me Biased?" *New York Times*, October 29, 2008.

28. Samuel McNerny, "Jonathan Haidt and the Moral Matrix: Breaking out of Our Righteous Minds," *Scientific American* (blog), December 8, 2011, http://blogs.scientificamerican.com/guest-blog/2011/12/08/jonathan-haidt-the-moral-matrix-breaking-out-of-our-righteous-minds/.

29. Michael Dodd, Amanda Balzer, Carly M. Jacobs, et al., "The Political Left Rolls with the Good and the Political Right Confronts the Bad: Connecting Physiology and Cognition to Preferences," *Philosophical Transactions of the Royal Society* 367 (2012): 640–49.

30. John T. Jost, Dana R. Carney, Samuel D. Gosling, et al., "The Secret Lives of Liberals and Conservatives: Personality Profiles, Interaction Styles, and the Things They Leave Behind," *Political Psychology* 29, no. 6 (2008).

7. SHIFTING TO NEUTRAL

1. Gary Langer, "Poll Tracks Dramatic Rise in Support for Gay Marriage," ABC News, March 18, 2013, http://abcnews.go.com/blogs/politics/2013/03/poll-tracks-dramatic-rise-in-support-for-gay-marriage/.

2. Jeff Stone and Gordon Moskowitz, "Non-Conscious Bias in Medical Decision-Making: What Can Be Done to Reduce It?" *Medical Education* 45, no. 8 (2011): 768–76.

3. Howard J. Ross, *ReInventing Diversity: Transforming Organizational Community to Strengthen People, Purpose, and Performance* (Lanham, MD: Rowman & Littlefield, 2011), 153–69.

4. Timothy D. Wilson, *Redirect: The Surprising New Science of Psychological Change* (Boston: Little, Brown, 2011).

5. Wilson, *Redirect*, 176.

6. Calvin K. Lai, Maddalena Marini, Carlo Cerruti, et al., "Reducing Implicit Racial Preferences: I. A Comparative Investigation of Eighteen Interventions," *Social Science Research Network* (October 2, 2012), http://papers.ssrn.com/sol3/papers.cfm?abstract_id=2155175.

7. Herbert Benson, *The Relaxation Response* (New York: HarperCollins, 1975).

8. Jacobien van Peer, Philip Spinhoven and Karin Roelofs, "Psychophysiological Evidence for Cortisol-Induced Reduction in Early Bias for Implicit Social Threat in Social Phobia," *Psychoneuroendocrinology* 35, no. 1 (January 2010): 21–32.

9. Rollo May, *The Courage to Create* (New York: W. W. Norton, 1975), 100.

10. Gordon Allport, *The Nature of Prejudice* (Cambridge, MA: Perseus Books, 1954).

11. Lai, Marini, Cerruti, et al., "Reducing Implicit Racial Preferences: I. A Comparative Investigation of Eighteen Interventions."

8. INCUBATORS OF CONSCIOUSNESS

1. George Seltzer, *Music Matters: The Performer and the AFM* (London: Scarecrow Press, 1989), 215.

2. William Osborne and Abbie Conant, "The Representation of Women in European and American Orchestras," Update 2009, http://www.osborne-conant.org/orch2009.htm.

3. Claudia Goldin and Cecilia Rouse, "Orchestrating Impartiality: The Impact of 'Blind' Auditions on Female Musicians," *American Economic Review* 9, no. 4 (September 2000): 738.

4. Mary Elizabeth Williams, "Conductor: 'A Cute Girl on a Podium Means That Musicians Think about Other Things,'" *Salon*, September 3, 2013, http://www.salon.com/2013/09/03/conductor_a_cute_girl_on_a_podium_means_that_musicians_think_about_other_things/.

5. Elliott Aronson, *The Jigsaw Classroom* (New York: Sage, 1978).

6. Brett W. Pelham, Matthew C. Mirenberg, and John T. Jones, "Why Susie Sells Seashells by the Seashore: Implicit Egotism and Major Life Decisions," *Journal of Personality and Social Psychology* 82, no. 4 (2002): 469–87.

7. Scott E. Page, *The Difference: How the Power of Diversity Creates Better Groups, Firms, Schools and Societies* (Princeton, NJ: Princeton University Press, 2008).

APPENDIX

1. . Marianne Bertrand and Sendhil Mullainathan, "Are Emily and Greg More Employable Than Lakisha and Jamal?" National Bureau of Economic Research, NBER Working Paper no. 9873, July 2003.

2. . Frances Trix and Carolyn Psenka, "Exploring the Color of Glass: Letters of Recommendation for Female and Male Medical Faculty," *Discourse and Society* 24, no. 6 (November 2013).

3. Christine Wennerås and Agnes Wold, "Nepotism and Sexism in Peer Review," *Nature* 387 (May 22, 1997): 341–43.

4. . Susan D. Hosek, Amy G. Cox, Bonnie Ghosh-Dastidar, et al., "Gender Differences in Major Federal External Grant Programs," RAND Corporation Technical Report 37, 2005.

Index

ABC News, 66, 104
Allport, Gordon, 118
American Association of Medical
　Colleges, 91
American Bar Association, 87
American Journal of Psychology, 20
American Psychological Association, 3
amygdala, anterior cingulate cortex
　response, 22–23, 98
anchoring bias, focalism, 55–57, 57, 65
Angelou, Maya, xi
anti-immigrant sentiment, xvii
Aronson, Elliot, 130
assumed, demonstrated power, 73
attribution theory, 45

BAE Systems, 136–138
behavioral standards, xii
behavior, transformational change,
　105–119
Being There, 50
belongingness, 31–32
Bennett, William, 63
Benson, Herbert, 114
bias: constructive versus destructive effects
　of, 8–10, 9; defined, 4; domains of,
　8–10, 9; in everyday thinking, xiii;
　gender, 4–5, 55, 105–106; in-group/out-
　group, 6; logical fallacies versus, 4; as
　normal part of human experience,
　107–109; primacy bias, 124; as

protective mechanism, 5–7;
　qualifications versus, 8; recency bias,
　124; self-esteem and, 16; types of,
　11–13; unconscious, xi, xx–xxi, 2, 3–4;
　warmth versus competence basis of,
　11–12. *See also* networks of bias;
　unconscious patterns
bias elimination, 102–104; awkwardness,
　discomfort and, 118; bias as normal
　part of human experience, 107–109;
　constructive uncertainty, 116–117;
　feedback and data, 119–120; group
　engagement and, 118–119; human
　consciousness development and,
　142–144; paradigm shifts and, 141;
　PAUSE acronym, 116–117; progress
　in, 139–141; self-observation, 113–115
brain functioning, 22–23, 29, 31, 33–34,
　34, 98
Brown v. Board of Education, 54
Buddha, 114
Bush, George H. W., 95, 102
Bush, George W., 95

Cain, Herman, 63
Clinton, Bill, 95
CNN/Opinion Research Corporation poll,
　97
coercive power, 72
Cognizant test, 111

179

About the Author

Howard J. Ross is the founder and chief learning officer of Cook Ross Inc. and has served for almost thirty years as an influential business consultant to hundreds of organizations across the United States and in dozens of other countries, specializing in leadership, diversity, and organizational transformation. A recognized thought leader on exploring and addressing unconscious bias, Howard was the 2007–2008 professor of diversity-in-residence at Bennett College for Women, the first time a white man has ever served in such a position at a historically black college or university. Howard is a recipient of the 2012 Leadership Stars Who Mean Business Peer Award from Diversity Woman, the 2013 Winds of Change Award from the Forum on Workplace Inclusion, and can be heard monthly on NPR as a regular guest on The Kojo Nnamdi Show. His first book, *ReInventing Diversity: Transforming Organizational Community to Strengthen People, Purpose & Performance*, was published in 2011 by Rowman & Littlefield in association with the Society for Human Resource Management. A former educator, and rock n' roll musician, he lives in Silver Spring, Maryland, with his wife Leslie Traub and has four sons and six grandchildren.